AN IRON HAND
UPON THE PEOPLE

AN IRON HAND

UPON THE PEOPLE

The Law Against
the Potlatch
on the
Northwest Coast

DOUGLAS COLE & IRA CHAIKIN

Douglas & McIntyre
Vancouver/Toronto

University of Washington Press
Seattle

Douglas & McIntyre Ltd.
1615 Venables Street
Vancouver, British Columbia V5L 2H1

Published in the United States of America by The University of Washington Press, P.O. Box 50096, Seattle, Washington 50096-5096

Canadian Cataloguing in Publication Data
Cole, Douglas, 1938–
    An iron hand upon the people
    Includes bibliographical references.
    ISBN 0-88894-695-3
    1. Potlatch.   2. Indians of North America—Northwest Coast of North America—Rites and ceremonies.   3. Indians of North America—Northwest Coast of North America—Legal status, laws, etc.   I. Chaikin, Ira.   II. Title.
E78.N78C64   1990   390'.089'972   C90-091391-6

Library of Congress Cataloging-in-Publication Data
Cole, Douglas, 1938–
    An iron hand upon the people : the law against the potlatch on the Northwest Coast / Douglas Cole, Ira Chaikin.
        p.   cm.
    Includes bibliographical references and index.
    ISBN 0-295-97050-2
    1. Indians of North America—Northwest Coast of North America—Rites and ceremonies.   2. Potlatch—Northwest Coast of North America.   3. Indians of North America—Northwest Coast of North America—Legal status, laws, etc.   4. Indians of North America—Northwest Coast of North America—Government relations.
I. Chaikin, Ira.   II. Title.
E78.N78C632   1990
394.2–dc20

This book has been published with the help of a grant from the Social Science Federation of Canada, using funds provided by the Social Sciences and Humanities Research Council of Canada.

Cover photograph: Kwagiulth Raven mask from the Potlatch Collection of the Kwagiulth Museum and Cultural Centre, cat. no. 988.5.53. The mask, originally owned by Billy Assu of Cape Mudge, was one of the ceremonial artifacts confiscated by the Canadian government in 1922. It was returned to the Kwagiulth people by the Royal Ontario Museum in 1988. Photo by Bill McLennan of the University of British Columbia Museum of Anthropology is used courtesy of the Nuyumbalees Society, © 1990.
Design by Arifin Graham
Typesetting by The Typeworks
Printed and bound in Canada by D. W. Friesen & Sons Ltd.
Printed on acid-free paper ∞

Contents

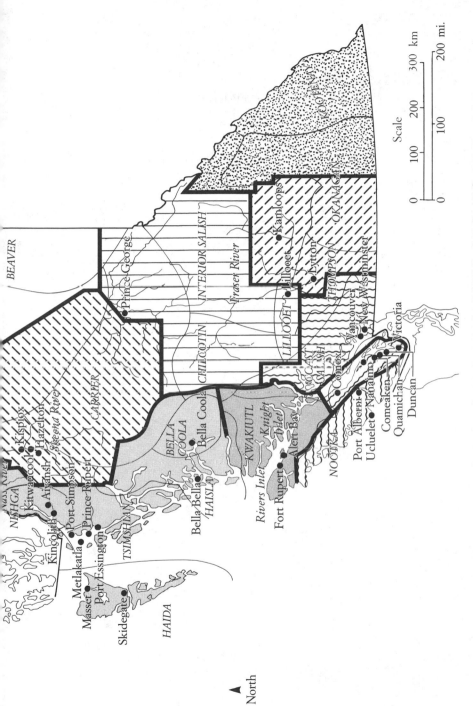

BRITISH COLUMBIA INDIAN AGENCIES AND LINGUISTIC GROUPS PRE-1905

To Arnold, Celia, Ron and Tamara
I.C.

To Don, Neva, Christy and Steve
D.C.

Preface

THIS BOOK BEGAN in 1983 when one of the authors was asked to give a lecture on the potlatch law at the Seattle Art Museum. The lecture was one of a series held by the museum in conjunction with its Box of Daylight: Northwest Coast Indian Art exhibition curated by Bill Holm. Forrest E. La Violette's *The Struggle for Survival,* the only account of the law against the potlatch, had been written when only a minimum of documentation was available, and it became apparent that the story, its complications and its ambiguities could usefully be retold using material that had more recently become available. The presence, after 1985, of both authors at Simon Fraser University allowed the project to begin in fruitful collaboration. The generosity of the Secretary of State, Multiculturalism Canada and a Molson Research Prize permitted its continuation.

Acknowledgements are due to Jill Rullkoetter and Bill Holm for their initial inspiration and to those who kindly read the manuscript or portions of it: Bill Holm, John Hall, Aldona Jonaitis, Robin Fisher and the anonymous Social Science Federation of Canada readers. Sheliza Lalji, Steven Hicks and Paul Mend assisted with the initial research. Finally, the skill and patience of our editor, Barbara Pulling, guided this work to its final form.

Introduction

IN 1885 THE Canadian government outlawed the potlatch, that seemingly profligate and ruinous gift-giving ceremony of many British Columbia Indians. Only in 1951 was the "potlatch law" dropped from the statutes. That law, with its associated provisions, and the Indian response to it are the subjects of this book.

The legal suppression of the potlatch became a symbol, in both native and white communities, of the Canadian treatment of British Columbia Indians. The potlatch was a central institution to many Northwest Coast Indians and they quickly saw the law as an instrument of injustice and intolerance. Second only to the taking of land without extinguishing Indian title, the outlawing of the potlatch can be seen as the extreme to which Euro-Canadian society used its dominance against its aboriginal subjects in British Columbia. Only the repression of native languages among Indian schoolchildren can compete with the potlatch law as an example of the assault on indigenous culture. The potlatch law "tore away most of the traditional social fabric" of the Kwakiutl Indians, writes Peter Macnair of the Royal British Columbia Museum.[1] The law was enforced to persecute native people, not to prosecute for offences.[2] This view has been well expressed in an excellent film, *Potlatch!: A Strict Law Bids Us Dance,* produced in 1975 by the U'mista Cultural Society of Alert Bay, and in a documentary collection prepared by Daisy Sewid-Smith, a Kwakiutl, and published by Cape Mudge's Nu-yum-balees Society.

An Iron Hand upon the People is essentially a re-examination of the history of the potlatch, the law and the Indian response to the legislation. Our approach reflects a current, widespread movement in recent writing to avoid viewing native people merely as passive objects of external forces. British Columbia's Indians, even when subjected to a paternalism that became increasingly authoritarian, remained significant participants in their own cultural destiny.

The conflict between white and native over the potlatch was a clash of values. The ceremony was seen by many missionaries, Christian Indians and Department of Indian Affairs field agents as a barrier to the assimilation of the native peoples into European and Christian society. To most Indians, on the other hand, their potlatch was a time-honoured and beneficial institution that did no harm.

Values, usually legitimate within their own frameworks, are difficult to reconcile, and B.C. Indians had a number of different responses to the antipotlatch legislation. Some abandoned the potlatch altogether. Some altered many features of their ceremonies so that they became more western in appearance, while others, notably the Kwakiutl, made adaptations but refused to compromise the most salient features of the potlatch system.

The government made its own adjustments. Faced with Indian defiance, it decided to rely upon church and school rather than police and prison to effect the change it desired. After 1913, however, the mutual accommodation broke down when the government, impatient with the continuation of the Kwakiutl potlatch, decided to enforce the law.

The Kwakiutl protested, but, as a disenfranchised and powerless group, a minority even within native society, they could not alter the will of an unsympathetic bureaucracy. Unable through legal channels to have the law modified or repealed, they resorted to thwarting it. By stealth, disguise, surreptitiousness and an ingenious use of legal loopholes, they continued an underground resistance that stymied all efforts at enforcement. The government was again forced to relent, to trust that time would bring an end to the ceremonies.

The Indians had once more managed to reconcile the conflicting values of traditional and modern society. The potlatch, though it declined and even disappeared in some areas, never died out. Recent years have seen a resurgence of the ceremony, even in areas where it was seemingly lost. The potlatch continues to occupy a significant place in native culture, reinforcing values both indigenous and adapted.

While the antipotlatch law was an instrument of coercion, its power and effect can be overemphasized. The "iron hand" never quite worked. For the most part, British Columbia's Indians found their own solutions.

A Note on Nomenclature

Throughout the manuscript, we have chosen to use widely accepted terms for Northwest Coast groups, even though these are often inaccurate and not what the peoples concerned now prefer to call themselves. The Southern Kwakiutl or merely Kwakiutl, for example, are more properly termed Kwakwa ka'wakw, the Bella Bella, Heiltsuk, and the Nootka (or West Coast, as they were briefly known), Nuu-chah-nulth. While it would be more appropriate to use these names, we fear that to do so would confuse readers accustomed to the older ones, which, however inaccurately and regrettably, have received a measure of sanction by long usage in English. Similarly, we have used several terms—white, Canadian, European and Euro-Canadian—perhaps equally inaccurate or imprecise, to characterize the intrusive settler groups.

1

"A Very Complex Institution"

THE NORTHWEST COAST potlatch was the occasion at which a traditional name, rank or hereditary privilege was claimed through dances, speeches and the distribution of property to those invited. The group hosting a potlatch displayed certain of its hereditary possessions, which included songs, dances and masks, recited the origins of these rights and the history of their transmission, and bestowed the new rank and name upon the member now entitled to use them. The ceremony was completed by distributing gifts, really payments, to the guests. The guest group, by witnessing the claims made, validated and sanctioned the status displayed and claimed. This was vital; the claims had to be publicly witnessed to be valid. At the same time, there was reciprocity to the ceremony. The guests were confirmed in their own status by the order in which they received their gifts, by the amount presented to them and often by the seating arrangements.

The occasions for such validations and confirmations were many. Potlatches were most usually held at significant points in the life cycle—the naming of a child, the acquisition of a traditional family name, a girl's first menses, marriage and the redemption of a bridal payment, and death, with the raising of a memorial pole and the assumption by a relative of the name and position of the deceased. Potlatches also occurred at the winter ceremonials, similarly to accompany the acquisition of new privileges or rights. Other events, such as the wiping away of shame from some misfortune, might also occasion a potlatch.

Potlatching was "giving away," but it was invariably accompanied by feasting and dancing, and by the more or less regulated festivities inherent in the assembling of people for a festive occasion. Sports, gambling (Northwest Coast Indians were inveterate gamers), talking and gossipping, some lovemaking, and, after white contact, sometimes drinking, accompanied the more formal ceremonies.

While this basic description is adequate, the potlatch was "really a very complex institution"[1] and any brief account inevitably does it an injustice. To begin with, no Indian used the word, except to outsiders, to describe his or her own giving-away event. The term was an invented omnibus word, originally from the Nootka *patshatl,* "gift" or "giving," and entered into general use through the Chinook trade jargon in the 1860s or perhaps even a little later. Orthography remained uncodified for some time, with "patlatch" and other variations vying with "potlatch" even after the latter entered the statute books in 1884. The term was probably adopted by whites to characterize the common feature of gift distributions by Indians, with native people employing it in their conversations with whites and probably with Indians speaking another language. Each native group would have had its own words for the various ceremonies and feasts. The Salish would have used *klanak* or some other term depending upon the occasion, the Tlingit had *Xu'ix* and *Tutxu'ix* ceremonies, the Kwakiutl *P!Esa'* and so on.

While every coastal group—and many interior groups—had ceremonies that included payments or gifts on an extensive scale, each acted somewhat differently. Major Tlingit and Haida potlatches occurred at the death of a chief, with a funeral and memorial ceremony for the deceased and a validation of the accession of the successor. Among the central coast Kwakiutl and Bella Coola, occasions for potlatches were more numerous, following a succession of events in the life cycle of an individual—birth, puberty, winter ceremonial initiation, marriage and death—all of which meant the transferral of privileges, names and ranks. These differences reflected variation in the social structure, kinship and descent systems of the groups involved. The variations and patterns are complex and elaborate, but they involve, among other things, the matrilineal descent system of the northern coast tribes and the ambilineal descent of the central and southern coast, the preferred pattern of marriages, and variations in the division of the group by moiety, clan or kinship.[2]

Marriages among the Tsimshian, Tlingit and Haida, because of the social structure of these groups, were not, as elsewhere, usual occasions for potlatching. With matrilineal descent and fairly fixed marriage-pattern rules, marriage did not involve a great change in social status. Thus the validation function of potlatching was relatively unimportant. Among ambilineal groups, where important rank and prerogatives could be attained through marriage (and where, as with the Kwakiutl, multiple marriages could increase the opportunity fourfold), marriage-related potlatches were of great importance.

Potential for competitive potlatches—tests of status and privileges between two individuals and their supporting groups—was present everywhere, but realized itself most significantly among the Southern Kwakiutl. Actual practices varied greatly. Coppers—plaques of beaten copper—played a prominent part in most Southern Kwakiutl potlatch transactions, but were not a universal feature on the coast and were used only later by the Lekwiltok Kwakiutl, who employed canoes in a similar manner. Among most groups, gifts were distributed according to the rank of the guests, though the Coast Salish favoured a general scramble—blankets tossed from a platform to the guests below—for all but the highest ranks.

As significant as group variations were the dramatic changes in potlatching over the historical period. These changes may have played a role in creating the regional variations in the historical potlatch complex as well as spreading certain commonalities between groups. For all the study that the potlatch has evoked among scholars, almost nothing is known of the phenomenon before the coastal Indians came into contact with the European economy.[3] John Jewitt, a New England sailor who was taken captive by the Moachat Nootka in the late eighteenth century, gives the first printed description of a wolf ceremony with accompanying gifts, but that necessarily naive account provides little insight.[4] From what is known, it seems likely that, with surplus food more abundant than surplus goods, feasting was more characteristic than gift-giving. The goods distributed would have been blankets of fur, goat hair and cedar bark, and mats, canoes and slaves, the precious commodities and trade goods of precontact society.

Feasts and gift-giving probably served several functions. One might well have been to compensate for the variability of food supply between groups.[5] Feasts and gifts also provided a means by which a chief could attract and hold a labour force, forming a way to compensate commoners for their participation in the harvesting of his or her resources. And, of course, feasts and potlatches legitimatized and bolstered the privileges and wealth of the chiefs and nobility.[6]

The fur trade stimulated native ceremonial life. The custom and ceremony of the potlatch, which may have existed largely among north and central coast groups before contact, became more fully developed there and, through the increased intensity of intertribal communications, spread southward. According to native tradition, the Quinault of the Olympic peninsula held their first potlatch around 1800. The Lower Columbia people probably did not possess any elaborated gift-giving ceremony even by 1830, acquiring it only later.[7]

The greater wealth brought by the fur trade made possible larger and more frequent potlatches. In precontact times only the highest ranking chiefs potlatched, and so the ceremonies were infrequent, with the potlatch gifts being assembled by the entire kinship group. As contact and trade intensified, potlatches changed. Access to non-traditional sources of wealth gave nonchiefs the opportunity to potlatch; the invited guest group became larger and the value of the gifts increased.

The size, frequency and importance of the Coast Tsimshian potlatch increased with contact. Helen Codere, in one of the few intensive studies of potlatch history, concluded that, before Fort Rupert's establishment in 1849, the potlatch was relatively unimportant in Southern Kwakiutl life. Once a trading post was operating in the area, a dramatic increase occurred in the size and frequency of potlatches, a change she attributes to their becoming substitutes for warfare among the Kwakiutl. Until 1849 the Kwakiutl were still using native blankets in gift-giving ceremonies, but these were replaced by the Hudson's Bay Company's woollen ones. Wayne Suttles notes similar but earlier substitutions of potlatching for warfare and of woollen blankets for native ones among the Salish.[8] There seems to have been a complex interrelationship in which access to new wealth, the availability of blankets and the decline of warfare, all stemming from the establishment of European trading posts, tended to stimulate the potlatch among most groups.

Other potlatch-related ceremonials spread as well. Some of the so-called secret societies spread both north and southward from the central coast, their probable centre. Chief Concomely on the Columbia seems to have brought a secret society from the north, perhaps from the Quinault. The Southern Kwakiutl, who developed the winter dance complex most highly, seem to have borrowed its core elements from their northern neighbours, the Haisla and the Heiltsuk, perhaps as late as the early nineteenth century. The Tsimshian, the Tlingit and the Haida were on the northern fringe of this development, and in early historic times were in the process of borrowing a number of the dance orders or societies from the south, although the new secret society dances never attained, among the Haida and the Tlingit, the importance they had in Kwakiutl and Tsimshian life.[9]

While cultural practices and ceremonies expanded and increased among some groups, they did not persist everywhere. George Gibbs reported in 1850 that the potlatch had fallen into disuse among Indians in western Washington and Oregon who associated regularly with whites. Only more remote tribes such as the Lummi and the Klallam continued the practice, and then on a considerably reduced scale.[10]

The disturbances of contact—the end of intergroup warfare, depopulation from disease and alcohol, the enormously increased availability of surplus wealth and the use of European tools to create poles and ceremonial regalia—seem to have intensified potlatching during the greater part of the nineteenth century. By the end of the century, however, these and other factors of contact—religious conversion, European-inspired work patterns and emulation—seem to have brought about a decline of the ceremony among many groups. Here generalizations falter. While potlatching virtually disappeared in much of Washington State, on the Queen Charlotte Islands and among many northern groups, it carried on strongly among the Gitksan Tsimshian and increased among the Southern Kwakiutl.

While subject to these variations over time and among groups, the potlatch was nevertheless a common system among the Northwest Coast Indians. The public distribution of gifts, linked with some elevation in status, was, at least in the mid-nineteenth century, a central part of native society. It served as the mechanism for recognition of the rank and prestige that were fundamental to Northwest Coast social systems.

Native society on the Northwest Coast was organized into a complete series of ranks graded relatively, one for each individual.[11] All tribes were characterized by a clear development of the idea of rank, perhaps more so than in any other area north of Mexico. These grades of prestige were hereditary, with a name carrying a social evaluation based on its traditional origin and on the honour of its previous bearers. These distinctions of birth were most marked in ceremonial life. A potlatch always served as an "announcement-of-standing" ceremony, a way of claiming one's accession to a social distinction. While hereditary, any name, rank or distinction ultimately rested upon the ability of someone to command the wealth to claim it, and then to continue to live up to that status by giving liberally at formal occasions. Although a person might have a right to it, a name could not be assumed without a public distribution of goods. Social position was thus determined by the linked factors of heredity and wealth. Either of two Tsimshian cousins might, for example, have claim to a vacant chiefship; the one who was able to gather the wealth, not only by his or her own endeavours but also with the help of kin, and host the requisite potlatch, could successfully claim the position. Even once a position was claimed, however, it was not enough for one of high birth to rest on hereditary glory; at frequent intervals the rank needed to be reasserted by displays of wealth lest it risk losing the place it properly commanded through inheritance.[12]

The potlatch could operate at the nexus of the entire social system, determining, through liberality of giving, the reputation and status of every individual. It confirmed not only current standing but heritage. Among the most fundamental Northwest Coast ideas was that one's "patrimony" (and "matrimony") should be kept intact. The name and honours that an individual held belonged not only to their current bearer, but to the ancestors and descendants; the present generation was of less importance than the tradition that they happened for the time to represent. The fear of falling short, in splendour and liberality, of the standards set by predecessors, did much to spur an Indian to efforts to protect the prestige and even gain new privileges for the hereditary line.[13]

In a society where all were ranked, but where the gradations remained fluid, assertions of higher status might be possible through an increase in disposable wealth. While one could rarely acquire rank by potlatching alone, one could not claim entitlements without a ceremony. In most groups, one could not claim a rank to which one was not entitled, but a potlatcher could, through wealth, attempt to secure a vacant rank to which the potlatcher had a real but distant, or even dubious, claim. Among the Kwakiutl, some potlatchers whose wealth and liberality gave them a status inappropriate to their heredity were allowed to claim the "eagle" rank, though it was also a position belonging to some head chiefs. One Fort Rupert half blood was given such status, put there by the wealth and prestige of his Indian mother because he had no place in the tribe. Such mobility was, of course, a historical phenomenon. Prior to contact, wealth was derived almost solely from territorial resources controlled by chiefs. Contact provided new, nonterritorial sources of wealth that allowed potlatches to become the road to greatness, the path to glory.

The association of wealth with prestige is, as Philip Drucker has pointed out, common to both Northwest Coast and western societies. In both cases wealth and its acquisition occupy a large share of people's thoughts; "there, however, the similarity ends." In western society prestige rests on accumulation, on "making money," or on its mere possession, on being "a millionaire"; in Northwest Coast society prestige was enhanced not by accumulation or possession alone but by the distribution, even the destruction, of wealth. Distribution was the only justification for accumulation. The object of giving it away was not merely to show philanthropy or liberality, but to confirm or enhance prestige and satisfy pride. Wealth and goods were of use only to be given away by the ambitious, by those wishing to "better themselves." Among central coast groups, at least, one potlatched as often as possible to "bring out" names and other prized claims and titles, the ideal person always looking for an excuse to potlatch. A true Oweekano Kwakiutl chief always died poor because he would have potlatched as much as possible. The idea of hoarding or accumulating wealth for any other purpose except to give would have been regarded as abnormal, unthinkable, even shameful. What was valued was not wealth but rank, privileges, names and crests, all of which endowed prestige and which were claimed, validated and upheld by the giving away of wealth in a measure befitting the status of their claimant. Paradoxically, "to give away wealth was to be wealthy," though not in any material sense.[14]

Linked as it was to social stratification, the potlatch was much more than an ostentatious festival. It was fundamental to class, rank and privilege, even to economic and social exploitation. Wrapped up in claims based on kinship, it was often integral to marriage. "The guiding themes of social organization were hereditary transmission of status and privilege." Marriages were arranged in accordance with the system of rank, involved the normal demonstrations of rank and defined, indeed were arranged to designate, the social status of the offspring.[15]

The tamananawas dances, also the subject of the Canadian legislation of 1884-85, were similarly complex institutions. The term "tamananawas," like "potlatch," was an omnibus word. Derived from a Lower Chinook word meaning "being endowed with supernatural power," the term had come to mean both shamanistic acts (including a differentiation between healing or "white tamananawas" and witchcraft or "black tamananawas") and all performances belonging to the so-called secret societies.[16] These winter ceremonials might include, among the Tsimshian-speaking groups of the north coast, "dog-eating" rites involving the mutilation of a dog, usually living. The central-coast Kwakiutl, Bella Bella and Bella Coola possessed a special initiation ceremony involving ritual cannibalism. Both ceremonies (less is known of dog-eating) seem to have incorporated conceptions of demonic possession that is constrained and overcome by nondemonic forces. Both, then, were expressions of repugnance at practices unacceptable in human society, but were acted out in realistic ways horrifying to white society. On the central coast, the possessed novice took bites from the arms and chests of witnesses and human corpses were used in ceremonies, but there is no conclusive evidence that any flesh was ever actually ingested.

Distinctions between European and native conceptions are central to the problem of the potlatch and the law. Brought into proximity by the advancement of settlement and by the extension of Christian proselytization, the two societies clashed in various ways. Land and resource use were the most important fields for conflict and dispute. Here the Indians often found the Christian missionaries, less often the federal Department of Indian Affairs, on their side in opposition to white settlers and the provincial government. In the clashes occasioned by differing customs and values, such as that over the potlatch, the sides changed. Settler society and the provincial government showed little concern with potlatching while missionaries and government officials usually opposed it. Indians were found on both sides of the question. Because the potlatch law represented a clash of values, judgements on the issue depended upon subjective standpoints. They still do. If the following pages contain any overriding theme, it is this diversity of values and the ambiguity of judgement.

2

"A Worse Than Useless Custom"

ON 7 JULY 1883 the Canadian cabinet was advised by the prime minister, Sir John A. Macdonald, acting in his capacity as superintendent general of Indian affairs, that measures should be taken to suppress the potlatch. Cabinet accepted his recommendation that, pending the introduction of legislation at the next session of Parliament, the governor general issue a proclamation discountenancing the custom and requesting that Her Majesty's Indian subjects abandon it.[1] Less than a year later, on 19 April 1884, an amendment to the Indian Act made engaging in the potlatch a misdemeanor. Outlawed at the same time was the tamananawas dance. Both ceremonies were to be declared offences effective 1 January 1885.

In a sense, the suppression of the potlatch was not new. Missionaries and federal officials had actively opposed the custom since they first set foot in British Columbia. Their request for the full authority of legislative proscription marked the ineffectiveness of their efforts. Their concerns, transmitted to the Department of Indian Affairs in letters, reports and petitions since 1873, were responsible for moving Ottawa's official mind to legal sanction.

The baneful aspects of the potlatch had been brought to the attention of the dominion government soon after Ottawa assumed control of Indian affairs in the newly confederated province of British Columbia. In January 1873, only months after his appointment as Indian superintendent in Victoria, Dr. I. W. Powell commented that potlatches, "quite common" on the coast, retarded civilizing influences and encouraged idleness among the less worthy Indians.

Wise administration, he trusted, would in time make them obsolete.[2] Other officers made similar statements.

George Blenkinsop, an agent with the Indian Reserve Allotment Commission on a fact-finding tour of Barclay Sound, reported that, until the local Indians were cured of their propensity for potlatching, "there can be little hope of elevating them from their present state of degradation." Feasting and giving away property took up too much time and interfered with other, more industrious pursuits. "These people," he wrote, "are the richest in every respect in British Columbia and were a proper disposal made of their immense gains they could furnish themselves with every comfort they could possibly wish for."[3]

Equally important, perhaps, in awakening Ottawa officialdom to the potlatch problem was the independent advice of Gilbert M. Sproat. As the joint federal-provincial appointee to the Indian reserve commission, Sproat had worked in close association with many groups of British Columbia Indians since 1876. In October 1879 he addressed a letter to Sir John A. Macdonald expressing doubt as to whether the federal department "fully appreciates the giant evil which in this inveterate and most pernicious custom has to be met and overcome." The potlatch was "the parent of numerous vices which eat out the heart of the people." It produced indigence and thriftlessness, forced women into prostitution and "promoted habits inconsistent with all progress." "It is not possible," he wrote, "that the Indians can acquire property, or can become industrious with any good result, while under the influence of this mania." Sproat was shocked that the federal government, after eight years of administering Indian affairs in the western province, had done virtually nothing to aid missionaries in their fight against such a soul-corroding system. He urged Ottawa to warn, rebuke and, if necessary, "lay an iron hand upon the shoulders of the people" in order to eradicate an evil that sprawled "like a huge incubus upon all philanthropic, administrative or missionary effort for the improvement of the Indians."[4]

In the face of such reports, Ottawa decided to accept Sproat's recommendation. The deputy superintendent general, Lawrence Vankoughnet, issued instructions to Superintendent Powell, James Lenihan, his newly appointed counterpart in New Westminster, and

Sproat himself to discountenance "the foolish, wasteful and demoralising custom." One means to the eradication of the potlatch, Powell hoped, would be through the influence of band councils, created under the 1881 Indian Improvement Act. He had no doubt that councillors would be chosen from among "the younger and more advanced Indians" who would be willing to exercise "a vigorous civilizing power" by introducing bylaws or regulations against potlatching. Nevertheless, Powell informed his newly appointed Cowichan agent, with or without a council, the Indians could not be permitted to continue the custom. No law, he admitted, prohibited the practice; its cessation rested entirely upon the persuasion of the agent.[5]

Ottawa's awareness of the difficulties presented by the potlatch were reinforced by a North Coast petition received early in 1883. The petition came from chiefs of the Coast Tsimshian and Nishga mission fields at Port Simpson, Kincolith, Greenville and elsewhere. Transparently inspired and written by Methodists Thomas Crosby and A. E. Green, perhaps with the collaboration of Anglican Thomas Dunn at Kincolith, the petition demanded that the government review the pernicious effects of the potlatch and officially suppress the practice.[6] Powell responded to a department request for comment by stating that the appointment of resident agents to that still unsupervised region and the establishment of Indian councils and bylaws would "contribute materially" to the suppression of donation feasts. More effective in halting the vice, however, would be a federal law prohibiting the potlatch and other "reprehensible customs." Many Indians, both Christian and heathen, Powell wrote, would "gladly welcome and assist in enforcing such a regulation." The loyalty of the Indians and their great respect for the Queen's law would ensure its effect.[7]

Powell's response decided the government. Vankoughnet advised Macdonald that, pending legislation, an Order in Council should be passed enjoining the Indians to discontinue the potlatch and "other heathen celebrations." Macdonald accepted the suggestion and directed his deputy to prepare a minute for council describing the evils of the system, recommending legislation and, in the meantime, a proclamation stating that "the Queen desires her Indian people to abandon the Custom."[8]

Vankoughnet's memorandum, quoting generously from the

Sproat and Powell letters, followed within the week. Cabinet obliged. Just over two weeks later, on 7 July, the proclamation to "enjoin, recommend, and earnestly urge" the Indians to abandon the potlatch was signed in the Queen's name by Governor General Lord Lorne and conveyed to Powell, who in turn conveyed it to his agents.[9] Powell himself doubted the value of the proclamation. For years he had been making the Indians aware of the "Queen's objections" to the potlatch. Without legal support, however, he felt that the proclamation would have little effect.[10]

The government intended just such support. Its intent was bolstered by further advice from British Columbia. Early in 1884, William H. Lomas, Cowichan Indian agent and a Vancouver Island resident since 1862, concluded that legal sanction was necessary to stop the potlatch and dances that were so serious a problem in his district. His views were endorsed in letters solicited from Cowichan's Catholic missionary, G. Donckele, and the Methodist missionary in Nanaimo, Cornelius Bryant.[11]

The intentions of Macdonald and Vankoughnet were reinforced by this continued unanimity of opinion among departmental officers and clergymen, who had judged it "absolutely necessary to put this practice down."[12] On 12 February 1884 the prime minister tabled legislation in the House of Commons that would make anyone participating in a potlatch or tamananawas dance guilty of a misdemeanor and liable to imprisonment for two to six months. Macdonald introduced debate in committee by noting that the government had received strong representations from both agents and missionaries. These testified, he emphasized, that attempts at introducing orderly habits were "utterly useless" where the potlatch existed.

Edward Blake, leader of the Liberal opposition, agreed that the potlatch was an "insane exuberance of generosity." Anyone who had read descriptions could not doubt "that it has a very demoralizing tendency in a great many ways." He warned, however, against Draconian measures. The custom was "a very old and a very inveterate one" and the government should be cautious in attempting suddenly to stop it by the harsh process of criminal law. Blake suggested that the bill's minimum penalty of two months imprisonment be altered so that nominal punishments might be imposed initially. The point, he urged, was to make the Indians gradually see that the practice was contrary to the law, and warnings of much more severe punishments might repress the potlatch without inviting calamity.[13]

Senate debate on the bill went to greater length. Minister of Justice Sir Alexander Campbell introduced the amendment with quotations from the Lomas, Donckele and Bryant letters. A few senators were skeptical. British Columbia Senator W. J. Macdonald felt that it was "entirely work for missionaries" to stamp out this vice and feared that ineffectual enforcement might lead to contempt for the law or a gunboat reprisal that could spark an Indian war. Senator W. J. Almon, a Nova Scotia Conservative, imperialist and surgeon to the Halifax field battery, strongly opposed any law that interfered with the customs and prejudices of natives lest it provoke a reaction similar to India's Sepoy Mutiny. He doubted the law could be enforced in an area where "there are neither jails nor jailers" and was happy to "leave these matters to the missionary and let time work any reformation that is needed." His provincial colleague, R. B. Dickey, agreed that moral suasion would be more effective than coercion.[14] Despite this expression of sober second thought, the amendment passed the Senate without a roll call or recorded vote.

The decision of the dominion government to take legislative action against the potlatch and the tamananawas dance was based on numerous arguments submitted to it by missionaries and Indian officials. They were varied, but may be roughly divided into three categories: health, morality and economics, although to the nineteenth-century mind these easily overlapped.

Health was perhaps the most immediate issue. Missionaries and agents were concerned about the spread of disease among large numbers of Indians gathered at close quarters in temporary, unsanitary accommodation over an extended period. George Blenkinsop, by now agent to the Kwakiutl, judged that such conditions were a major reason for "the terrible decline now taking place." Lomas described potlatching as "the principal cause of the decrease of population" in his Cowichan agency. In every tribe around Cowichan and Nanaimo where dancing was kept up, Father Donckele wrote, there was a general complaint of sickness. "Alas, how could it be otherwise, when for about two months they hardly take a night's rest, and when they indulge whole days in ceaseless vociferations." Lomas considered the potlatch the main cause of sickness and death among Indian children. Six out of every ten infants died, he told the

Quamichan band council, because "you take little infants with you [to be] roasted during a dance and then bring them out with scarcely any clothing [into] the coldest nights." Blenkinsop faced a similar situation in the Kwawkewlth agency. Late in 1881 he reported the Kwakiutl had "surrounded themselves with boxes of property all ready for the 'potlatch' on which their whole souls are now fixed," but turned "a deaf ear to any suggestion to purchase a little rice, tea or sugar for their suffering progeny." The old suffered almost as much as the young. Lomas told the Quamichan council how he had found only "old and helpless creatures" left in the villages after the first snow without food or fuel—often "with a single blanket to cover them and in many cases not a stick of wood to burn." The potlatch, wrote Bryant, was "a principal cause of the destitution and misery of the aged."[15]

Moral issues, at least in a narrow sense, were hardly mentioned in the petitions or reports that led to the proclamation and the law against the potlatch. Alcohol might occasionally have been present during the ceremonies, but it seems to have been a minor problem. Much more serious was the encouragement that the potlatch system gave to prostitution of native women as a source of funds. "Worst of all," wrote Sproat, "a man will say to his wife, nay to his maiden daughter, that before the spring or other appointed time he must have so many dollars for his proposed 'Potlach.' " In this way, more than from any "licentious desire," women were forced into prostitution.[16]

The tamananawas dance, on the other hand, was condemned almost entirely on moral grounds. Biting the arms of spectators and tearing apart dead dogs or exhumed human bodies with the teeth were "orgies of the most disgusting character." Here, however, missionaries and Indian agents had been able to exert some influence. Some of the most offensive practices of the secret society ceremonies had been either modified or eliminated by the 1880s. Mutilation of the dead, human or animal, disappeared among the Indians at Port Simpson and Metlakatla, and on the west coast of Vancouver Island where missionary influence was strong. Blenkinsop managed to control it among the Kwakiutl by threatening prosecution for assault, at least where his threats had force within the sprawling Kwawkewlth agency.[17]

Condemnation of the potlatch's demoralization of the Indians was much less on ethical grounds than on economic. Far the most frequent and serious arguments against the potlatch were those that touched on the system's incompatibility with settled habits of labour and industry: the loss of time from agriculture, ranching and even fishing, and the potlatch's destructiveness of the accumulation of savings. Work and savings were directed, not towards material progress, but to hoarding and then the extravagant dispersal of money and goods. Even the West Coast agent, Harry Guillod, who found the Nootkan potlatch largely inoffensive, agreed that it was "much against the habits of saving" and Lomas, who estimated that his Cowichans had earned over $15,000 in the 1881 Fraser River fishing season, regretted that the greatest portion of this sum would be spent on blankets to be given away. Improvident habits, commented Rev. Bryant, were already too common among the Indians, but they were "sadly fostered" by the potlatch system. Blenkinsop had reported in 1883 that potlatches and feasts at Fort Rupert lasted until July, which meant that "the most valuable portion of the fishing season was lost." Few would have disputed Sproat's judgement that material progress was impossible while the potlatch existed. "It produces indigence, thriftlessness, and a habit of roaming about," he wrote, "which prevents home associations and is inconsistent with all progress."[18]

One further indictment of the potlatch reached Ottawa, one that grew in intensity and strength with the passing years: schools could not flourish where the potlatch held sway. "During the whole winter," wrote Rev. Donckele, "schools are deserted by all those children whose parents attend the dances." Once winter was over and the Indians had squandered all their summer earnings, they were "compelled to leave their homes and roam about in their canoes in search of food, and thus neglect cultivating their lands and sending their children to school."[19]

From official and missionary points of view, the potlatch possessed scarcely a redeeming feature. Powell might muse that it was in principle no different from practices among "more civilized beings," but its universality and the extent to which Indians deprived themselves and their families divorced it from such a comparison. Guillod, far the most sympathetic of officials, saw it as "a bond of union" between the West Coast tribes, bringing them into mutual acquaintance on occasions they seemed thoroughly to enjoy. Doubtless there was some waste, but the poorer Indians reaped benefit from it and all carried away what they could not eat. But Guillod's comments were exceptional. To everyone else, the potlatch was, as Vankoughnet summed up for cabinet, a "worse than useless custom."[20]

This near unanimity of opinion deserves emphasis. Sproat, Powell, Blenkinsop and Lomas were knowledgeable observers. All were long-term residents in the province: Sproat intermittently, Powell and Lomas continuously since the 1860s, Blenkinsop since the 1840s. All had expertise in Indian relations: Powell since his 1872 appointment, Blenkinsop from his long Hudson's Bay Company service, Lomas as a catechist and settler in the Cowichan valley, Sproat as the reserve commissioner and perceptive author of *Scenes and Studies of Savage Life*, an impressive monograph on the Nootka. To this experienced and knowledgeable group can be added George M. Dawson, a geologist and ethnologist, perhaps the most outstanding Canadian scientist of his generation. Dawson, who had made British Columbia his field, wrote a memorandum in 1885, apparently for his own use, judging the Kwakiutl potlatch as "pernicious" because every member of the tribe was drawn into the system. Wives would even rob husbands to support a blood relative in amassing blankets preparatory to a struggle for social preeminence. The great gatherings led "not only to waste of property & time but to all sorts of trouble," with "all becoming miserly & saving but to no good result."[21]

These judgements were correct within their own assumptions and frames of reference. Those concerned with the welfare of the Indians of British Columbia sought their uplift and their reform. They wanted to alter the lives of native people into a pattern both acceptable to and within the mores of western society. The potlatch was seen as a hindrance to the health and prosperity of the native population. If the Indians did not recognize the harm they were causing themselves, the thinking went, they needed to be helped, even by the full thrust of criminalization, towards ends that were for their own benefit.

While the late-twentieth-century skeptic might discount the views of Christian missionaries such as Bryant, Donckele, Crosby and Green, it is more difficult to do the same with the opinions of men like Sproat, Dawson, Blenkinsop, Powell and Lomas. They were

neither stupid nor badly informed. They possessed, like the missionaries, a first-hand knowledge of the lives of British Columbia coastal
Indians that is irretrievable today. Their judgements were based on
close observation and experience and upon a strong desire to advance the condition of the Indians by rectifying social evils patent to
their European views. This unanimity, this overwhelming corrobo-
ration of contemporary witnesses, forces one to pause before assuming our judgement superior to theirs.

While Guillod reported that the potlatch was becoming increasingly
harmless on the west coast and similar reports were received of a decline in the Fraser Valley, Ottawa heard largely of the incorrigibility
of other Indians and of an increase in potlatching and offensive
dances. Attempts to restrict the ceremony had been fruitless except
in places like William Duncan's Metlakatla and Thomas Crosby's
Fort Simpson villages, where rigorous mission methods had brought
far-reaching reform. The younger men seemed willing, even eager,
to abandon the practice, but the influence of chiefs and old men was
too strongly entrenched. Native opponents, wrote Lomas, did not
have the moral courage to stand up for their beliefs in the clear light
of day; unable to withstand the taunts and jeers of their elders, they
buckled into conformity.[22]

The proclamation and the law against the potlatch were adopted
on the basis of such indictments of the system. To agents, missionaries, government and Parliament, it stood in the way of Indian economic progress, contributed to the drastic decline in native population, prevented regular schooling of Indian children and fostered
prostitution. The simultaneous ban of the tamananawas dance was
motivated by a basic moral repugnance towards the cannibalistic
and dog-eating features of some winter ceremonials.

There were cavils. As discussed earlier, Edward Blake and three
senators were concerned with Indian reactions to the law and the
possibly catastrophic results of rigorous enforcement in an area
where government authority rested as much upon the power of gun-
boats as with loyalty to Her Majesty. Among the senators who
thought matters should be left to the moral suasion of missionaries,
however, only Senator Macdonald knew the local situation. And
even he, in holding up William Duncan as the only missionary who
had succeeded (and some might doubt if Duncan's instrument was

entirely suasion), was transparently riding a personal hobbyhorse as a partisan of the controversial lay missionary who had divided church and public opinion by his disregard of any authority or view other than his own.

To the government, the case against the potlatch and winter dances was compelling. No responsible policymaker could have ignored the problems these customs raised and none could deny the virtually unanimous condemnation by those closest to the situation and most concerned with the welfare of the Indians. None could spurn the advice of experienced government and church officials who judged that only legislative sanction would succeed where persuasion had proven powerless. The aim of the potlatch legislation was, moreover, within the framework and assumptions of Canadian social and Indian policy.

Since the 1830s, Canadian Indian policy had been built (however imperfectly) on the twin pillars of protection and advancement. Indians were placed on reserves, largely to free their land for settlement, but also to protect them from the rapacity and evils of white society and to teach them to abandon their old ways for those of the ascendant culture. The Indian question would end when every Canadian Indian was absorbed, by education and intermarriage, into the general population. Amalgamation—the disappearance of Indians as a distinguishable subgroup of Canadians—was the goal. The policy was professedly paternalistic. Native people were wards of the government, to be put out of harm's way and encouraged, through example and education, eventually to advance from their "primitive" level to that of the whites who surrounded them. Ancient encumbrances that hindered upward progress, such as the potlatch, needed to be discouraged, even outlawed. This civilizing policy would later earn condemnation as "enforced acculturation," even "cultural genocide," but it did aim at admitting the native to full Canadian citizenship.

We are dealing here, of course, with Canadian policy and European concepts of industriousness, education, capital formation and progress. We are dealing, too, with European definitions of the repugnant. Of the latter, little need be said. Few readers, native or white, will not feel a similar revulsion at the biting of arms and bodies by hamatsa initiates, at the tearing apart of human corpses or of living dogs with the teeth. Like laws regulating slavery, prostitution, bigamy, child marriage, abortion, infanticide or even pugilism, such impositions of societal values upon minorities is common and defensible, though not without ambiguities. Ceremonial dog-eating and cannibalism were made criminal offences in 1885; were they practiced today, they would probably again be subject to criminal prosecution.

The potlatch law fits into a different category. It was passed as reform legislation, intended to promote the health and the economic and social progress of British Columbia's Indians. In this respect it falls within the western liberal, philanthropic, reform tradition. In many ways its supporters represented all that was best and most noble in Euro-Canadian society. The law was in the tradition of imperial reform—of William Wilberforce and Exeter Hall, of the Aboriginal Protection Society, of the abolition of slavery and the slave trade, and of the suppression of suttee in British India. That the proponents of the law prohibiting the potlatch and the tamananawas dance suffered from all the failings of this philanthropic and reform tradition should not blind their descendants to the fact that they also shared its virtues. "To an extent that is seldom recognized," John Webster Grant comments, "the assault on Indian culture bemoaned by social activists today was led by social activists of an earlier era."[23]

3

"The Law Is as Weak as a Baby"

THE INDICTMENT OF the potlatch was compelling within the assumptions of Euro-Canadian government and society, but British Columbia's Indians, who did not share such assumptions, remained unpersuaded. The great majority of the coastal Indians, while often willing to rid their ceremonies of features objectionable to Europeans, wanted to continue their customary system and could see little reason not to do so. They sought to avoid conflict with the law, to bend its interpretation and to temper its enforcement, even to seek its repeal. If none of these were successful, however, many were prepared, certainly with a sense of their own strength and the government's limitations, to defy it.

Indian dissatisfaction with the government's attitude, even resistance to it, was evident long before the actual ban. The Indian affairs circulars of 1879, made in response to Sproat's letter, had served notice that the potlatch was to be "discountenanced," and Powell and some of his agents had acted as if the policy were law. In the Kwawkewlth agency, George Blenkinsop reported "a most determined opposition" to the policy, principally from elderly chiefs. He noted "a general tone of despondency" at the threat of "being obliged to give up this old custom." Among the Cowichan, Lomas's efforts to introduce band council bylaws against the potlatch failed. His councillors refused the proposal and he could identify only a handful in his agency who were willing to give up the ceremony.[1] More tellingly, Bella Bella chiefs, fearing that the 1881 census was a guise for the government to interfere with dancing and giving away

property, refused missionary C. M. Tate permission to enumerate
their villages.[2]

Everywhere along the coast the agents' opinion seemed the same:
the Nootka would have to be educated before they would see the
folly of the potlatch; the Kwakiutl doubted the wisdom of doing
away with it; the Cowichan said it would be wrong for the government to prevent it.[3] The most complete statement of an Indian viewpoint prior to the law was transmitted by the sympathetic West
Coast agent Harry Guillod. After hearing the government's position
and the meaning of the new proclamation, the Nootka replied:

> It is very hard to try and stop us; the White man gives feasts to his
> friends and goes to theatres; we have only our "potlatchs" and
> dances for amusement; we work for our money and like to spend it
> as we please, in gathering our friends together and giving them food
> to eat, and when we give blankets or money, we dance and sing and
> all are good friends together; now whenever we travel we find
> friends; the "potlatch" does that.[4]

Once the law was on the books and its enforcement became immi-
nent, native opinion crystallized. The native response to the ban is
harder to analyze, though, since it was usually filtered through missionaries, agents and officials.

Indian support for the potlatch was most often expressed as a desire to maintain an important tradition. The ceremony, wrote the
Nass River Indians, "has been a custom prevalent among our people
for many generations." The Cowichan considered it "our oldest
custom," and Indians on the northern coast honoured it as "the oldest and best of our festivals." A Hudson's Bay Company official regarded Indian persistence in the potlatch as a mark of tenacious de-
votion to the religion of their forefathers.[5]

Native people also cherished the potlatch as an institution that
sustained other social needs and traditions. Like a fair, the gatherings provided an opportunity for Indians to exchange handicrafts
and other products. More importantly, they allowed an enlarged
network for arranging marriages according to custom and provided
a forum where matters affecting property, rank and precedence
could be settled. To West Coast agent Guillod, the potlatch was

both "a bond of union" and "a bond of amity" between neighbour-ing bands.[6]

A particular concern, and certainly an expression of native values, was the need to avoid disgrace by redeeming debts in public. "How can I pay my debts unless they are all here to witness?" asked a Cowichan shaman. "It cannot be wrong to pay what we owe," said the chief of the Comeaken, "& this is the only way to do it, we are not like White people, and it is one of our laws that these payments shall be done in public." Chief Ken-a-wult of Qaumichan was frank: "I shall be shamed by all Indians if I do not pay what I owe in the old manner, that is in the presence of all others." Public giving-away conformed, wrote a Skeena magistrate, "to the publicity of all their tribal affairs."[7]

Customary and honourable, the potlatch was also defended as a harmless institution. It was an "innocent pastime of a nature similar to that indulged in by their white brothers." It did no more injury than European customs, which also made presents "often for some past, or the expectation of some future favor." For those without theatres and unable to read, the potlatch provided their only diver-sion. It was important as a "winter amusement," "the only amuse-ment left them." C. W. D. Clifford, the Hudson's Bay Company manager on the Upper Skeena, wrote that "unless the Dominion Government expect the Indians to suck their paws like bears all winter I do not see well, how they can get along without their feasts."[8]

Indeed, the potlatch was "an assurance or benefit society" that aided the old, crippled and destitute. It repaid the elderly for all they had provided in their more productive years. Were it stopped, many would not have enough to live on. Clifford likened the pot-latch to a primitive system of banking: "Old people and infirm are fed and clothed during the long winter months, who otherwise would starve."[9]

Indians insisted that they had already abandoned many of their ancestral ways, but should be permitted to continue the oldest and best of their traditions. "We have given up fighting with each other," wrote the Cowichan chiefs. "We have given up stealing, and many other old habits, but we want to be allowed to continue the 'Potlach' and the Dance."[10] Maquinna, displaying his mask and paraphernalia, told how the Nootka had given up all their bad customs, such as fighting, slavery, stealing and tribal feuds, at the request of white chiefs,

> but it was very hard to ask them to give up a custom which was inter-mixed with all their thoughts and feelings, an incentive to industry, a great help to the white trade in Victoria, which encouraged friendly relations with other tribes, being an occasion for amusement and re-joicing, and had been handed down to them by their ancestors.[11]

The Kispiox were willing to send their children to school, to stop eating dogs and to do everything else the government asked, "but to give up the Potlach they could not." The Talio Bella Coola and the Oweekano, arguing that they had already renounced all their other ancient customs, asked permission to continue what they called the "modern potlach," a ceremony that omitted the "wild heathen dances of old" and retained only "such dancing as conduces to their amusement."[12]

The Indians' most earnest appeal was to fairness. The law was simply unjust. The ceremonies now were always peaceable, orderly and free from lawlessness. They could not see why their social gath-erings should be stopped when they did not in any other way break the law. Did not the whites celebrate Christmas, give feasts, dance and distribute presents? The potlatch was a social custom like Christmas, only on a larger scale. "We believe," wrote a group of Nass River chiefs, "that it is our right just as much as it is the right of our white brethren to make presents to each other."[13]

This appeal was part of an insistent desire to live within the law and a regret at being forced outside it by a statute they could neither understand nor respect. "We are trying to live in peace," wrote the Mamalillikulla Kwakiutl, "and want to be friendly to all." On the Nass River, Indians were willing to keep the law of "our Great and Good Mother Queen Victoria whom we all love," but felt "very keenly this interference." The Cowichan asked for the law's repeal, "that we may not be breaking it when we follow customs that are dear to us."[14]

Some Indians promised to accept the law if the government pro-vided an alternative. A Nanaimo chief asked if there would be "any other means of diversion" provided for his people. Sukwete, a

Kwakiutl chief, agreed to give up the potlatch if the government bought his coppers; otherwise "he would have to lose many hundred blankets and he could not be expected to do that." Three villages of Nass River Indians felt five thousand dollars would be sufficient to settle their claims. On the Upper Skeena, however, the Gitksan disdained such agreements and asked what the government proposed to substitute for their ancient and popular institution.[15]

The conclusion of some was that the new law was a tragic mistake. "The White Chief does not understand our ways," said Cehawitawet of Comeaken, and the Nass River chiefs complained that "the aim and object of the Potlach is apparently misunderstood by the White people who made the laws."[16]

Some natives, it is true, dissented from these views. An 1879 gathering of Interior Salish at Lytton adopted bylaws prohibiting the potlatch, but only after a long and inconclusive debate led them to allow Sproat a deciding opinion. Dissent came largely from the converted. On the Nass, Christian Indians asked Powell to forbid the custom among the heathen outside their villages[17] and the 1883 petition from the same area called for the potlatch's legal abolition. The Christian Indians, however, represented only a minority; the great majority wished to continue their customary potlatch system.

Officials blamed Indian resistance on those who had debts outstanding or were owed a potlatch, and on old men who clung to tradition. "Many of the old Chiefs," declared Powell, "being wedded to old and ignorant customs, discourage the ambition to progress which prevails among the young men of the band." Such resistance, noted Lomas, was encouraged by self-interested storekeepers and whites who saw the potlatch as a harmless, amusing fair where they could buy Indian curios. The authorities placed their greatest hope in the younger Indians, who were thought willing to abandon the custom and even support its abolishment. A great many Indians, Lomas felt, cared nothing about the potlatch itself, but were simply attracted by the excitement of large gatherings. Victoria was certain that, with the passing of the old people, the custom would die.[18]

Lomas's Cowichan agency was a slightly special case. Many chiefs, reported the agent in 1882, owed blankets and other property to distant tribes, but had promised to return only what they owed and not to lend any more. There would be one or two large potlatches hosted by these debtors, "given as a kind of final flash," before the custom died out. By Christmas 1884, with the law's implementation only days away, Lomas noted that many Cowichan were "very discontented." Almost all had outstanding potlatch debts, and chiefs, otherwise anxious to end the potlatch, wanted only to return what they or their band owed. Under the circumstances, he advised that enforcement of the new act be delayed or that each band be "allowed by special license to hold one returning 'Potlach' with the distinct understanding that no additional property shall be lent."[19]

Superintendent Powell was unconvinced. "There will," he wrote Ottawa, "always be the same objection which is urged by Mr. Lomas." On the other hand, one or two potlatches among the Cowichans might pass without notice on the understanding that they would be the last. But Ottawa would have none of it. The department could not sanction what the law prohibited.[20]

By now, however, Lomas's problems were mounting. The law had created an "unsatisfactory feeling" among the Cowichan that he thought "ought to be remedied without delay." The situation was volatile, and he appealed for help. It would be utterly impossible, he told Powell, to imprison the three or four hundred Indians who would take part and to arrest one "would only stir up the rest to resist."[21] Unable to quell Indian discontent and in a poor position to enforce the law if the Indians defied it, he requested that Powell appear personally at Comeaken to pour oil on troubled Cowichan waters.

The focus of discontent was Lohah (or Lohar), chief of the Comeaken. He had been cooperative if a little errant, for years supportive of Lomas and of great assistance to him in settling disputes. He was one of those who had promised to host a final potlatch to repay his debts but to lend no more. The illness of his son, however, had prevented his "final flash" before the law's implementation. Now, in early 1885, he wanted to settle both his own debts and those of his dead son. "My son Benoir before he died begged me to return all property that he owed, as well as my own debts," Lohah implored in a petition. "If I do not do it my heart will always cry. I will die of grief." This would be his last potlatch, but he owed over 800 blankets and nearly as many dollars in other property. If he was not allowed to hold the gathering, the disgrace would be greater than he could bear. "I should be sneered at by every Indian," said Lohah, adding that he had always supported Powell and the government, often against the whole of the Cowichan bands, and "now I am likely to be the first to be punished [by the law]."

His plea was supported by those of Benoir's widow and others, most significantly a younger son.

> My father Lohah has always helped White men against the old or bad Indians, and if Dr. Powell does not help him now he will always be laughed at. When he came back Monday from seeing Dr. Powell, the other Chiefs laughed at him, saying he was like a baby or a slave, doing always as his White masters said, and they never did anything for him.

Lomas and Powell were caught in the midst of a traditional status battle, with their most important Cowichan allies appealing for exception and support. "Now if Dr. Powell will try to get permission for him to hold his return potlach," the son wrote, "Lohah will be lifted up above the others, and they will see that the Doctor thinks well of his conduct."[22]

The good grace of the petition did not mask the fact that Lohah and his friends intended to hold a potlatch regardless of the law. The Indians' hostility and determination, unmatched by any police support at Powell's command, decided the issue. Against a back ground of Metis, Cree and Assiniboine discontent on the prairies and the armed conflict of the Northwest Rebellion in late March and early April, Powell quickly realized that enforcement would be both unwise and futile. His resolve collapsed. He capitulated.

The government had no wish to act unjustly, Powell told the assembled Cowichan, or to promote injustices among them. So long as the meeting was merely to return gifts, there would be no interference. "I explained," he told Ottawa, "that a Potlach meant the donation of property in order to get back the original and interest, and that an assemblage such as they now desired did not constitute a Potlach as referred to in the Act." Having thus defined a potlatch as not a potlatch, he put an even better face upon his obvious retreat. Powell boldly assured his superiors that, by clearly stating that further loans would be unrecoverable under the new law, his visit had "pretty well stamped out the continuance of the Potlach system in the District."[23]

That was bravado. Powell knew he had backed down, and he defended his actions at some length to Ottawa. "It is impossible," he continued, "to effect much in the way of rapid reform." The period between passage and implementation of the law, he argued, had been far too short; Indians required up to five years to accumulate enough property to repay their potlatch obligations. Moreover, he was totally without influence on the north coast and, as long as the Indian Act was not enforced everywhere, great care should be taken with a law that the majority of Indians opposed. White traders vigorously objected to a law that might lessen their sales to potlatchers; their influence meant that the law did not have the sympathy of the provincial government. His own appropriations were inadequate to maintain Indian constables. With the provincial government unwilling to provide assistance and the federal government unwilling to provide funds, Powell had "no means of properly enforcing the Indian Act."

Powell concluded his litany of difficulties with a frustrated confession of "the helplessness one experiences in attempting with the means at command, to enforce any law such as that prohibiting the Potlach." Fortunately, the Indians had shown themselves "amiable to moral suasion" and the excitement had been quieted. He had every reason to believe that a majority would conform in time. The system, he wrote in his annual report, "will cure itself." Ottawa accepted Powell's rationale: his decision appeared justifiable under the circumstances.[24]

In the first test of the law, the Indians had won. The Cowichans had threatened to defy the act and Powell, fearing that defiance, had pursued a "conciliatory course"[25] by defining their potlatch as within the law, though ruling recurrences as illegal. He introduced his interpretation as policy when he circulated new instructions to agents. They accepted his orders without comment, but the circular provoked the wrath of Rev. A. E. Green, a Methodist missionary toiling among the Nass River Nishga.

Green supported the ban against the "nefarious" potlatch and believed the majority of Indians had received the new law kindly and would abide by it. Powell's post-Comeaken circular, however, sanctioned open violation and created "a terrible state of affairs." By announcing that the act was not intended to restrict the repayment of debts, Powell totally undermined the law's intent. The return of previous presents, Green wrote, "is really the vital point of the potlach, for, as at each time they meet, they give presents, this potlaching must go on for ever." The Indians were quite right when they stated that they had the superintendent's authority for their actions.[26]

Green was asserting what Powell already knew. The point, however, as Powell made clear, was the discrepancy between the government's desire to impose the law and the Indians' resistance to it. A large majority of Indians regarded the law "as a great innovation upon their liberty." Powell, undoubtedly conscious of Louis Riel and the Indians in the territories, felt it important "not to deal too suddenly or harshly in compelling immediate obedience." Sufficient time should be allowed for the repayment of all debts before enforcing the law. Without some leniency, Powell was certain that the majority would defy the ban and, with "no sympathy and little assistance" from the province, he almost totally lacked any means of enforcement.[27]

Indian resistance and government powerlessness were evident not only at Comcaken. "I do not see any way to successfully enforcing the law," reported Harry Guillod from Ucluelet. With few exceptions, "all are in favor of the potlatch, old and young." His only assistance in preserving order among the estimated 3500 Indians of his agency were the chiefs and native policemen, and the latter were subordinate to the strongly pro-potlatch chiefs. The Kwakiutl at Mamalillikulla and Fort Rupert, where R. H. Pidcock had replaced the intemperate Blenkinsop as agent, were "very defiant in the matter." The Fort Ruperts told Pidcock that they would hear nothing he had to say on the subject, and potlatches were being openly prepared at Alert Bay and Mamalillikulla. Pidcock wanted to enforce the law, "the only effective way of ending speedily this most demoralizing practice," but "the determination with which they cling to the custom, makes me think the opposition at first will be very strong." With a jail, a white constable and local assistance, Pidcock felt he "might be able to carry out the law," but he would not risk failure.[28]

Further north the situation was no different. Charles Todd, the agent in the newly created Northwest Coast agency, discovered that the great majority of the tribes were determined "to stick to what they term 'the oldest and best of their festivals.'" A minority, led by missionaries, clamoured for enforcement but, with most Indians in favour of the practice, it was "almost useless to attempt to abolish it by law." He possessed insufficient force to do so against the will of the people, most of whom were otherwise good and law-abiding.[29]

According to Franz Boas, a young anthropologist who visited British Columbia Indians several times in the 1880s, the law could not be enforced "without causing general discontent." Enforcement, moreover, was beyond the government's ability. Indian settlements were so numerous and the agencies so large that "there is nobody to prevent the Indians doing whatsoever they like." Boas illustrated his point with the example of Lomena'kulu, or "Cheap," a Xumtaspi Kwakiutl whom Pidcock had appointed a constable and given a uniform and flag. "It was made his special duty to prevent dances and feasts," wrote Boas, "and since that time he dances in his uniform and with the flag."[30]

The law, once so urged upon Ottawa by officials on the coast, went without application. The overwhelming opposition of the Island Salish, the Nootka, the Kwakiutl and the Nishga, paired with the utter inability of the Department of Indian Affairs to enforce its own proscriptions, meant that the ban could not be enforced. The department's feebleness came in part from lack of local police support, a symptom of the recurring disagreement between provincial and dominion governments over most aspects of Indian administration in British Columbia.

The provincial government, while accepting its responsibility to enforce federal criminal law, maintained that the Indian Act was solely a federal responsibility. Victoria went so far as to refuse Indian agents the use of its jails or its police to render them any assistance.[31] The federal government, having no police force of its own, was totally dependent upon the province for enforcement of the Indian Act. If the province refused to cooperate, the department had no means of imposing its will.

With no understanding between dominion and local authorities governing the preservation of peace in Indian districts, the enforcement of any section of the Indian Act, not just the potlatch amendment, became impossible. Powell might appeal to the provincial secretary for "mutual cooperation," but to no avail. Federal Indian laws, he complained, "are virtually inoperative and the Agents are helpless to carry out their provisions." His authority and that of his agents was reduced to moral suasion, confessedly "of little account among Indians with no exhibition of power to sustain it."[32]

The impasse was broken only in 1888 when Ottawa and Victoria agreed that the province would administer the enforcement of the Indian Act in return for being allowed to keep the money from fines collected under the act's liquor clauses.[33] With police support now available, the department lost no time in urging the provincial government to "cause measures to be taken to put in operation the law for the repression of the 'Potlach.' "[34]

The first arrest under the potlatch amendment occurred almost a year later (and almost four years after the law's implementation), ironically without provincial assistance. On 1 August 1889, Agent Pidcock arrested Hamasak (or Ha-mer-ceeluc) of Mamalillikulla for twice calling various Indian tribes to a potlatch. He was arrested in his village at night by Pidcock and two native constables. There were protests and a minor scuffle, but no serious resistance. Hamasak was brought before Pidcock, who also acted as justice of the peace. Hearing the charge read to him through an interpreter, Hamasak pleaded guilty and was sentenced to the maximum penalty of six months' imprisonment. Here, however, confusion ensued, for, at the same time, Pidcock (or perhaps the superintendent's office) committed the defendant for trial in Victoria.

On 17 August, Hamasak's friends applied for habeas corpus. The presiding judge, Chief Justice Sir Matthew Begbie, granted it on the grounds that, having already been convicted in Alert Bay, the man could not be tried again. Much more seriously, Sir Matthew went on to demonstrate the legal difficulties of the 1885 amendment.

Begbie was an established British Columbian, having arrived in Victoria in 1858 as the colony's sole judge. He had travelled the coast and interior and knew a great deal about the Indians. He wondered now if the nature of the charge had been explained to Hamasak. "From all I know of the gatherings," he said, "I think it would be very hard to explain." Different people had different notions of what "potlatch" signified; under the same name, very different practices and objects might be intended. If Parliament "desired to create an offence previously unknown to the law there ought to be some definition of it in the Statute." It would be an abuse of justice, Begbie judged, to take advantage of a guilty plea from "an ignorant Indian who speaks no word of English and allege that he has pleaded guilty to an offence, the facts constituting which we should ourselves be unable to set forth."

The same applied to the tamananawas dance prohibition. It was, Begbie said, "utterly unknown here," and an Indian might plead guilty to such a performance after having taken part in some quite innocent dance which Parliament never intended to ban. Unless a defendant knew what actions were illegal, how could he say whether or not he had committed them? "I think," the justice concluded, "these considerations show that there would be some difficulty in convicting at all under the Statute."[35]

Pidcock was appalled, the department concerned. To the Kwaw-kewlth agent, the release of Hamasak was "very unfortunate." The arrest had "caused a marked improvement" in the behaviour of the Kwakiutl. In Ottawa, the department immediately asked the deputy minister of justice if Begbie's judgement could be reversed on appeal. His reply scuttled any hope: no provision existed for an appeal by the prosecution. Moreover, if Begbie's statements about the ambiguity of the word "potlatch" were well founded, "it would be difficult, and probably impossible, to sustain a conviction under this provision of the Statute at all."[36]

In the face of Begbie's shattering *obiter dictum,* the potlatch law was, as Pidcock later acknowledged, "a dead letter." "To attempt what the law will not support," Lomas frankly told his superintendent in Victoria, "can only create a feeling amongst the Indians antagonistic not only to their Agent but to the Indian Department generally." Ottawa realized this as much as the local agents. Under the circumstances, Vankoughnet dodged. Responsibility for enforcement rested with the local government and not with the Indian agents. "It would not appear," he wrote, "to be absolutely incumbent upon the Indian Agent to take any measures to prevent the celebration of the potlach festivals"; unless there were formal complaints, an agent "need not take steps in the matter."[37]

The provincial government, told of its responsibility, fell back to its old position. The federal Parliament had passed the law; it should prosecute violations. Federal opinion continued to be that the constitutional duty rested with the province but, should the province fail, it was up to the federal department to determine whether or not it should incur the expense of enforcement or "allow the law to become a dead letter." The result was renewed instructions that agents interfere only after consultation with local authorities and a similar request to the province that they consult with Indian agents.[38]

Federal policy settled into this retreat. Rather than amend the law to clarify its ambiguities or repeal it altogether, the department decided to leave the defective statute in place. It could, of course, redraft the law to make it judicially enforceable, but to what end? The province was clearly unwilling to lend its assistance and the reports and advice from British Columbia pointed to the wisdom of avoiding strict enforcement.

One such report came from Captain Napoleon Fitzstubbs, stipendiary magistrate at Hazelton on the Skeena. In a letter sent to the provincial attorney general and copied to federal Indian authorities, Fitzstubbs politely but firmly said that any enforcement of the potlatch law on the Upper Skeena would require "much prudence" in order "to avert serious difficulties in the way of preserving law and order." The potlatch was an ancient and highly valued institution that would be very difficult to suppress by force. Indeed, any attempt to enforce the law in too summary a fashion might provoke general disobedience. His letter contained a supporting memorandum from C. W. D. Clifford of the Hudson's Bay Company that was less oblique: "Any attempt to forcible [*sic*] put down potlaching here," the trader wrote, "will prove disastrous to the tranquility now prevailing."[39]

Fitzstubbs's advice fell into a pattern acceptable to Arthur W. Vowell, the new superintendent in Victoria. Powell, suffering from ill health which neither English specialists nor a European holiday could relieve, was superannuated in 1889 from the post he had held since 1872.[40] His successor brought few immediate changes to Indian administration in British Columbia, least of all on the potlatch and tamananawas issues. As a relative newcomer to Indian affairs (though a long-time provincial official), Vowell sought counsel on the matter from his agents in the field. All, except Pidcock among the Kwakiutl, advised a moderate course. Guillod continued to insist that the West Coast dances were not objectionable and denied that the tamananawas was practised among the Nootka. In the Northwest Coast agency, Todd felt that enforcement would be "folly" since the Indians would surely resist law officers or ignore any court summons. Pidcock, on the other hand, reiterated his wish to stop the Kwakiutl potlatch. "It is quite certain," he wrote, "that so long as this demoralizing custom prevails, little or nothing can be done for the good of these Indians." Lomas, who in 1884 had been the most vocal and influential of advocates for a law, had tempered his views since the crisis at Comeaken. Except for the time that was wasted, he wrote, there was little he now found objectionable about the potlatch. Indians met friends and relatives they otherwise never saw, debts were paid, articles were bartered and deceased friends were mourned. Dances among the Cowichan were "mainly given for the amusement of the guest" and the tamananawas scarcely existed.[41]

Vowell's recommendation to Ottawa reflected the majority view of his agents. In two 1895 letters sent just as the government was considering an amendment that would meet Begbie's objections of six years earlier, he wrote that "special legislation would appear to be, at this stage, unnecessary." Most striking, however, was the extent to which Vowell's views reflected the native viewpoint. The customary potlatch had been practised for generations. The old people "would sooner die than renounce a custom so ingrained in their natures from their infancy, and handed down from generation to generation." Such instincts were natural and the custom would surely pass with these old people. Its nature was essentially friendly, "something the same as our Christmas or holiday gatherings, only on a larger scale." He characterized the celebrations as the only relaxation in a life of frequent privation, continuous toil and constant exposure to the elements. During these "happy occasions" troubles were forgotten "and all was feasting, dancing, and good-natured merriment." Of course, the absences from their villages meant that the natives paid little attention to their gardens and other interests, but to no lesser extent than those who attended the large native retreats conducted by Catholic missionaries in the interior. Such absences could be viewed as outrageous or praiseworthy depending upon one's viewpoint.[42]

By 1895, then, the law was not only "a dead letter," but was judged by most local officials as virtually unnecessary, perhaps even unjust. Within four months of its implementation, the Cowichan Indians had forced its practical abandonment. The provincial government continually refused to support its enforcement, and most agents judged such enforcement as unwise and impossible. The British Columbia superintendent saw the potlatch as a natural and friendly amusement, defending it in terms few Indians could express better.

The Indians had triumphed. Aided by the judgement of Justice Begbie, by the intransigence of the provincial government and, perhaps, by storekeepers who profited from the existing situation, they had thwarted the best intentions of federal Indian policy.

British Columbia's Indians had strong advantages. They were numerous—in most areas of the province, more numerous than Europeans. The scattered settlers in their midst prized the loyalty and peacefulness of their native neighbours and did not want the unnecessary provocation the potlatch law might bring. The provincial government, in addition to its usual truculence towards its federal counterpart in Indian matters, shared this view.

The position was clear. Even after the government amended the law to meet Begbie's objections, Ottawa realized that its "ability to retain the law must depend on the exercise of discretion with regard to its enforcement." It feared that some, especially missionaries, might "from excellent motives" be tempted to act indiscreetly. The Kitwanga Indians were probably right: the potlatch law, they had told Fitzstubbs in 1890, "was as weak as a baby."[13]

■ Lohah (*top left*), chief of the Comeaken and "paramount chief" of the Cowichan, wearing a medal presented by Governor General Lord Lansdowne for assisting in quelling disquiet caused by reserve surveys. Lohah insisted in 1885 on holding a potlatch to redeem his and his dead son's debts. The Cowichan agent, W. H. Lomas (*top right*), whose reports had helped secure passage of the law against the potlatch, was unable to persuade Lohah and the Cowichan to obey the new law. The British Columbia superintendent of Indian affairs, I. W. Powell (*left*), called to Comeaken by a frightened Lomas, backed down before the three hundred defiant Cowichan and allowed Lohah's potlatch. Redeeming debts was not really illegal, he said, understanding that this would be Lohah's last potlatch.

Photo credits: *Royal British Columbia Museum* (RBCM), *No. 5935; British Columbia Archives and Records Service* (BCARS), *No. 56423;* BCARS, *No. 6626*

■ Kwawkewlth agent R. H. Pidcock (*top left*) arrested a Kwakiutl chief in 1889 for potlatching. Chief Justice Sir Matthew Begbie (*top right*), pictured here in 1875 wearing his royal court uniform, dismissed the case on a technicality, but judged that the potlatch law was so drafted that convictions would be impossible. Only in 1895 was it redrafted. A. W. Vowell (*left*), B. C. superintendent of Indian affairs between 1889 and 1910, maintained a policy of discreet tolerance of the potlatch, insisting that it had become largely harmless and was gradually dying out.

Photo credits: BCARS, *No. 45456;* BCARS, *No. 51325;* BCARS, *No. 7453*

NOTICE.

We, the undersigned, being chiefs and others of Kispiox, wish
it to be known:

1.   That we desire that there should be no more potlaches
held in this village of Kispiox.

2.   That we want no more old fashioned feasts, but if
any feasts are held, then we desire them to be set out with
clean tables and everything made up-to-date.

3.   We desire that there be no calling of names if any
money is dispersed at a feast given in memory of a dead chief
or any other person.

4.   We want all dancing to be abolished at our feasts.

5.   We desire that there should be no more dressing up
in old heathen and old fashioned costume, or any painting of
the face.

■ Dances, such as this 1895 Sxwayxwey ceremony (*top*) at the Songhees Reserve under Victoria's Johnston Street railway bridge, and potlatches continued openly under Vowell's superintendency. Many Christian Indians, however, opposed the potlatch and a few banned it from their villages. A group of Kispiox, Gitksan of the
upper Skeena River, published this ban of their own about 1908 (*bottom*).

Photo credits: RBCM, *No. 6492-B;* BCARS, *C. M. Tate Papers*

4

"The Very Best Discretion"

IN JULY 1895, as part of a package of eight amendments to the Indian Act, Parliament rewrote the antipotlatch and dance law to meet Justice Begbie's objections in the Hamasak case of six years earlier. Any person, stated the new Section 114, who celebrated or assisted or encouraged another to celebrate "any Indian festival, dance or other ceremony of which the giving away or paying or giving back of money, goods or articles of any sort forms a part, or is a feature, whether such a gift of money, goods or articles takes place before, at, or after the celebration of the same" was guilty of an indictable offence. Similarly guilty was anyone engaging or assisting in "a celebration of which the wounding or mutilation of the dead or living body of any human being or animal forms a part or is a feature." The penalty, two to six months imprisonment, remained unchanged.

The revised wording seems to have been made by departmental headquarters. While Ottawa sought from Vowell information about the distinction between the ordinary potlatch and the tamananawas, it ignored his view that "special legislation would appear to be, at this stage, unnecessary."[1] In fact, the impetus behind the new drafting was not the potlatch in British Columbia so much as the sun and thirst dances of the Indians on the Canadian prairies.[2] The new wording could apply to both areas.

Vowell accepted the tightened wording and was even willing to act upon it, yet he continued to walk his narrow path. The revised clause was sustainable in court, but he remained circumspect. In a circular dated 4 September 1895 he informed the local Indian agents of the new amendment and cautioned them that "great care should be observed in inforcing [sic] the law." He did not consider that social gatherings where Indians met "for a friendly and harmless interchange" or occasions when they distributed "food and clothing etc." were meant to be prohibited and advised that in such cases the law "should not be too strictly applied."[3]

He was willing to prosecute, however, when things went too far and where events could be controlled. In January 1896 he accepted Fraser River agent Frank Devlin's suggestion that action be taken against Bill Uslick, a Stalo Salish at Tzeachten Reserve near Chilliwack. Uslick was a "bad Indian," one who still wished "to keep up the old habits and customs and would like to be a leader among the Indians of the neighbourhood." Uslick's potlatch, Devlin reported, had left the man practically destitute. Uslick had sold his cattle, horses and oxen and then borrowed to the full extent of his credit in order to give away, over three days, "everything he had in the world except his wife, and a few potatoes, which nobody wanted." At Vowell's urging and with Ottawa's consent, Devlin arrested the offender and on 1 February, sitting with S. Mellard, J.P., tried and sentenced Uslick to two months' imprisonment. There were no incidents, though almost all the Indians in the district felt that Uslick should not have been interfered with. According to a newspaper report, "the most threatening individuals" were subdued by Devlin's threat to make an example of them.

The Uslick case was exceptional. The man had given away all he had, some of which was not his, and had "nothing left to pay his debts."[4] Vowell sanctioned no other prosecutions; Uslick's was part of a calculated policy of discretion applied to a settled area where the agent could exercise authority. The remote northern coast was different. There the department possessed little authority and its approach to enforcement of the law led to confusion and difficulty.

The Nass and Skeena rivers were home to the Nishga and Gitksan. Located in the mountain valleys, their villages were remote from major settlements and thinly populated with Euro-Canadians. The Skeena was navigable only to Hazelton and had been a route for gold miners to the Omenica gold fields in the 1880s, but since then had been settled by only a few whites. The neighbouring Nass was beyond even the mining frontier. Unnavigable except by canoe, it remained in the 1890s home only to the Nishga and their missionaries.

Indian affairs in the north were already difficult enough. The Metlakatla dispute of the early 1880s, pitting missionary William Duncan and the majority of Indian followers against their bishop and parent Church Missionary Society (CMS), had aggravated the northern natives' insistence upon aboriginal land title. Duncan's supporters refused to recognize the authority of Indian agent Joseph W. MacKay or the Indian Act. Duncan argued that his Indians were Christian and civilized and that the Indian Act was not relevant to them. Magistrate A. C. Elliot, already at Metlakatla, was given acting power as Indian agent and the rejected MacKay reposted to the Kamloops-Okanagan agency, but the discontent continued and the concern for land rights grew.[5] Federal authority over the Indians remained tenuous even after the posting of Charles Todd, a permanent Indian agent based at Metlakatla. On the Nass it was made more complicated by Anglican and Methodist rivalries and the divergent tendencies of the two churches towards land and government. The Anglican Church Missionary Society had established posts at Kincolith, Gitlakdamiks and Aiyansh in the previous two decades, the Methodists at Fort Simpson and Lakkalsap (later Greenville). The Methodists, represented by Thomas Crosby and A. E. Green, almost immediately concerned themselves with the native land question, and, having established a model village complete with its own municipal government, shied away from any intrusion of federal authority into their realm. They, like Duncan, did not want an Indian agent or the application of the Indian Act to their domain.[6]

The situation was exacerbated in 1888 when a government force, sent to pursue the "outlaw" Kitwankool Jim, met with Indian defiance and threats. Things settled down, but officials worried about the "baleful teaching" spread by native Methodists. Actuated by the land question, Indian missionary William Pierce vilified government officers who, in turn, feared that the message might "fan a race antipathy into race hatred." Methodist Indians, Anglican J. B. McCullagh charged, had been "freely indoctrinated" with the belief that the government was "an organized system of land robbery" and that all civil authority "was of the devil and should be resisted."[7] Unlike their Methodist counterparts, Anglican missionaries were unconcerned with land questions and sought to apply the weight and authority of the government and its agents.

By the 1890s the Nass valley had become "one seething mass of disaffection and discontent owing to the Potlatch,"[8] the scene of bitter contests between a zealous antipotlatch party and traditionalists intent on defending their way of life. In the winter of 1886–87, what McCullagh called "a rabble" of native Methodist antipotlatchers invaded Gitlakdamiks, the largest and most inland of the upper Nass villages, to promulgate the law among the village's unconverted Nishga. McCullagh protested their "taking upon themselves to do what they had no authority to do" and effectively chased them back to Greenville. The conflict had reached a high in February 1894 when the Methodist Chief Quksko (Matthew Nass) attempted to stop a Gitlakdamiks potlatch by rushing the host, Chief Nishyok, with a knife. McCullagh, vested with the authority of a justice of the peace, found Quksko guilty of assault, but, in view of the issue precipitating the hostilities, declared that all future potlatches would be dealt with according to the law. On the other hand, he foolishly allowed Nishyok to finish his feast, a concession that allowed the potlatchers to claim full victory.

The Nishga, "greedily swallowing the slightest excuse" (as McCullagh put it), took up the custom again with alacrity. McCullagh vainly tried to close the door but, unwilling to act alone and unable to secure assisting magistrates, his summonses were allowed to lapse. This merely aggravated the situation in which inconsistency, lack of civil authority and "Indian craft and cunning" were at the core.

The potlatchers had already been led to believe they had successfully intimidated the government into inaction because of Agent Todd's ineffectual promulgation of the law. Certainly they had frightened off James Welsh, a justice of the peace who had issued summonses to several tamananawas dancers at Gitwinkshilqu. "So confident were they by that time in their own strength and so convinced of the feebleness of the law," wrote McCullagh, "that they pursued the magistrate in a canoe some distance down the river and so successfully intimidated him that he took no further steps."

The 1895 revision of the act had led both McCullagh and the Nishga to believe that it would be enforced. Potlatchers among the Nishga became so concerned they dispatched a delegation of eight chiefs to Victoria with a petition protesting McCullagh's interferences and proclaiming their right to practise "the custom prevalent among our people for many generations." They departed from their interview with a rebuke so mild that they accepted it as licence. According to McCullagh, the delegates brought back news that they could "go on potlatching as much as they liked" and that the authorities did not intend to enforce the new law. Certainly Vowell's circular, dated five days after their meeting, gave support for a continuation of "social gatherings" with "friendly dances" and feasts. To McCullagh, not quite rude enough to accuse Vowell of softness, the delegation's "unmistakable craft and cunning" had the same effect as if their report were true. Soon, even the Christian converts at Aiyansh resumed potlatching. McCullagh quickly suppressed this lapse through his municipal council and extended it by civil prosecutions against the heathen chiefs Skaden and Nishyidiksh of neighbouring Gitlakdamiks.[9]

McCullagh's actions prompted another delegation of potlatchers to Victoria. Composed of three Nishga chiefs, two of whom had been among the previous delegation, they claimed to represent 153 chiefs and to have $15,000 at their disposal. Their eloquent statement and subsequent petition to G. E. Corbould, Member of Parliament for New Westminster, received ample coverage in the press, instigated a flurry of letters to the editor, both pro and con, and perpetuated a war of words between Nishga potlatch and antipotlatch factions.[10]

The antipotlatchers, in a series of petitions between 1896 and 1900, claimed to represent 65 to 75 per cent of the Indian people. Their appeals for enforcement had missionary backing, but their language and tenor often carried a strongly indigenous flavour. The petitioners condemned the custom as "a cruel monster" that was "injurious to our race" by its effects on the health of infants and children during the bitter winters. More pressing, however, was the desire to be unburdened by the potlatch. "We want to advance in civilization and knowledge," they proclaimed.[11] Such were the standard condemnations from missionaries and government officials, but now they were joined by a native voice.

Even more recognizably native was the outrage expressed towards the efforts of potlatchers to usurp the ranks and positions which nonpotlatchers could no longer defend. In July 1896 a petition was marked by nine Nishga chiefs who claimed "we have been robbed of our name and title both of which we are justly proud and both of which are as dear to us as the birthright of an [*sic*] noble-man." The potlatchers were viewed as part of a system of unjust cor-ruption by which "our names, fishing streams & hunting grounds are taken away from us." The "lawless" potlatchers, complained three Christians in 1898, were men of "abnormal ambition" who "expected to be great." Stanley Osterhout, a Methodist missionary at Fort Simpson, summed up this grievance when he wrote that am-bitious youths were "trying by presents and bribes to increase their own authority and often to usurp the authority and birthright of others."[12]

Two systems were at war on the northern coast. The antipot-latchers were converts, some Methodist but mainly Anglican. Hav-ing embraced Christianity and accepted federal authority, they ap-pealed to the government to complete that authority. "The principle [*sic*] objection amongst the Christianized Indians to the potlatch," judged Agent Todd in 1899, "is the fact that it is in reality the old Indian Chief 'form of Government' and they argue that it should not be tolerated by the White Man's Government, that wherever it is allowed to exist, no other government is respected or obeyed by the Indians only through fear of punishments." Todd's impressions were soon confirmed by a letter from the Nass chiefs. "We want to follow the Queen's law and the Indian Act," they wrote, "but the Potlatch law will not agree to the Queen's law."[13]

Potlatchers, assuming a licence from Victoria, pressed forward a little too hard. Luke Nelson, son of Chief Skaden of Gitlakdamiks and chief councillor at the CMS village of Kincolith, testified that the potlatchers were flooding the river with their whiskey. Indeed, the winter of 1898–99 had seen more liquor on the Nass than there had been for years. The liquor problem was a major reason for several chiefs turning against the potlatch. Early in 1899, three chiefs—Moses Oxican, Peter Ka-ya Calder and Nathaniel Lai Robinson—had moved to the mission village of Lakkalsap (now Anglican) to es-cape the "drunken festivities." The free flow of alcohol, wrote Cal-der, had made the winter dreadful. "Whisky is dangerously free on our river now and lives are in danger," complained Oxican, "be-cause of the workings of whisky and the potlatch, and one will not stop without the other." Robinson added that "whisky cannot be stopped unless the potlatch it's [*sic*] father is first destroyed."[14]

By 1899, the tide had turned strongly in favour of the antipotlatch interests. Their claim to represent the majority was accepted by Vowell, and the potlatchers were reduced to a rump who now sent their own delegation seeking governmental protection from oppression by Christian Indians. Insulted and subjected to "an onerous system of espionage" by the majority, the potlatchers were promised by Vowell that Agent Todd would protect them against "unauthorized aggression." By this time, though, Ottawa was wondering if the moment had not come for Vowell to enforce the law in the Nass district.[15]

Through the storm, Vowell kept his policy intact. He had reiterated it early in 1897, reminding the agents that "when the Indians only meet together for a friendly and harmless interchange of kindly and social relations they should not be unduly interfered with." Occasions when food and clothing were distributed among the aged and destitute, with no property destroyed or otherwise wasted, should not be considered as coming under the amendment. He urged that "the greatest discretion be observed" to guard against creating serious disturbances between officers and natives. Should it be deemed expedient to put the law in force against an Indian wilfully defying it, arrests should be made only after the offence had been committed and only when the Indians had dispersed.[16]

Vowell's reminder was issued following an injudicious attempt at enforcing the law in precisely the way he was trying to discourage. On 2 January 1897, the Methodist missionary at Cape Mudge, R. J. Walker, disturbed by the empty schoolrooms of his mission, secured from Kwawkewlth agent Pidcock a warrant to arrest two Salmon River Kwakiutl. The local justice of the peace, M. Manson, proceeded with four special constables to the Wiwaioukai and Wiwaiaikum where they sought to arrest Johnny Moon and his father, Chief Harry. They encountered resistance and, after a brief struggle between constables and natives, Chief Harry escaped. Moon, however, complied with the warrant and was taken, with witnesses Billy Assu and Jim Nak-nak-nim, to Nanaimo county court, only to be discharged because the depositions carried no proof that the potlatch had actually taken place.[17]

To Vowell the incident was clear proof "that it would have been infinitely better had these Indians at Salmon River not been interfered with at the time and in the manner narrated." Pidcock's indiscretion was his inability "to resist the importunities" of zealous persons "desirous of stopping the Potlaches at any price."[18] The incident, with the other disturbances in the province, led to a serious attack upon the law. It came not from Nass potlatchers or defiant Kwakiutl, though they contributed to it, but from the Legislative Assembly of British Columbia.

In April 1897 Henry Dallas Helmcken introduced a resolution in the provincial legislature noting that the Indian Act's potlatch clauses had caused the Indians to be "greatly disaffected" and enforcement was "likely to cause serious trouble." The resolution urged the immediate repeal of the law so that the Indians could "enjoy such customs unmolested." Helmcken, son of John Sebastian Helmcken, the former Hudson's Bay Company physician, and a grandson of Sir James Douglas, was a member of the assembly for Victoria and, as a lawyer, counsel to the delegations of Nishga potlatchers. He told the assembly of the Nass chiefs' visits and how they had advised that there would likely be trouble if the law was enforced. Seven members spoke on the issue, the majority obviously in favour of allowing the Indians to retain "this harmless old custom." C. B. Sword, member for Dewdney, moved an amendment that modified the resolution by requesting repeal of the antipotlatch law only if an inquiry by the federal government determined that the grievances were well-founded. Sword's amendment carried fourteen to thirteen, and the modified resolution passed without recorded dissent.[19] The Helmcken-Sword resolution underscored a central fact: the law did not have the support of either the provincial government or the public.

Though Protestant missionaries and many Indians strongly supported the ban, they were now isolated, distrusted by both the provincial government and by DIA's British Columbia officials. The latter, like their counterparts elsewhere in Canada, were embarrassed by the missionaries' enthusiastic interference with customs that gave them little trouble when left alone.[20] There were also the store keepers and traders who profited from the large amount of trade goods used for potlatching. These merchants, as Dr. Powell had noted in 1885, had votes and could influence provincial government policy.[21]

A year earlier the Methodist missionary Cornelius Bryant had denounced the "selfish purpose" of local traders "whose business interests have been temporarily benefitted by the potlatches." Similarly, Father Donckele thought the custom might have abated if not for "a host of wicked white advisors" in the area "who for the sake of scanty emolument persuaded the Indians to continue their old customs."[22] To the modern reader, it sounds a little like the scapegoating of "outside agitators." Moreover, the accusations were almost always vague and anonymous. The only storeowners ever named in writing as encouraging the Indians in their potlatching were the Hunt family of Fort Rupert, and few merchants lobbied the government against the law or its enforcement.[23] The allegations did have inherent plausibility, however.

Beyond the small number of self-interested traders, the white community seems to have viewed the potlatch largely as a harmless and colourful diversion. Lomas reported in 1890 that the Cowichan potlatch had the moral support of the local white population "who see no harm in them, but look upon them as a kind of fair at which they can be amused and buy baskets and other Indian curios." By this time Cowichan potlatches were becoming something of a local institution to whites at Duncan and Nanaimo. Free of drink and disorder, they had the flavour "of a county fair." Jim Sil-ka-met's 1895 Nanaimo potlatch was visited daily by hundreds of whites, "both Ladies and Gentlemen and even little children." The ceremonies were considered a form of local entertainment. All objectionable features had been eliminated from "the programme." "In the native costume the Indians look very picturesque," was a newspaper comment on a 1902 potlatch near Duncan. The length of the gift distribution could make the potlatch itself "rather tedious," but the dances were "very exciting and interesting." Victorians could watch potlatches at the Songees reserve across the harbour and observe there a picture "which artists who love quaint phases of art, would have gone miles to see."[24]

Under this impression of the potlatch as a harmless entertainment, the public feeling seems to have been that the government had no reason or right to interfere when no other laws were broken. "I believe the majority of the people of this province are opposed to any forcible interference with the harmless customs of the natives," wrote William Dwyer in the *Province*. He seemed to represent an attitude shared by almost all. A group of Nass chiefs told Vowell that, in the opinion "of many intelligent and good white men," clerical meddling was uncalled for. Lomas judged that popular feeling in his district held that "we have no moral right to interfere in these harmless Indian customs."[25] Letters to provincial newspapers seem to confirm the isolation of the missionaries on the issue. When Rev. C. M. Tate condemned the evils of the potlatch—prostitution, disease, immorality, unprogressiveness and truency—laypeople joined the Nootka chief, Maquinna, in controverting the indictment.[26]

For most whites, the overriding issue was the continuing fear of Indian disaffection. The Indians of British Columbia had been extraordinarily peaceful, law-abiding and effusive in their expressions of loyalty to British law and Crown. But peace had been maintained as often by gunboat and show of force—and the heterogeneity of native society—as by Indian acceptance of white intrusions upon lands, resources and customs. Old land grievances and new restrictions on fishing and hunting were testing the limits of Indian tolerance. Enforcement of the potlatch law, Lomas felt, would "add to the steadily increasing strain which is now being felt against both the Dominion and Provincial Governments caused by 'Fishery Regulations', 'Game Acts' and the general hard times which are at present really oppressing the Indians."[27] By the late 1890s white British Columbians were reasonably secure, but they saw no reason to alienate a native population simply because it insisted on wasting time and giving away money and goods that were its own. The potlatch law was seen as quite an unnecessary irritant.

Ottawa, already aware "that the sympathy of a large portion of the community is extended to the Indians when attempts are made to put a stop to the ceremony," took the Legislative Assembly's resolution very seriously. It instructed Vowell to secure full particulars on the extent of enforcement and native disaffection. It was prepared to consider repeal, though that would be seen by many as a "retrograde step" and good reasons would have to be made for such a course.[28]

Vowell responded by reiterating the wisdom of his policy of discretion. His reports on the subject had already made Ottawa aware "that to a certain extent the Indians are very much dissatisfied with the law," but, by taking "the greatest precautions," he had avoided serious conflict. As long as "prudence and good judgement" were used, he could see no cause for difficulty. He was certain that his instructions to his own agents would prevent them from acting inadvisably, though justices of the peace over whom he had no control might, from ignorance, prejudice or pressure, create serious trouble. Repeal would cause considerable dissatisfaction among Protestant missionaries and would, moreover, undermine native respect for government. "In dealing with the Indians," he reminded Ottawa, "firmness is of all things the most necessary qualification to ensure success; vacillation always produces disrespect and thorough want of confidence in the source from which it emanates." Should the law stand, he urged that the provincial government be asked to instruct its magistrates and constables to use the "very best discretion."[29]

Ottawa followed Vowell's recommendation. The government went further, asserting that the potlatch had "a most demoralizing effect" upon Indians, but accepted that, for the reasons given by Vowell, the law should not be repealed but should be used with discretion and great care. The solution was in line with Superintendent General Clifford Sifton's limited faith in the power of law to enforce morality. The government could discourage but hardly prohibit such occasions; when they were held, it could only "take all possible steps to preserve order and decorum." Trusting that the young and progressive Indians were largely opposed to the potlatch, the department presumed that the custom would gradually disappear. In the meantime, agents were to continue to use the law with "great care and moderation" and the provincial government would be requested to instruct its magistrates to use "their very best discretion" in dealing with the law. The department made its position clear to the provincial attorney general in the spring of 1899. There was no question about the necessity of abolishing the revolting features of the tamananawas, such as the mutilation of human bodies and of dogs, or of the wasteful destruction of property associated with the potlatch, but it would be imprudent to "draw the line too closely all at once." It recommended that reforms be introduced gradually rather than by "over-zealousness with an appearance of harshness or arbitrariness." Because the native religious and economic system was involved in the potlatch, because of the strong sympathies of the white community and because of the difficulties of enforcement in many localities in case of resistance, the utmost caution should be maintained. Patience and education were proving successful and the festivals, when held at all, were "gradually assuming the character of harmless social gatherings from which the most objectionable features have disappeared, and giving away has been in the main confined to the relief of the aged and the destitute."[30]

Vowell was content. His policy held firm. He avoided prosecutions, Uslick's being the only potlatch case recorded in the decade after the 1895 amendment. Secure in the wisdom of caution, education and suasion, he leaned heavily towards a program of noninterference. He kept his agents in close check, rebuking Pidcock for yielding to the zealousness of Rev. R. J. Walker in the Salmon River incident, and doing his best to restrain McCullagh and other missionaries who were inclined to use their magisterial authority in a way he considered indiscreet. When matters went beyond a "harmless interchange of kindly and social relations," however, he was prepared to act. He drew the line, loosely, at the destruction of property and, more firmly, at mutilation of dogs or humans.

"I would rather that these meeting [*sic*] should be discontinued," Vowell wrote in 1903, but he practised a quiet tolerance. He maintained the boundaries of his discretion, letting ceremonies pass if they were orderly and free of alcohol, the mutilation of humans or dogs and the threat of epidemic. He ordered the Cowichan agent to send some LaConner Indians back to Washington State for fear they might spread smallpox into the province through a Saanich potlatch. School attendance was also a concern. Lomas was instructed to tell the Kuper Island Indians that if truancy continued the dances would be stopped and the participants punished.

When the department prodded Vowell about enforcing the law on the Nass, he made gestures of compliance, but noted that "what the Indians distributed was neither Government nor Departmental property but entirely the result of their own labour, that at least some of the goods, etc., disposed of went to the needy amongst them, that nothing was destroyed, and, lastly, that the enjoyment derived from performances associated with the Potlach was about the only real pleasure these hardworking and more or less simple minded people had to look forward to from year's end to year's end."[31]

By 1900 the potlatch system did seem to be on the retreat throughout most of the province. The law was one factor. It had survived the challenge of public opinion and provincial opposition. Enforced by only a single court conviction, it nevertheless stood as a proscription and a threat. While it was not invoked through summonses, it loomed large behind the agents' admonitions. But government policy—Vowell's policy—had shifted the onus of the potlatch law from legal enforcement to moral suasion. "Persuasion," he wrote Rev. McCullagh, was "the most efficatious [*sic*] means of doing away with such festivals." The prosperity afforded to those abandoning the custom was "a strong argument" against those wishing to continue it.[32] More important than the law, however, was the accelerating pace of Christian conversion.

Most of British Columbia's native population was now within the orbit of Christian influence. Missions could be found at Masset and Skidegate on the Queen Charlotte Islands; at Port Simpson, Metlakatla, Kincolith, Greenville, Aiyansh, Kispiox and Kitwanga among the Tsimshian speaking northerners; at Alert Bay and Cape Mudge among the Southern Kwakiutl and at Bella Bella among the northern; at Duncan, Nanaimo, Vancouver and Chilliwack among the Coast Salish; at Ucluelet, Clayoquot and other places among the Nootka. All along the coast missionaries laboured among the converted and sought to extend their influence over a declining number of heathen. Their influence was uneven and they witnessed frequent "backsliding," but the extension of Christianity had been continuous until, by 1910, the vast majority of British Columbia Indians were adherents of one Christian church or another.

This widespread shift to missions in a matter of two or three decades "is one of the most striking phenomena in the post-contact history of British Columbia."[33] The embracing of Christianity was a result of voluntary conversion, itself a reaction to the massive change taking place in and around Indian communities. Motives varied among both individuals and groups. Material advantage was one factor. Since many missions operated stores, they were a potential source of cheaper trade goods. Missionaries also possessed medicines against diseases impervious to traditional remedies, and could offer expertise in technology, especially in sawmilling. They were opponents of disruptive forces, especially liquor, that threatened communities. And they were often mediators and advocates for native people in the new systems of land and resource regulation that increasingly impinged upon the Indians. In some places they might offer high-ranking families an opportunity to continue their authority, in modified forms, under conditions in which traditional leadership was eroding; elsewhere nonranking men and women might see missionaries as allies against traditional authority. Most commonly, the missionary offered a new way of life which many sought as an answer to the crisis brought by the erosion of the old. The Christian mission might promise a defence against the depopulation, social disorganization and demoralization that threatened native life.[34]

Useful though the missions were, they extracted a price for their intervention. Heathenism and most of its attachments had to go. Some missionaries, like William Duncan at Metlakatla, demanded total conversion; others permitted compromises if they seemed compatible with their faith. The Indians often found their own compromises. In most areas of missionization, elements—perhaps whole complexes—of native practice were transformed into conduct that, while European in appearance, continued traditional patterns of behaviour. The ceremonial changes adopted by the Haida of Masset on the Queen Charlotte Islands are a good example.

Among the Massets, the potlatch disappeared almost without resistance, certainly without defiance, soon after the turn of the century. Ostensibly responsible for this apparently great change were the Anglican missionaries, the first of whom had been called there in 1876 at the request of the Haida.[35] The winter dance complex went first. CMS missionary W. H. Collison managed to secure, without great difficulty and within a few years of his arrival, the substitution of hymns for the spirit possession dances. The disappearance of the potlatch took only slightly longer.

The missionary convinced some Haida chiefs to neither give nor attend further potlatches, and publicly chastised those who did. Since the Haida relied on the missionary to order potlatch blankets from Victoria, he claimed to possess "the greater influence over the people so that they readily comply with what I say and so no blankets are distributed." While smaller potlatches may have continued in stealth for a time, the great public assemblages disappeared within sixteen years of the missionaries' arrival. The last totem pole raising was held in 1890, with the amount of goods given away a pitiful shadow of the abundance of the past. Florence Davidson's recollections include a "big doings" at Dadans about 1907, then a secret distribution of china washbowls to celebrate her own first menstruation in 1908 or 1909, but there was, she thought, nothing on the occasion of that of her younger sister's. "We became like white people then," she stated.[36]

Did the presence of a single missionary really have such a sweeping effect upon the legendary "Warriors of the North Pacific"? The case is inherently dubious. More plausible in explaining the rapid disappearance of the northern Haida potlatch is the drastic decline in Haida population at the time, which put severe constraints on potlatching, especially on the important *walal* potlatch.[37] With this decline it became more difficult to find the required number of people of proper affiliation to assist with the prerequisites of the ceremony, notably house construction. For this and doubtless other reasons, by 1883 there were no traditional houses being built, while four new-style frame cottages were under construction. By 1890 Masset had something like sixty built or nearly built one-family English-style houses. No potlatch accompanied the completion of a frame house and none of the dwellings were given names. "The demise of the walal potlatch can be sufficiently explained," Margaret Blackman believes, "as a product of demographic changes in combination with directed changes initiated by missionaries and the federal government."[38]

The "directed change" initiated by the federal government, that is, the antipotlatch law, probably had little to do with the demise of the potlatch. No Indian agent was posted to the Charlottes until 1910 and Charles Todd, in whose district the islands lay before then, scarcely visited the Haida.[39] The only possible governmental action that may have hastened the demise of the Haida potlatch was the abolition of slavery long before Confederation. Slaves were an important mark of chiefly rank and among the most symbolically valuable material property of Haida chiefs. The ending of slavery may have acted in concert with the demographic and house-building changes that undermined both chiefly prestige and the *walal* potlatch.[40]

If there was a central factor in the decline of the Haida potlatch, it came from the Haida themselves. In their effort to cope with the crisis of population decline and their threatened dissolution, they turned to the model of material advantage they saw at Metlakatla. The Masset Haida embraced Christian leadership and the western way of life, discarding traditional customs deemed incompatible with the new life. Northern Haida moved willingly to Masset, made little objection to having their children taught in the Christian faith, began to spurn arranged marriages, freed their slaves, abandoned labrets and tattoos, and even preferred their church services in English. Conversion reached across all levels. Younger men and those of lower rank seem to have been the earliest to build new-style houses, but it was through the "untiring energy" of Chief Albert Edward Edenshaw, who died in 1894, "that the Haidas finally cast off heathenism, adopted a more civilized mode of life, and acquired a respect for the laws of the Empire," wrote Charles Harrison in retrospect.[41]

Beneath the apparent changes a great deal of old Haida culture remained. Crests, songs, dances and myths died away, but names and titles were retained. Feasts substituted for potlatches on most occasions, especially at deaths, but also on completion of a house and even in place of the traditional face-saving potlatch. However, gift-giving was prevalent at mourning and memorial feasts, and the feasts and gifts functioned in the traditional way. As indicative of continuity was the preservation of some features of the old mortuary potlatch. The Haida, after an initial distaste for earth burial, "eagerly took to the idea of purchasing tombstones to replace their traditional mortuary totem poles." Anglican ritual was grafted onto the mortuary potlatch to a point where the Haida no longer thought of their ceremony as a potlatch. Tombstone raising replaced the mortuary potlatch, yet the ceremony, while seeming quite different, remained "structurally and functionally unaltered."[42]

Elsewhere in the north, the potlatch had by 1900 been tamed in a somewhat similar fashion. The Skidegate Haida went through much the same process as the Masset Haida, though under Methodist auspices. The Coast Tsimshian, under mission influence at Metlakatla, Port Simpson and Kincolith, had all but abandoned the custom. Feasting among the Gitksan, Nishga and Tsimshian expanded and was enveloped within Christmas, Easter and other holy and secular holidays. Labelling the distribution of goods and money as a feast rendered innocuous a ceremony discouraged by the churches and forbidden by law. Here too there was a substitution of feasts, tombstone raisings and memorial services for the traditional potlatch, done either independently or by mutual emulation and example.[43] The changes remained uneven and incomplete, however; the Gitksan continued to feast, dance and potlatch throughout the period, erecting poles almost continuously into the 1940s.

Christianization, much more than the law, was the instrument of this transformation. Northwest Coast agent George W. Morrow credited the change to missions and schools, agencies that had brought in "something to take its place and interest them." "By raising the Indian step by step," the missionaries and their schools "had more to do and will have more to do, in civilizing and raising the Indian above his old customs, than any possible law or punishment that can be enforced."[44] By 1894 all Queen Charlotte Haida were nominally Christian; by 1904 McCullagh could declare that no heathen remained on the Nass. The degree of understanding and the depth of faith may have been doubtful, the success of the conversion process broken from time to time by sporadic outbreaks of traditional ceremonialism, but the process of conversion to Christianity and to western practices was ineluctable and in large part irreversible.

The Haida and others concluded that the old potlatch system was out of keeping with the times. This, rather than the Indian Act provision, seems the major factor in its demise. Persuasive here is the example of southern Alaska, an American territory where there was neither law nor Indian agents, but where the Tlingit had traditionally potlatched much along the lines of their Haida and Tsimshian neighbours.

By the turn of the century many Alaskan Tlingit were ready to abandon the potlatch. Over 140 signed a petition urging that the ceremony be outlawed, and 80 Sitka Christians renounced their old laws and customs and demanded that Governor John G. Brady "command all natives to change and that if they did not they should be punished." Brady, himself a former Presbyterian missionary, resisted the plea for legal sanctions, both from these natives and from the powerful Presbyterian Sheldon Jackson. He ranked the potlatch among the worst of all Tlingit customs, but encouraged a general conference of Panhandle Indians that would convene for a last, grand potlatch. In December 1904 Killisnoo, Hoonah, Juneau, Chilkat and other Tlingit groups gathered in the territorial capital for a potlatch, the "last of its kind given by Sitka Indians." The ceremony was long and festive and, during its course, Governor Brady hosted his own ceremony at which Tlingit chiefs came forth to renounce their old customs and to present the governor with a raven

hat said to be from the eighteenth century. While it persisted in remote Yakutat and even at Hoonah for a time, the Tlingit potlatch
was disappearing, its passing unaffected by any law prohibiting it.[45]

Among the Nootka and the Coast Salish of Vancouver Island, the
pattern was slightly different from that in the north. Here the potlatch continued with something of its prelaw zeal, but divested of
whatever repulsive features it might once have possessed. West
Coast agent A. W. Neill noted in 1904 that the Nootka potlatch had
lost its objectionable features and the Wolf Dance its former "ter-
rors." The "final flash" Lomas predicted never occurred. Salish potlatches were often integrated into Christian occasions in the latitudi-
narian Catholic culture to which most Cowichan and Nootka had
become attached. At the reserve near Duncan, major potlatches
were held during the June Corpus Christi celebrations. Feasting and
potlatching sometimes extended over a week or more, but the weekend was reserved for adopted festivals. On Sunday morning Bishop
Bertrand Orth of Victoria would follow native brass bands in a pro-
cession of hundreds of celebrants to high mass at the Tzouhalem
church. The afternoon became a sports day on the convent field
with foot and pony races and a baseball game (the Saanich team
devastated the Kuper Island nine in 1903). Each day brought tour-
ists and others to witness the varied and interesting program. The
Somenos reserve was only a short distance from Duncan "on good
bicycle roads," though by 1906 the local livery stable contemplated
running a stage for greater convenience. On a little ridge above the
playing field, a white entrepreneur might raise a flag-decked tent to
sell lemonade and sweets to Indians and their guests. Rev. C. M.
Tate, the Methodist missionary then labouring among the
Cowichan, was annoyed at the encouragement the large numbers of
white spectators gave to the continuation of the demoralizing
dances, and scandalized by ball games after solemn Sunday worship
("What shams for religion"), but even he sometimes found the potlatch gatherings convenient for his own purposes. Two thousand Indians assembled at Duncan meant no daytime services, but his evening ones were packed every night with a large crowd arriving after
the conclusion of the day's potlatch. Cowichan dances, judged
Agent W. R. Robertson, no longer contained anything of an objectionable nature.[46]

Even among the Salish, however, the potlatch was disappearing,

especially in the Fraser Valley. One factor was the increasing importance of summer work in the berry fields and the canneries, work
that made the traditional long summer Salish gatherings less convenient. The last potlatch there took place about 1915.[47]

Superintendent Vowell could feel vindicated. As Ottawa told him in
1904, it appreciated "the significance of the fact pointed out by you
that potlatching has almost disappeared" in the province "under a
policy of patience and moral suasion rather than of coercion."[48] The
exception to Vowell's success, as Ottawa also knew, were the
Kwakiutl of the central coast. Among the Southern Kwakiutl the
potlatch was as strong as ever, perhaps even stronger now than before the enactment of the law. Here too the outlawed tamananawas
dance was still practised and, in 1900, brought the first prosecutions
under the act's prohibition of the mutilation of human flesh.

5

"The Incorrigible Kwakiutl"

THE SOUTHERN KWAKIUTL, inhabiting northern Vancouver Island and the adjacent mainland, were regarded as the most "incorrigible" of all British Columbia groups. Powell wrote of their "almost intractable character," remarking that they had "always been and are inferior to any other in the Province in respect to morals and habits generally." A Catholic mission to the tribes congregated at Fort Rupert abandoned the effort. A departing priest told W. H. Collison that, though he had worked among several tribes, none were so bad as the Kwakiutl: "I can do nothing amongst them." "The testimony of everyone I have met," wrote Anglican A. J. Hall on his 1878 arrival at Fort Rupert, "is that they are a bad set." A year later he told Powell that they "were a most difficult lot to civilize"; the superintendent thought that Hall's efforts had not had much effect.[1]

The Kwakiutl were behind few others in exploiting the economic opportunities offered by the European economy. They entered commercial fishing and cannery work, hired on as sealers, did hand logging and other wage labour and took to the hop fields of Puget Sound. Kwakiutl women also worked as washerwomen and prostitutes in the cities and camps.

The Southern Kwakiutl were industrious, but their "incorrigibility" persisted. They lagged behind other Indians in the adoption of Christianity, in sending their children to schools and in personal and community hygiene. European-style frame houses, even when built, were only slept in, the rest of the day being spent in the traditional multifamily lodges "wanted for the gatherings which they hold on every possible occasion."[2] "The energy which they display in collecting property is certainly remarkable," Blenkinsop wrote in 1883, though he noted that much was squandered. If only the evil influence of the potlatch could be done away with, Agent William Halliday wrote over twenty years later, the Alert Bay Kwakiutl "would forge right ahead."[3]

While grasping economic opportunities, the Kwakiutl resisted imported values, exploiting the new culture for their own ends. To a degree almost unknown elsewhere, the people "completely shut themselves off from the European." They "appear to desire to resist, inch by inch, so to speak," wrote Powell in 1883, "the inroads of civilization upon old savage custom." Blenkinsop, who had been among Northwest Coast people (including the Kwakiutl) for decades, wrote that "the Kwawkewlths evince no desire for improvement; they see plainly that innovation will destroy their old, much-prized domestic institutions, and hence they cling to them with more pertinacity than ever." So they remained to departmental officials: "antagonistic toward the white race" and "opposed to any thing and everything advanced by the white man."[4]

Agents Blenkinsop, Pidcock, DeBeck and Halliday referred again and again to the importance of the potlatch to the Southern Kwakiutl. Their letters and reports are replete with comments on the "determined opposition" by the Kwakiutl to attempt to end the potlatch. "I was told by the older men," wrote Pidcock in 1895, "that they might as well die as give up the Custom."[5]

The exceptional conservatism of the Southern Kwakiutl is not easily explained. Certainly they were remote enough from settlement to be spared some of the intense acculturating pressures on the Salish of the Fraser Valley or southern Vancouver Island, but this was true of most central and northern coast groups. For reasons that can only be guessed at, probably involving kinship, marriage and inheritance, the Southern Kwakiutl took a different course.

Every group on the coast adapted differently to the intrusion of Europeans upon them. Certainly there are common patterns of adaptation to be found, but cultures were different and contact was uneven, so responses were unpredictable and distinct. All groups were selective in their adaptations, but their choices varied. Not enough is known about the historical development or the cultures of aboriginal peoples to pin down the ways in which individuals, let alone groups, responded to the European infiltration. More ethnographic information exists about the Southern Kwakiutl than any other group, yet it does not explain the course that they—one speaks hesitantly here, since not all, even among the Kwakiutl, acted in unison—adopted.

The Southern Kwakiutl seem to have been like most other coastal groups in the precontact era. They possessed a decent abundance of natural foods and so often gave feasts to those with whom they were in frequent contact and with whom they intermarried. Potlatches were probably few; while food was plentiful, transferable wealth—in the form of carved bowls, oil, animal skins and canoes—was modest. Only the highest (and perhaps the second highest) chief of a lineage group (the *numaym*) potlatched, with the assistance of the entire numaym behind him.

Contact changed this in several ways. The gradual imposition of peace—that is, the diminution of warfare under British dominance—increased intergroup relations, especially intermarriage, and thus the exchange of crest privileges. This allowed for an expansion of the guest group invited to feasts and potlatches. At the same time, employment and trade brought an increase in transferable wealth. A further change, perhaps the most telling of all, was the dramatic decline of population from a variety of introduced diseases and alcohol. There are no accurate statistics, but the population may have fallen by as much as 75 per cent between the 1830s and 1880s.[6]

While the exact process is unclear, it is plain that depopulation, increased wealth and the end of native warfare brought profound modifications to the Kwakiutl social system. Kwakiutl society was based on hereditary rank; there were over seven hundred named positions among the Southern Kwakiutl. The loss of population meant that there were more positions than individuals clearly marked by heredity to fill them. Unconventional adjustments were necessary, including the elevation of women to high rank. There was "almost a veritable overthrow of the old order of things," and, in addition to validating inherited rank, the potlatch became a means of accession to positions where inheritance was cloudy.[7] With this, the potlatch became democratized to a degree: lower-ranked people, even commoners perhaps, could, by amassing wealth, claim positions to which they had only a tenuous hereditary link. The availability of transferable wealth items, almost entirely European trade goods acquired through wage and piece labour, commercial fishing and prostitution, brought "une perversion profonde du système ancien."[8]

The profound change became evident in the years following the 1849 founding of the Hudson's Bay Company post at Fort Rupert. Situated at Beaver Harbour, the new coal, timber and trading post provided the nearby Kwakiutl with increased wealth, especially those who moved to the site to act as middlemen and labourers. Potlatches flourished as never before, increasing in frequency, in the number of guests invited and in the amount of goods distributed. The traditional ranks lost much of their old significance, but retained their prestige and acquired a new significance—other ranking Indians could emulate a chief through potlatching. They could acquire wealth items, in the form of blankets and other trade goods, as easily as chiefs. This challenge to chiefly prerogatives "primed the potlatch inflationary cycle" as chiefs struggled to retain their prestige and commoners sought to imitate it.[9]

What probably made the Kwakiutl potlatch exceptional was a combination of the hazy gradation in ranks, especially among neighbouring groups brought into closer relations by postcontact developments, and the ability to obtain rank by marriage, even by multiple marriages. Among the Tlingit and Haida, marriages were unimportant as vehicles to alter rank and gain prerogatives; among the Kwakiutl and Bella Coola, marriages became the major vehicle for enhancing prestige, and the Kwakiutl not only permitted but honoured serial marriages.[10] Yet it is likely that for all the change and expansion, there was no deviation from the primary purpose of the potlatch: the formal presentation of a claim to a hereditary right to a specific social status.[11]

The Kwakiutl turned the altered circumstance of increased wealth to their own ends. Instead of adopting the social values of their European employers and customers, they used their earnings to reinforce the most significant aspects of their social system. "By the latter part of the nineteenth century," notes one study, "the Southern Kwakiutl were going to extreme lengths to hold together what they regarded as the most important part of their social structure." They might have allowed the means of claiming and validating rank to be individualized and democratized, but they were un-willing "to permit changes in their system of formal social rank, which it was the basic function of the potlatch to define." Mission-aries, agents and the presence of a proscriptive statute could not stamp out the custom. Indeed, there was perhaps a counterproduc-tive element in efforts towards this end. "It is quite clear that the potlatch became even more esteemed and cherished, acquiring overtones of defiance of the unwelcome authority of the agent, defi-ance of the laws of white civilization that the Indians felt were clos-ing in on them." An element of nostalgia, of the value of tradition it-self, was perhaps present, making the potlatch "at once a symbol of defiance and a reminder of the good old days."[12]

Elsewhere, Christianity, economic change, education and moral suasion had ended the potlatch system or rendered it relatively in-nocuous, but these "agents of civilization" had had little effect upon the "recalcitrant" and "unprogressive" Kwakiutl. Instead of declin-ing, the potlatch continued to intensify, with repercussions that were felt throughout Kwakiutl life.

Most British Columbia agents were content with the policy of dis-cretion initiated by Powell and refined by Vowell, but, amidst the blooming Kwakiutl potlatch system, the Kwawkewlth agents were as exceptional as their wards. Blenkinsop was intent on enforcing the law within the measure of his ability; Pidcock actually enforced it against Hamasak and complained about the "dead letter" pro-duced by Justice Begbie. But it was G. W. DeBeck, Kwawkewlth agent from 1902 to 1906, who became so enraged by the flagrant transgressions against the law that he took stern action to stamp out behaviour he saw as evil.

In March 1902 R. H. Pidcock, Kwawkewlth agent since 1886, died in a Victoria hospital. His successor was George Ward DeBeck, a fifty-three-year-old lumberman a little down on his luck. Pidcock, though irritated and frustrated by the "intractability" of the South-ern Kwakiutl, had reluctantly complied with Vowell's stubborn in-sistence that education, moral suasion and time would erase the pot-latch among the Kwakiutl just as they had done elsewhere. DeBeck, more accustomed to an independent business career in milling, tim-ber cruising and property speculation than to bureaucratic subordi-nation, became completely exasperated by the ambiguities of discretion. This brought him into conflict not only with his Kwakiutl wards but also with his superior, Vowell, who remained as intransigent in his policy of toleration as the Kwakiutl were in pursuing the custom DeBeck found so disturbing.

Following his arrival in April, DeBeck had noticed very little potlatching among the Indians. At the approach of winter, however, he reported "preparations going on for quite an extended business in that line." He was determined "to check the growth of this most detestable practice." The Kwakiutl paid little attention to his admonitions: "Any advice or talk one may give them seems to run off them like water off a slate roof." By January 1903 the season was "just getting into full swing" with Indians from Fort Rupert, Tanuntiano, Klamtsis, Matilpi, Sen-auk-to and Mamalillikulla assembling at Alert Bay for feasting, dancing and potlatching. DeBeck asked Vowell for guidance: Should he force them to leave the Alert Bay reserve? The superintendent's reply referred DeBeck to earlier circulars and instructions that explained the department's policy of cautious discretion. DeBeck was scarcely satisfied: "It strikes me very forcibly that coaxing, threatening, exhorting or advising is simply a waste of breath." But, he supposed, "there is nothing else for me to do." The next October, after receiving a similar request, Vowell told his agent that he could use Section 21 of the Indian Act to force the departure of Indians who were "unduly trespassing upon reserves not allotted for their use," though he preferred the use of "all the moral power vested in you as Indian Agent" to secure the abandonment of objectionable practices.[13]

DeBeck, by this second winter of his tenure, was convinced that something should be done about the potlatch and decided to invoke the trespass provision to do it. At one gathering, he summarily forced the visitors to leave Alert Bay. "At less than 24 hours notice," one witness reported, "at the height of festivities to which they had been invited, two tribes were scared into leaving notwithstanding that the weather was so rough & squally that two canoes each worth about $100 were split from end to end in getting off the beach." On 21 March 1904, on a tour through the agency, DeBeck notified eight to nine hundred Indians gathered at Fort Rupert for Dave Hunt's potlatch that they must leave by 4 April. He expected that they would ignore his order—some had boasted that they intended to stay until the salmon run began at the end of June—but he was determined to "break up this pernicious practise."[14] With Constable Walter Woollacott and a special constable, DeBeck returned to Fort Rupert to enforce his command. Three chiefs were arrested for trespass and, despite a "show of fight" from the Indians, were taken aboard his gas boat, the *Gicume*,[15] for trial in Alert Bay. There he dispatched a wire to Vowell asking for the immediate assistance of a government steamer at Fort Rupert and, acting as justice of the peace, fined Mah-kwa, Klo-klal-so and Naai-guene $10 each for trespass.[16]

Hearing nothing from Victoria about the departure of the *Quadra* or the *Kestrel* to Fort Rupert and knowing that the three arrests had failed to disperse the gathering, DeBeck returned with Woollacott to take further action.[17] The constable secured one man but the Indians would not let him leave with the prisoner. With "a rush, whooping and yelling," they hemmed in agent, constable and prisoner. One Tsawataineuk man was so aggressive that he too was arrested, though agent and constable remained powerless in the midst of the crowd. Finally, after a "hard struggle" of over two hours, they were able to get to their boat with three prisoners. Despite fines of $30 ($10 for each day of trespass) levied on two men (the third man was dismissed), DeBeck reported that the Indians at Fort Rupert were "still defiant and under the impression that they have beaten me out."[18]

DeBeck did not renew his attack on the Fort Rupert potlatchers that winter. Concluding that the department did not approve of his actions, he stopped all proceedings. He felt beaten, betrayed by a lack of support from Superintendent Vowell who had made no move to back his efforts. If a boat had been sent (according to Vowell, neither government vessel was available), DeBeck believed that he could have put a permanent stop to the potlatch. "A very little show of assistance, or backing, from the Department would have completed the job," he wrote later, "and put an end to their nonsense for all time." Instead, the Indians "seem to have gotten an idea into their heads that an appeal to headquarters would be favourably considered."[19]

This impression stemmed partly from a separate incident in which DeBeck, seeking the "ringleaders" of a cannibal dance at Quatsino Sound, had asked Vowell to dispatch Thomas Deasey, the federal constable in Victoria, to assist. Deasey, arriving in Alert Bay too late to accompany the agent to Quatsino, used his time to tour the surrounding area, arresting a few women for unnamed offences and securing material for a long article for the Victoria *Times*.[20] Deasey's tour and his article, which pictured the Kwakiutl potlatch as a harmless good time and blankets as preferable to whiskey, irritated DeBeck enormously. "One thing is certain," he fumed. "The effect of it on the minds of the Indians has been anything but advantageous to the Agent, or conducive to the best interests of the Indians."[21] Deasey's "indiscreet talk and actions" among the Indians had been "largely responsible for the trouble at Fort Rupert." DeBeck awaited the coming winter season anxiously. Uncertain of the wishes of the department and of the backing Vowell would extend, he nevertheless remained intent on suppressing the potlatch in his agency. His uncertainty soon turned to rage and a sense of full betrayal.[22]

Instead of giving guidance to his subordinate, Vowell gave encouragement to the Kwakiutl. With the assistance of lawyer S. Perry Mills of Victoria, a number of Kwakiutl led by Willie Harris drew up a petition complaining about their treatment and presented it to Vowell. The superintendent replied in his usual way. His letter to the petitioners, wrote an angry DeBeck, "virtually assured them that they will not be interfered with." "Quite a ripple of pleasurable excitement has been created among the old, most ignorant, and savage of the Indians by your action in giving them permission to go on with their potlatch," DeBeck wrote in scorn, while "a directly opposite feeling has been aroused in the breasts of most of the young men, & those who had been trying to better their condition in life."[23] The Harris letter, on top of the Fort Rupert difficulty and the Deasey affair, was too much for DeBeck. He appealed over Vowell's head to Ottawa.

DeBeck's letter to the superintendent general poured out his frustrations with his superior. He had approached Vowell "time & again" about the potlatch, "but have never yet been able to get any satisfaction." He believed that the superintendent "did not want to have anything to do with me." The potlatches hampered his work among the Indians. "These social gatherings," he wrote, "are not the harmless, little reunions that some people imagine them to be." He insisted on precise instructions: "If the Department wants me to suppress the potlatch or any other of their heathenish or unlawful

practices, I'll do it, do it quick, and with the least possible expense."
If the custom was to be allowed to continue without interference, he
should be so informed and not left in the unenviable position in
which Vowell's "peculiar work" placed him.[24]

The department was understandably cautious. It had no new instructions to give Vowell about his discretion in enforcing the law; it
sympathized with "the Agent's zeal for the remedy of the condition
of things" and hoped that the superintendent would "carefully consider whether any prudent measures can be devised for assisting him
in what is certainly a very laudable object." Though mildly repri-
manding Vowell for giving inadequate guidance, the department
nonetheless came down solidly on the superintendent's side.[25]

The Vowell-DeBeck imbroglio was a clash between Vowell's continuing policy of patient moral suasion and the conscientious zeal of
a self-made man unaccustomed to bureaucratic discretion. Behind it
lay the exceptionalism of the Kwakiutl. Potlatching, Vowell insisted,
had "almost entirely disappeared" in British Columbia without
"persecution or drastic measures." Superintendent Vowell was not
blind to what was happening in the Kwawkewlth agency. The potlatch there was still carried on extensively, he admitted to Ottawa,
but he excused it as "no worse" than it had been in earlier days
among other British Columbia groups. While Vowell was content to
await his policy working itself out among the Kwakiutl, DeBeck was
unwilling to sit quietly in Alert Bay and let his wards continue practices that he considered "a disgrace to everybody concerned" and
destructive to the Kwakiutl themselves.[26]

The feasts and potlatches, Debeck believed, were "fast decimat-
ing" the Kwakiutl. Reporting on a number of deaths in the summer
of 1903, he expressed a firm belief that these were caused "by their
herding together here last winter." At Fort Rupert potlatches the Indians lived in filthy, overcrowded conditions. Pneumonia, the most
prevalent disease in his agency, was always at its worst during and
immediately after a big potlatch. Doubtless there were other aspects
of the potlatch that gave rise to DeBeck's insistence on being placed
"in a position to make them do what I know is best for themselves,"
but at the heart of his opposition seems to have been a concern for
the health of his agency, which did, in fact, continue to suffer from
population decline. Already reduced to about 2300 souls in 1883,
the Southern Kwakiutl numbered only about 1300 in 1905. Deaths

and low replacement were due largely to consumption, pneumonia, influenza and other pulmonary diseases.[27]

DeBeck was responsible for another move aimed at undermining the potlatch. He had a portion of the land reserved for the industrial school surveyed into lots in 1904, and these were set aside for Indians "wishing to abandon the old heathen and savage customs forever." The idea found little favour. "Though every influence except force" was brought to bear, only five people responded by 1914.[28] Another measure was to order non-Nimpkish out of Alert Bay. A number of Hunts fell victim to his removal decrees.[29]

By the winter of 1905–06 Vowell was fed up with DeBeck and his insubordination, and DeBeck, in turn, was frustrated beyond measure at the impossible position in which his superiors had placed him. It is unclear from the record whether he left voluntarily or was pushed, but he resigned in April 1906, departing for Vancouver, there to tend his revived city property and to enjoy retirement in suburban Ebourne. DeBeck was, remembered a missionary, a very fine man, "the unfortunate victim of circumstance."[30]

The new agent at Alert Bay, W. H. Halliday, was an established resident of the area and no newcomer to the potlatch. He had come to British Columbia as a boy in 1873. His father was a schoolteacher at Yale, then a principal in New Westminster and Victoria. In 1883 the family moved to a farm in the Comox district where William, then in his teens, saw his first potlatch under the guidance of Agent W. H. Lomas. In 1894, his brother preempted farm land in remote Kingcome Inlet and Halliday moved there, about two miles from the reserve of the Tsawataineuk Kwakiutl. In February 1897 he settled in Alert Bay as a trades instructor under Rev. A. W. Corker at St. George's residential school, then moved on to teaching positions at Duncan and Victoria. He was appointed Kwawkewlth agent in May 1906, and remained in the position until his retirement in 1932.

Halliday's observation and experience, in both Kingcome Inlet and Alert Bay, gave him some knowledge of the difficulties he would face in his new job. W. A. Stevens, who had acted as agent in the brief interlude between DeBeck's departure and Halliday's arrival, warned of trying times for the new agent: "I know this disease of the potlatch, or whatever it might be called, has a firm hold upon the people and is on the increase."[31]

Even so, Halliday was a more circumspect man than DeBeck. He did not rock the boat very much, either among the Kwakiutl or with Superintendent Vowell. He broke up, with little trouble, a gathering in Gwayasdums in March 1907 but left the potlatches, if they were orderly, largely alone. Such gatherings, he told Vowell, perhaps tailoring his words to the views of his superior, were "comparatively harmless; potlatches waste a great deal of time generally but as a rule do not do much harm."[32]

Also at issue in the Kwawkewlth agency were two practices associated with potlatching: marriage customs, described by Agent DeBeck as a "feeder" to potlatching, and ceremonial cannibalism, the tamananawas dances of the original 1884 amendment.

In March 1900 Agent R. H. Pidcock and Constable Woollacott had instituted proceedings against two Southern Kwakiutl for offences under Section 114 of the Indian Act. Their alleged crime was not potlatching but participating in cannibalistic ceremonies, the only instance of governmental prosecution under "the wounding or mutilation of the dead or living body of any human being" section of the statute.[33] Vowell was a man of considerable patience and tolerance, but he did not extend these to such "revolting ceremonies." With Pidcock apparently having a good case, Vowell urged that everything be done to insure a conviction.[34]

Ceremonial cannibalism was an obvious target of federal Indian policy. Dog-eating ceremonies among the Tsimshian and ritual biting and eating of human flesh there and among the central coast Kwakiutl had long provoked horrified reactions in Europeans and Euro-Canadians. Reports of cannibalism went back to the eighteenth century[35] and their currency had prompted the ban on tamananawas dances as part of the 1884 Indian Act amendment that proscribed the potlatch.[36]

"Tamananawas" was a confusing term. Powell was never very clear on the meaning; his usage of the word included both "medicine dance" and "orgies of the most disgusting character, namely biting the arms of spectators or rather tearing to pieces dogs and human bodies (exhumed for the purpose), and occasionally, killing slaves with this object in mind." Cannibalistic practices had, he judged, largely disappeared. They were still carried out in various inlets along the coast (he cited the Nass, Kitimat, Oweekano and others among the Southern Kwakiutl) "though not on the same extensive scale" as formerly. Pidcock assumed that tamananawas referred to the "red-bark" or hamatsa ceremony of the Kwakiutl, though they assured him that it was a Flathead (presumably meaning the Straits Salish) practice unknown amongst themselves.[37] Justice Begbie compounded the confusion by declaring that the tamananawas was "utterly unknown" in British Columbia.[38] Terminological confusion was ended by the 1895 amendment that outlawed the mutilation of animal or human flesh.

Long before 1895, even before the 1884 amendment, missionaries and agents had sought to end the practices. Blenkinsop tried to control the biting of witnesses among the Kwakiutl by threatening prosecution for assault. Pidcock was able to make the Kwakiutl omit the worst features of the hamatsa wherever he was likely to be present, "but often they perform the dance at some distant Village where they feel secure from observation." The previous winter, he was told, Ne-na-kwis of the Nakwakto band had eaten portions of a human body at Quasa-la on Smiths Inlet, but Pidcock made no attempt to prosecute.[39] Now, early in 1900, he was certain he had evidence and witnesses that could bring a conviction against George Hunt, a forty-six-year-old half blood.

Hunt was the son of a Tlingit woman and an HBC man who had bought the Fort Rupert store from the company. He was raised virtually as a Kwakiutl and married amongst the people. He worked often for S. A. Spencer, the cannery owner at Alert Bay who had married Hunt's sister Annie. Fluent in both Kwakwala and English, and literate in the latter, Hunt often served as an interpreter and translator for officials, including Powell and Rev. Hall. In 1888 he met Franz Boas in Victoria and the young anthropologist began employing him as an assistant, a relationship that matured into a collaboration of great significance to them both.[40]

Pidcock charged Hunt with assisting in the mutilation of the body of an old woman dead for several years.[41] The offence had occurred in mid-February among the Klawitsis (or Tlawitsis) at Karlakwees. "There is little doubt from the evidence," Pidcock reported, "that a dead human body was taken into a house at Klawitsis village and there mutilated in a horrible manner." Hunt admitted that he had taken part in the ceremony, but maintained he was there to obtain information for Pidcock to act upon, a story Pidcock thought nonsense. Hunt's actions then and later did not sustain the excuse, since he had said nothing about the matter until charged.[42]

The accused was taken by Constable Woollacott to Vancouver aboard the *Coquitlam,* along with a number of Indian witnesses. Hunt, after being lodged at the New Westminster jail, was released on bail (his brother-in-law, S. A. Spencer, put up the necessary $500 and secured a lawyer, W. J. Bowser). The trial date had to be postponed so that Hunt could return to Alert Bay to arrange for witnesses to appear on his behalf. The trial took place in Vancouver County Court on 17 and 18 April before a jury, with Chief Justice Angus John McColl presiding.

Native witnesses for the prosecution claimed that the hamatsa had come in with a dead body covered with evergreen.

> The body was placed on a box and two chiefs stood up and spoke, calling on prisoner to come and do the carving. Hunt got up and a red cedar turban was put on his head, and he went over and went around the house singing in Indian and stopped at the body. The chiefs discussed what he should cut the body with. Saw him take a knife, took the evergreens off, and cut the legs off, then the head, and gave the three portions to a chief who handed them to the Hamatsa, named Wys-tla, who handed a piece to another Hamatsa, the trunk was given to a third and the legs to a fourth Hamatsa. They ate all the fleshy parts of the body. A chief gathered up the bones and put them on a buttoned blanket and wrapped them up. When the eating was finished prisoner stood up and advised people not to say anything about it, as it was a serious affair.[43]

Bowser, a leading Vancouver barrister and later attorney general and premier, told the jury that the allegations against Hunt were the result of a vindictive trap set by an enemy. Hunt, while acting as a special constable for Agent Pidcock, had come into rivalry with another constable named Plan-Hettie.[44] Bowser argued that the rival constable was behind the affair; Plan-Hettie had instigated the prosecution and every Crown witness except one was a relative of his. (Privately, Hunt said that he was a victim of "the missionary people.")[45] According to his lawyer, Hunt had attended the dance out of pure curiosity; he was an authority on tribal customs and had furnished information to scientists on questions of this kind. Hunt said that he had gone as a mere spectator and, even when called upon, had done no more than observe. Reports of his testimony stated that

> after the body had been brought in and placed in the centre of the room, he was called by name to come and see it. He did so, and when he saw what it was and was turning away the Hamatsas and bear and dog dancers snatched the body and ate, or pretended to eat, it.

The jury doubted the Crown's version; after about twenty minutes' deliberation, foreman George Fletcher brought back a verdict of not guilty.[46]

Although the mutilation section of the statute proved ineffective in its only court test, it remained, like the potlatch ban, a proscription and a deterrent. Pidcock, though disappointed at having again lost a case, thought that the prosecution had been worthwhile. Hunt, according to Pidcock's successor, avoided being present "at any more of these heathen feasts." Though he was acquitted, lawyer's fees and travel and accommodation for himself and witnesses had cost Hunt over $400.[47]

While cannibalism remained a concern of the agents, it was minor compared to what they saw as the more far-reaching effects of the potlatch's connection to sexual relationships. The potlatch's role in native prostitution had been cited at the time of the law's passage. The exodus of women to cities and camps remained a complaint of both Indians and agents in the following years. Agent Loring on the upper Skeena reported that mothers and aunts sent their daughters and nieces out to prostitute themselves for money for potlatch purposes, and Pidcock went so far as to order a group of Kwakiutl women bound for Victoria off the *Sardonyx* in 1889. Rev. Hall, acknowledging that the Kwakiutl were "morally worse" despite his ten years of labour among them, blamed the retrogression on "the wholesale migration of their young women to southern towns to procure by illicit [intercourse?] property which enables their male [relatives?] to carry on the 'Potlatch.' "[48] Anthropologist Boas, who, because he supported the potlatch as a valuable institution, would not have connected the prostitution problem to potlatching, was concerned enough at the effect of prostitution on coastal natives to write to Senator Macdonald asking for action against it.[49]

Vowell minimized the problem. There were, he reported to Ottawa, few Indian women living an immoral life in the province's towns and cities, and they were "less in number as a rule than that of their white sisters." This was probably true: there appear to have been only a handful of arrests of native women for street prostitution in Victoria between 1880 and 1910, fewer than those of white, Chinese and black women, and Senator Macdonald felt that the problem had declined by 1890. On the other hand, Agent Lomas was told that year by the Victoria police that, while no Cowichan were prostitutes in the city, northern and west coast Indian women were there constantly.[50] Vowell thought that it was only a matter of time before native women would, through example and teaching, be induced to abandon such "sensuous" and "barbaric" practices. Pidcock, responding to an inquiry on the question, left no doubt that the potlatch had a share in encouraging the practice, but he introduced another factor that would overshadow prostitution as a concern of Kwawkewlth agents. He thought that the Kwakiutl marriage law, "which allows parents or guardians to compel a woman to leave her husband unless he can furnish money or its equivalent, and then forcing the woman to take another husband as a means of raising money to carry on the 'Potlach,' " played a role in the immorality of Kwakiutl women.[51] Kwakiutl marriage practices became the great concern of Pidcock's successors, DeBeck and Halliday.

The Kwakiutl marriage system was anathema to Agent DeBeck. Marriage relations among the people, he wrote soon after arriving in Alert Bay, were in "a most deplorable condition." Hardly a day passed without the application by an Indian man for help in getting back his wife. The condition of DeBeck's agency could not improve so long as the custom of buying and selling women continued.[52] Halliday's great concern, at least while serving under Vowell's superintendency, was less the potlatch than the marriage laws of the Kwakiutl. If marriages were regularized, he thought, the potlatch would die a natural death. More important to Halliday, women would be saved from being sold like chattel for potlatching purposes, and young men would have a chance not only to woo and win the women of their choice but to disengage themselves from the tentacles of the potlatching system.[53]

This issue of the sale and purchase of wives was inflamed by press headlines such as "Girls Sold into Slavery," "Indian Fathers Sell

Their Little Girls," "Indian Maidens Sold at Auction" and "Girls Sold at Alert Bay Slave Market."[54] Halliday gave little credence to the newspaper stories which were often factually wrong and portrayed the transactions as open slave auctions when, in fact, matters were arranged privately with little or no bidding. On the other hand, he was outraged at the treatment of women by the arranged marriage system.

The marriage issue is a complicated one. Euro-Canadian historians can do little more than describe the objections to the Kwakiutl system, assess their truthfulness, and then describe the system itself, as depicted in the anthropological literature, hoping in the process to make both the Kwakiutl and the Canadian viewpoints understandable.

Franz Boas had already written in 1897 that "marriage among the Kwakiutl must be considered a purchase," but the object bought was not only the woman but the right of membership in her clan for future children of the couple. Kwakiutl practice was for alliances to be arranged by parents or families, often without the knowledge and usually without the consent of either bride or groom. The groom's family made a payment, usually in blankets worth from $500 to $1000, to the bride's family. Repayment by the bride's family to the groom and his family was required, however, with a partial payment being made at the time of the marriage and the rest following later, usually when children were born. Indeed, the preponderance of giving was done by the bride's side; in comparison, the bride price was "relatively unimportant," really only "an opening of negotiation."[55]

The charge of selling girls was, then, erroneous in the sense of a father profiting commercially, except in the very short run, from the "sale" of his daughter. On the other hand, the affair did have the air of a transaction, whether material, religious or ceremonial, because of both the initial bride price and the repayment, made in goods and, more significantly, through the bestowing by the bride's side of rank, privileges and names upon the groom's.

Bride price was not, however, the major complaint of either DeBeck or Halliday. They wrote of girls thirteen years or younger being sold without their consent, but both men realized that bride price required repayment. What bothered the agents much more was that, once repayment was made, the marriage was at an end. A couple, wrote Halliday, did not live together long. The man had to buy his wife again or she was taken and sold to someone else.[56]

The agents cited examples to support their complaints. Halliday wrote of a woman who came to Alert Bay for some winter shopping; on her return to her home village, she was met by a party of men who told her "that she was not to go back to her husband with whom she had been living very happily, but that she had been disposed of during her absence to another man." Her previous husband had been present at the negotiations, "but had no money to offer, to keep her." He also cited the case of two young men, "hard working decent young chaps," who were kept poor by the avarice of their wives' families; every time one of the men collected a few dollars he was immediately called on to pay it over. "These two young men are tenderly attached to their wives and would sacrifice anything to keep them," Halliday wrote. "If they refused to pay, the women would be sold to some one else."[57]

In these charges there was truth. Once the bride price had been repaid to the groom's side, Kwakiutl custom held that the obligations of the contracting parties had been fulfilled and the marriage was ended. If a wife remained with her husband, she stayed "for nothing"—a condition considered undignified. A new contract could be entered into by the original parties, though the payments were generally smaller. As often, after what Boas called the "annulment" of a marriage through repayment, the woman was married to another. After four marriages her rank was established and she was then expected to stay with her husband, though he was under no obligation, once repayment had been made, to keep her.[58] A Nakwakto woman described her marriages:

> When I was still a child, I was given in sham marriage by my father to a chief of another numayam. I was placed on a seat on a catamaran, the edges of which were set with skulls, and was taken across to the house of my husband. My father gave me the name Copper-around-the-Edges. I stayed for a little while in my husband's house. Then my father paid the marriage debt. He bought new canoes and all kinds of goods were placed on the catamaran on which I was seated. Coppers were laid across the canoe. As soon as the marriage debt was paid, I went home.
>
> When I was married to my uncle, I lived with him for two years; then my father and uncle paid the marriage debt. He gave me the

kelp house as part of the payment. The sun was painted in front of the house. After this, my father asked me to leave my husband, and I obeyed.

I did not know to whom he was going to marry me next. He wanted me to marry four times so that I should have a rank as high as that of my mother and aunts, for they were all noblewomen from distant times to the present.

Very soon I married a Gwasilla chief. Very soon the marriage debt was paid. Part of the payment was the carved house of my late uncle.

Next I married Paddled-to, and he was also given a house.

Finally, I was going to have a husband and married this Potlatch-Giver here. Soon the marriage debt was paid by my brother, and this house was given by my brother. The carved box with all our supernatural powers was put into this house, and it was opened here. I am obeying my late brother who asked me not to have any more husbands, for I am getting weak and everything has been done for me by my brothers. Now I shall not take any more husbands, and I am just waiting whether Potlatch-Giver may not drive me away.[59]

Some women's first marriages, like that of the Nakwakto woman, were "sham" marriages, done only for exchanges of privileges and unconsummated, but agents and missionaries were, nevertheless, deeply offended by the fate of the young men and women in their agency. DeBeck thought it cruel "to see a child of 13 or 14 years of age put up and sold, just like a sheep or nanny goat, to a bleary eyed Siwash, old enough to be her Grand-Father, for a pile of dirty blankets, which will in turn be potlached to the rest of the band and all to make the proud Father, a big Injun."[60] Rev. A. J. Hall successfully sought government funds for a new and larger girls' home at Alert Bay and the authority to compel any girl deemed neglected and needing protection to enter and remain there until she was at least sixteen. Halliday had seconded Hall's application. "Now, Sir," he wrote Superintendent General Frank Oliver, "there must be something wrong either in our laws or in our administration of them when a girl of tender years can be sold (for there is no other way to put it) to a man without her consent, in order that her father may have a little more to give away in potlatches." Opinions might differ on the advisability of taking away the Indians' old customs and habits, but, he wrote, when these customs are destroying them and lead them to demoralization in many respects, and when the happiness and even the lives of these girls are concerned it behoves [sic] us to do everything in our power to alter conditions so that these girls should be allowed at least to grow to maturity before being married and that they should have the right of every subject to choose for themselves.

The system of arranged marriages also undid the advancement of young men. "No boy," Halliday wrote, "who has been trained at the Industrial School can get a wife by wooing her and following the Ideas he has learned at school but must go back to the potlatch to buy one. One lad in speaking on this point said to me that one might as well be a eunuch as keep out of the potlatch."[61]

While they were concerned with the men, the agents' chief sorrow was the inescapable fate of Kwakiutl women caught in the web of the potlatch and marriage system. "At present the girls have no chance," Halliday wrote. They were seldom left in school after age twelve; instead they were sold into marriage, since it was a disgrace to keep a girl single after her first monthly flow. The women were so accustomed to the system that they rarely protested their family's arrangement or rearrangement of husbands. The system, the agents charged, gave old men a practical monopoly over young girls since they had superior leverage, both in wealth and prestige. Young men had "to put up with some worn out girl or wring in on another's wife." This left the young men very dissatisfied with the system, complaining that wives left them to get new husbands, usually old men who had gained influence by potlatching. According to DeBeck, it was next to impossible for a girl of thirteen or fourteen to be faithful "to an old brute of a Siwash 60 or 70"; eventually the girl got tired and left with another without paying back her obligations—"and then the trouble begins."[62] Halliday thought he could control the situation by registering Indian marriages, whether solemnized in a church or performed by Indian custom. Such a change would be welcomed by the younger Indians, he wrote, "as most of them are really sick of the potlatch but have not the moral courage to stand out against it." Vowell agreed and applied to the provincial government to have Halliday appointed as district registrar for births, deaths and marriages, which, after some delays, was done, but with no significant effect.[63]

Still, agents were troubled by the link between marriage and the potlatch. One of the worst features of the marriage contract, Debeck wrote, was that "it acts as a feeder to the Potlatch." Feasts, potlatches and marriages seemed to be "all blended & interwoven together, with their marriage law as the main spring." If the promiscuous practices could be stopped, Halliday believed, then "the potlatch would be a thing of the past. The two are so woven together that if the marriage part of it were properly adjusted the potlatch would lose its chief feeder."[64]

The Department of Indian Affairs appreciated the problem. "Nuptial unions are still in the most unsatisfactory conditions" in British Columbia, the deputy superintendent general commented in 1910, but interfering could make matters much worse. To deny the validity of any marriage would deprive a multitude of women who regarded themselves as married of their status and self-respect and render their children illegitimate. At the same time, attempts to force the issue might readily result in cohabitation without any pretense of marriage at all.[65]

Kwakiutl marriages did have most of the characteristics that bothered the agents, but they made their own sense.[66] Marriage, to the Kwakiutl as well as to other central coast groups such as the Bella Coola, was neither a mere economic arrangement nor strictly a way to regulate relations between the sexes. Its important feature was that it governed the status of the children. Family crests and privileges being their most important possessions, central coast Indians wished to have their descendants firmly established within their proud lineage. Marriage, as T. F. McIlwraith phrased it for the Bella Coola, "is not primarily a matter of affection but of the ancestral eligibility of the contracting parties." The choice of a woman to bear the children who would carry on the traditions of the ancestral family was "a matter of too great importance to be entrusted to any young person." The parents arranging the marriage approached it from a business standpoint, albeit a largely nonmaterial one. "Proud of their own ancient lineage, they would not demean themselves by allowing their son to marry a girl who could not trace her ancestry back to the first people, or with one whose forbears had disgraced themselves by marriage with slaves." The ability of the husband to potlatch depended largely on the wealth contributed by his wife's immediate family; wise parents eliminated a girl whose brothers were lazy. Their son's children would receive prerogatives from their maternal grandparents, so it was desirable to choose women from families who had prized dances or other valuable rights.

The repurchase or "buying out" of the wife by her family was obligatory. It also represented an honour to the wife and her children. It "made her heavy." In this way, remarriage made sense to both sets of parents. Once repurchased, the woman was proud and, if the marriage was terminated, she did not feel jilted.[67] A very young girl, as in the case of the Nakwakto woman, might be "married" to an influential chief. He benefited financially; at repurchase he would get more, in both material goods and ceremonial prerogatives, than he gave. For her part, the bride gained prestige by having been married to a man of note; the bride's family was fully compensated for the financial loss by the status gained in having their daughter the wife of a mighty chief.

A woman was especially honoured among the Kwakiutl (though not among the Bella Coola) by being married and released by payment of the marriage debt several times. Thus a woman married (either to the same man or to different men) and freed by payment of property four times, the honoured Kwakiutl number, bore the title of *o'ma* and was entitled to wear a painted hat and abalone earrings. Indeed, the Kwakiutl system was so open to remarriage that it could be exploited by the ambitious as the surest and easiest way to acquire capital and prerogatives. A ruthless man once went down the coast marrying a woman in nearly every tribe, divorcing her after she was bought out, and then passing on to another group and another wife. The higher his rank became, the more difficult it was to refuse a bride to him, even though it was known that he was following a definite, long-term strategy.[68]

The system did display some of the problems complained of by the agents. Young men might become restless at seeing girls for whom they had an eye married out from under them. To an extent the loose sexual standards regarding adultery, especially for men, alleviated some of this frustration (though not the agents' moral sensitivities). Tensions nevertheless emerged, at least by the turn of the century. Willie Harris, a Fort Rupert Kwakiutl of high rank, wanted to marry a commoner's daughter, a match objected to by parents on both sides. Not long after their refusal, he was found hanging from a tree, perhaps (as many thought) the victim of a drunken row; more likely, as Charles Nowell thought, dead by his own will from disappointed love.[69]

The marriage customs of the Kwakiutl had their internal coherence; the agents' complaints were by and large true. The agents probably mistook some "sham," investment-type marriages for real ones (the Kwakiutl had different words for the two relationships), and they exaggerated the bride price and understated the repurchase. But on the major points—women sold and repurchased, no permanence to the marriage bond and adultery as a common feature of Kwakiutl life—they were unsympathetically correct.

The persistence of cannibalistic ceremonial and marriage practices was symptomatic of the difficulties that the Kwakiutl presented to Canadian Indian administration and to Vowell's policy towards the potlatch. Elsewhere the potlatch seemed to be on the decline or at least had become part of a relatively harmless social occasion. Among the Kwakiutl, however, "there is no decrease in the number of potlatches held," Halliday reported in 1912, "nor is its influence apparently less. Nothing short of a social revolution will entirely banish the potlatch, and until this is accomplished, it will always be a great handicap."[70]

■ Superintendent Vowell allowed the potlatch law to go unenforced. At Victoria's Songhees reserve, onlookers watch potlatch guests scramble for the gift blankets tossed from a platform.

Photo credit: RBCM, *No. 6808, photo by R. Maynard*

SUSAN
Yis-Po-donna
Daughter of
Chief Tallo
She Potlatched among
her friends $1600⁰⁰
before her death.

■ The Bella Coola sometimes recorded in epigraphs the generosity of their dead. Susan's potlatches were put on her headstone (*left*), Chief Clelamen's on a house front above three coppers and a European wood sculpture (*below*).

Photo credits: *National Museums of Canada, National Museum of Civilization, neg. no. 58614, photo by Harlan Smith, 1923;* BCARS, *No. 97940*

HE WAS HONEST ✠ IN MEMORY OF ✠ &RESPECTED BY
& WELL DISPOSED CHIEF. CLELAMEN BOTH WHITES AND
· WHO DIED JULY 1893 AGED 50 YEARS INDIANS
IN DEC92 HE GAVE AWAY WITH THE HELP OF HIS SONS ALEXANDER &
JOHNNY, PROPERTY IN BLANKETS CANOES &C VALUED AT 4,000 DOLLARS
THIS BEING HIS EIGHTH LARGE POTLACH & FEAST THAT HE HAD HELD

■ Until 1919, the Kwakiutl continued their potlatches without heed for the law. The following seven photographs, all taken between 1897 and 1914, show various types of celebrations. *Top:* Sacks of flour are piled at Alert Bay for distribution at Harry Hanuse's flour potlatch. *Bottom:* At this gathering on the beach, part perhaps of Johnnie Clark's grease feast, cans of oolachan oil are visible among the landed goods.

Photo credits: RBCM, *No. 10083;* RBCM, *No. 10024*

■ Blankets, the dominant potlatch item in late nineteenth-century Kwakiutl potlatching, are shown piled high in preparation for giving.

Photo credit: *Courtesy Department Library Services, American Museum of Natural History,
neg. no. 22861, photo by Harlan Smith, 1897(?)*

■ These two photos depict a single Alert Bay potlatch, reportedly hosted by Bob Harris. *Left:* The boardwalk is piled with basins and buckets while silver bracelets, strung on poles, are to the side. *Below:* Household goods, especially dressers and sewing machines, are displayed before their distribution.

Photo credits: RBCM, *No. 2307-b, photo by J. Welsh;* RBCM, *No. 1887, photo by J. Welsh*

■ *Top:* Another Alert Bay scene shows masks, bracelets and kitchen utensils on display under strung bolts of fabric. *Bottom:* At Koskimo, a Kwakiutl village across Vancouver Island, Yacoutlas gave away $600 pinned in one- and two-dollar bills to button blankets and poles.

Photo credits: *National Archives of Canada, neg. no. PA 74039; Vancouver Public Library, No. 14070, photo by B. W. Leeson*

6

"Those Who Breach the Law Must Be Punished"

WHILE THE KWAKIUTL continued in their "recalcitrant" ways, the administration of Indian affairs was changing. A. W. Vowell resigned as British Columbia superintendent in 1910 and Ottawa took advantage of the vacancy to reorganize the provincial administration. In place of the superintendency, three regional inspectorates were created, two of which shared responsibility for the coastal region. A. M. Tyson, based in Vancouver, became inspector for the northern region, divided in 1910 to include the Queen Charlotte Islands, Nass, Bella Coola, Stikine and Babine agencies. In Victoria, William E. Ditchburn took over Vowell's old office to become southwestern inspector, his jurisdiction including the New Westminster, Cowichan, West Coast, Lytton and Kwawkewlth agencies.[1]

Raised in Ontario, Ditchburn had been sensational at lacrosse, a game in which he continued to star after his 1890 move to Victoria. By trade a printer, his virtual professionalism at lacrosse brought work with the local press, first with the Victoria *Times* and later with the *Colonist*. Leadership in the Typographical Union but more especially his friendship with Liberal newspaper proprietors Hewitt Bostock, Walter Nichol and William Templeman, the latter a cabinet minister, together with his activity in the Victoria Liberal Association, were his qualifications for the southwestern inspectorate of Indian affairs.

Ditchburn, at forty-seven, was absolutely new to the field, but he was conscientious and began a schedule of regular inspections of the agencies within his jurisdiction. Important topical matters preoccupied him in his initial years of office: compensation to Indians from the International Pelagic Sealing Convention award, negotiations for the acquisition of the Songees reserve in Victoria and dealings with the McKenna-McBride royal commission on Indian reserves. His major ongoing concerns, reflecting continuing departmental priorities, were education and the suppression of liquor on reserves. Alcohol abuse, not aboriginal marriage or the potlatch, remained "the most important feature" of Indian "immorality."

Only in 1913 did the Kwakiutl potlatch begin to emerge as a concern to Inspector Ditchburn. The initial impetus came from an investigation he was obliged to conduct into Kwawkewlth agency affairs following complaints made against Agent Halliday, primarily by Rev. John Antle of the Anglican Church's Columbia Coast Mission. The allegations were personal and bureaucratic, largely unrelated to the condition or behaviour of the Kwakiutl themselves. Ditchburn's report conceded Halliday's difficulties in maintaining friendship with his white neighbours. As Indian agent, however, all agreed that Halliday "is doing the best he can with his Indians." "Though they have had the benefit of missionary influence among them for over thirty years," Ditchburn reported, they "are still very slothful and show no desire to advance in the scale of civilization." The same problem; the same diagnosis. The potlatch was a prominent feature of their lives, and "they are so wrapped up in this deplorable custom that they give no heed to any advice for the betterment of their condition."[2]

Ditchburn's report to Ottawa passed over the desk of the department's chief clerk who marked the paragraph and, in passing it on to Deputy Superintendent General Frank Pedley, added the comment, "It seems a great pity that we cannot do something to break up this abominable and wasteful aboriginal custom."[3] Chief Clerk D. C. Scott was a rising figure in the department and would replace Pedley within the year. His desire "to break up" the potlatch became headquarters policy even before his official succession. Thus began, with a complaint against Halliday and the ascendancy of Scott, a reversal in potlatch policy, a change to which Ditchburn's Victoria office would give its full support.

Duncan Campbell Scott was fifty-one when he assumed the deputy superintendency upon Frank Pedley's forced resignation over speculation in Indian lands. A son of the manse, Scott grew up within a cultured home in the small towns of Quebec and eastern Ontario. His father's livelihood did not permit Scott to realize his ambition for a career in medicine, but the elder Scott's Conservative connections secured for the seventeen-year-old a clerk's position with the federal Indian affairs department. Intelligent and capable, Scott possessed "a shrewd and supple political sense"[4] that advanced his career with the department. He rose steadily, becoming chief clerk and accountant in 1893, and when a new position of superintendent of education was created in 1909, Scott added this to his duties. When Pedley's difficulties left a vacuum at the top, Scott quite naturally filled it. He was the first permanent deputy in departmental history to come from within civil service ranks, and his appointment ratified a role he had effectively been playing since the Pedley scandal had begun months before.

Scott was a successful bureaucrat, "gifted with that mixture of guile and idealism that is the mark of the highest sort of civil servant."[5] Yet public recognition, then as now, rested upon his literary avocation. His calm, contemplative and polished poetry, something of a reflection of Scott's gracious and courtly charm, gained him a reputation as one of the country's foremost men of letters. Although by the time of his appointment in 1913 his work was seen as slightly old-fashioned, he was just attaining the height of his powers, becoming capable of verse that, at its most original, possesses a remarkable unity of emotional intensity and perfection of form.[6] That summer, just after Scott's elevation to deputy superintendent general, Rupert Brooke sought him out, with a letter of introduction from admirer John Masefield, as "the only poet in Canada."[7]

Scott's poetry and prose frequently utilized Indian themes and characters, often portraying native people as doomed figures, part of a noble but waning race. The literary image of the Indian merged with official policy. "The happiest future for the Indian race is absorption into the general population," wrote Scott, "and this is the object of the policy of our government." Agriculture and employment should supplant hunting, fishing and gathering; Christian ideals of conduct and morals should substitute for aboriginal concepts. Native culture and tradition would be overcome by "the great forces of intermarriage and education."[8]

These views were conventional and had been expressed by Scott's predecessors as well as most of his colleagues. They were also shared by most Canadians and were transferred to the Ukrainian, Jewish and other new immigrants who had entered Canada in the vast population movement of the 1896–1914 era. Assimilation was the keynote of public policy. "Cultural pluralism" and the "Canadian mosaic" were concepts that had hardly been born, ideals of a later generation facing different realities than those of Scott's own. Few would have challenged Scott's assertion in 1920 that "our objective is to continue until there is not a single Indian in Canada that has not been absorbed into the body politic, and there is no Indian question, and no Indian department."[9]

Scott believed that historical processes necessitated the death of the old order and that Indian culture was among these archaic forms. "The Europeanization of the Indians," the deputy superintendent general considered, "was simply a part of the story of progress." In implementing this integrationist policy, Scott put proof into the pudding. Departmental appropriations increased substantially during his tenure as deputy. Indian affairs, like all civilian departments, suffered severe cuts during the desperate strain of the war years, but recovered dramatically in the 1920s. Appropriations doubled in the decade between 1921 and 1931. The emphasis was on education and health services. In 1920 Scott introduced compulsory school attendance as an amendment to the Indian Act and he further strengthened the provision a decade later.[10]

Scott's policy was reformist, well within traditional government policy towards native people. If there was a new note, it lay in increased intervention to bring about more rapid integration. Paternalistic initiatives had long been part of policy. Now they were carried further than ever before, even—as more than one commentator has judged—shifting from paternalism to oppression.[11] Where education and moral suasion were not working or where their pace appeared slow, Scott was prepared to intervene with the full coercive power of the Indian Act as it stood. Where inadequate to his aims, he was prepared to amend it.

Scott's predecessors had deplored the sun and thirst dances among Canada's prairie Indians and the tamananawas and potlatch in British Columbia. These, wrote Deputy Superintendent General James A. Smart in 1900, helped to "keep alive habits and practices

which are most objectionable." Since these customs had religious
and economic significance, however, the department's policy had
been "to suppress the worst features and wait for time and other influences to do the rest." Frank Pedley had continued "to avoid ex-
cessive measures" and to allow moral suasion and education to
wean the Indians from objectionable habits and customs.[12] With
Scott came a new wind, an impatience with practices that in Confederation's fifth decade still hindered the integration of Indians
into the Canadian population. The new line played itself out in the
western prairies against the sun dance of the Blackfoot and the thirst
dance of the Cree; in British Columbia it aimed at the potlatch. In
the Pacific province, Scott's shift proceeded with little resistance
from Halliday and support from Inspector Ditchburn.

Ditchburn's report on the complaints against Halliday had restored the potlatch to Ottawa's attention. The department was concerned, as Pedley (prompted by Scott) wrote Halliday, by "the fact
that the potlatch is still a prominent custom among your Indians."
Elsewhere it had been done away with; "it should be possible to
achieve a like result in your Agency." He asked Halliday to suggest
the best means to overcome the evil.[13]

Although the initiative came from Ottawa, Kwawkewlth agent
William Halliday was very responsive. He had been responsible for
the Southern Kwakiutl for six years and noted little advancement.
His best efforts were frustrated by Kwakiutl social conservatism and
the web that the potlatch system spread amongst almost all his
agency wards. The necessities of life came easily enough, and money
from hand-logging and fishing was plentiful. The Kwakiutl, Halliday felt, were in a rut of apathy, getting through life easily and
finding their glory from giving a potlatch. Prostitution seemed on
the decline and intemperance had largely been checked, but schooling remained neglected. Once antagonistic to education, the
Kwakiutl had developed only to a point of "absolute indifference."
The Nakwakto were probably the least civilized, wrote Halliday, the
Tsawataineuk of Kingcome Inlet and Gilford Island the most conservative: they still thought that "customs that suited their grandfa-
thers should suit them." The potlatch remained deeply ingrained
among the Fort Rupert Kwakiutl; everywhere it kept down any individual desire for an Indian "to launch out" for himself. The evil influence of the potlatch, especially its relationship to marriages, per-

vades Halliday's reports from 1906 to 1913. "The potlatch and its ramifications" remained "the great stumbling block in the way of progress." Though there was some native feeling against the loss of time given over to the practice, "there is no decrease in the number of potlatches held nor is its influence apparently less."[14]

Halliday responded quickly to Ottawa's inquiry about how the potlatch should be dealt with in his agency. Were the existing statute not defective, he said, he would recommend that it be strictly enforced. Remarkable here is Halliday's impression, almost seven years after assuming the agency, that the act remained ultra vires as a result of a case "some years ago." He had no record of the matter, only "facts as they were told to me by outsiders." This was folk memory of the Hamasak case as handled by Pidcock and Begbie in 1889. Halliday's ignorance is testimony to Vowell's approach to administering the law and to Ditchburn's preoccupation with other matters. "I presume," the latter wrote in August, "that those in charge of Indian Affairs in British Columbia in the past have had their own good reasons for not insisting that [the law] be put in force."[15]

Halliday's recommendation received reinforcement from A. E. Green, the Indian schools inspector for the province. Green's view that the potlatches were "immoral and degrading, and interfere greatly with the educational work among the Indians and retard civilization generally" was not new. Since at least 1885 he had held that opinion, first as a Methodist missionary on the Nass and now as federal inspector. More important, perhaps, was his testimony that the Indians had gained the idea that the potlatch was no longer disapproved of by the department. "I regret to say," he wrote, "it is spreading." Departmental indifference had given Indians a feeling of licence. The Bella Bella had held their first potlatch in twenty-five years, giving away over $4000 in cash and $5000 in goods. It was increasing on the Skeena in the Babine agency and in the West Coast agency, and had reappeared on the Nass. The worst of all was, of course, the Kwawkewlth agency.[16]

Responding to these reports, Ottawa initiated a review and found "nothing to indicate that the legislation had ever been declared ultra vires" and assured Halliday that he need not hesitate in enforcing Section 149 as it now appeared in the Indian Act. He should of course proceed cautiously, warning first and making no threats of prosecution. If ignored, he should secure witnesses, lay information and, should evidence appear conclusive, commit the ringleaders for trial.[17] Similar letters went to other British Columbia agents.

The policy push was now in effect. Behind it lay both Scott's impatience with a custom that seemed to hinder the integration of Indians into Canadian life and the centralization of authority that abolition of the local superintendency had brought. Administratively, the Victoria office was no longer able to act as a buffer between native people and Ottawa's will, but this change would have come about in any case since Ditchburn, along with Halliday and Green, welcomed the department's newfound zeal.

To some extent, Ottawa's push was bolstered by other reports from the coast. The accuracy of those reports is difficult to verify. Charles C. Perry, the Nass agent, described a "growing tendency" at Port Simpson to feast and give presents, and the Methodist missionaries also expressed concern at the revival.[18] Records from other areas are too sketchy to indicate any tendency.

Scott's decision to press the law was in a sense personal, but behind it lay the shift of population and power on the coast. Demographics had altered significantly since Powell's 1885 retreat at Comeaken, even since the provincial legislature's 1897 resolution. Whites in British Columbia now outnumbered natives by almost twenty to one. In 1901 Indians had made up over 16 per cent of the provincial population; by 1911, they were only slightly over 5 per cent.[19] In Gitksan and Kwakiutl country the natives remained a substantial element in the population, but few settlers or politicians feared their disaffection. A new railway was taming the Skeena, steamships now penetrated the northern channels and rivers with great frequency, and gasoline launches were available to most police detachments and many Indian agents. More than any other development, the great growth of the salmon canning industry had brought the Indians into closer integration with the white economy. By 1913 British Columbia's native population was not something to be feared. Laws might be sometimes hard to enforce, prosecutions might poison the relationship between an agent and his wards, but no one need fear a Canadian echo of the Sepoy Mutiny or a British Columbia replay of American Indian wars.

At Alert Bay, Agent Halliday was "exceedingly glad" that the department was taking steps to enforce the law. "It will," he wrote, "make a great difference." Less than four months later, Halliday took steps of his own. When the Indians gathered at Alert Bay on their way to the canneries, as was their custom, he called a meeting to read out the law and lecture on the evils of the potlatch. The assembly of about two hundred men from six different tribes was, naturally, subdued. "They listened very quietly and patiently," reported Halliday, "and asked a few questions regarding the matter and then said they would think about what I said and let me know what they thought after they came back from fishing."[20]

The Kwakiutl had heard strong talk before and were uncertain whether the government was serious this time or not. By October some had "determined to put the matter to the test." Johnny Bagwany, a Nimpkish of Alert Bay, boldly stated that he was prepared "to see the matter through" by calling the Indians from Cape Mudge, Campbell River and Salmon River to Alert Bay for a potlatch. Agent Halliday warned him, but Bagwany was steadfast. He "was willing to make a sacrifice of himself as a martyr as he did not consider that the law had any business to interfere with their customs." Word of a large potlatch at Bella Coola, unhindered by the agent there, bolstered the view that Halliday's warning was mere bluff.[21]

Halliday ignored a number of small potlatches, but on the first day of November he walked through the village and observed three or four hundred Indians gathered for a potlatch. Derisive remarks came his way to the effect that "that was all the law amounted to." Several other small potlatches went ahead and Halliday felt that if he did not prosecute immediately the Indians "would accept the fact that the Indian Agent knew that the potlatches were being held and that all the warnings given meant nothing at all." He laid information against five Indians before Rev. A. W. Corker, J.P., then withdrew three of these to concentrate on the one ceremony he had himself witnessed and could positively prove: that for which Ned Harris and Bagwany were responsible. The two Nimpkish pleaded guilty to the charge and Halliday allowed release on their own recognizance pending trial in Vancouver. There they elected for a jury trial to be heard in the spring assizes.[22]

Indian reactions varied. By reasoning Halliday could not follow, some had the idea, because they were allowed to elect for jury trial, that "they have scored a victory and that they are free to go ahead and potlatch all they like."[23] Nevertheless, the Lekwiltok at Cape Mudge decided to await the outcome of the assizes before continuing. Uncertainty among the Nimpkish about their future ability to recall loans made them hesitant and accounted for the dearth of significant potlatches at Alert Bay. When Halliday and Ditchburn warned the Fort Ruperts, they were met by long speeches defending the system and a plain indication that the Indians "would set the law at defiance." The Indians gathered at Fort Rupert seemed engaged only in dancing and speeches, but they soon returned to their usual potlatching. Charles Nowell reported in April that "we had a good time. There were dances every night & potlatches every day." Halliday issued summonses against several at Fort Rupert and two Tsawatsaineuk at Gwayasdums, but the provincial police requested a remand until the Harris-Bagwany case was settled.[24]

Rex v. Harris and Bagwany was heard before Justice F. B. Gregory in the Vancouver County Court in the first week of May 1914. The two defendants, past middle age and appearing "particularly intelligent" with "features betokening strength of character," were represented by D. E. McTaggart. In his summing up Justice Gregory defined a festival as a religious gathering and a ceremony as something conducted by fixed rules. The jury, after three hours, disagreed on whether a potlatch was either. A second trial was held the next day at which the prosecution, A. D. Taylor, K.C., for the Crown, assisted by R. R. Maitland, K.C., for the department, pointed out that dances had been held at the "festival" in question. The jury returned a verdict of guilty within minutes, but accompanied it with a strong recommendation for mercy. Justice Gregory suspended sentence on the grounds that this was the first case of its kind since Begbie's time.[25]

The prosecution had been successful, although ending only in suspended sentences for the two men. The Kwakiutl were "very much disappointed." They held Halliday personally responsible, in part because they knew of no other agent taking a similar line. The outcome of the trial, Halliday wrote, had "not made the life of the Agent a bed of roses," but the law had been established. He judged that one further conviction would be necessary "before submission can be depended upon."[26] The next winter's season would be critical.

Halliday slipped in August 1914 when he allowed Harry Mountain to mourn the death of his father. He had understood that Mountain intended only to pay the mourners for attending, but it turned into a potlatch, by either misunderstanding or wilful misinterpretation. Halliday felt he had been had—"put in a false position" was his phrase. Determined to repair any damage, he reaffirmed the law in a circular to all chiefs. While no one wanted to put any Indians in jail, "the law must be enforced and those who break the law must be punished."[27] A Milwaukee anthropologist collecting at Fort Rupert noted that "there is a jinks on here now" with two constables "ready to step in at any time."[28] When potlatches were held again at Gwayasdums and Fort Rupert in January 1915, Halliday moved immediately to arrest the major actor in each.

The case against Cessaholis of Kingcome Inlet was disposed of quickly. Lawyer Frank Lyons insisted that his client had not really been potlatching, merely giving a little feast for the hungry and presents for the needy, but advised Cessaholis to plead guilty. From the dock, the defendant accepted guilt, but not before asserting the propriety of his actions. "I did not give a potlatch," he stated. "I gave a feast for poor Indians, just like white people in Vancouver give feasts for the poor people." Indians in the Kingcome region could not sell their furs that winter or get work in the logging camps. "I call my people together, give them a good feast and presents of food to take home with them," Cessaholis said. Vancouver County Court Judge W. W. H. McInnis delivered a suspended sentence. Fort Rupert was in Nanaimo County and Kiskwagila was taken there and elected for a trial at the spring assizes. In May the grand jury, persuaded that it was a trifling matter, found that there was no true bill of indictment. The jury, Halliday heard, "did not see any offence in potlatching."[29]

Halliday and Ditchburn had wanted convictions and penalties. Instead, three suspended sentences had been followed by an outright dismissal, leaving all four offenders free and unpunished. The campaign was stymied, Scott's policy ineffectual. Rev. F. W. Comley, principal of the Alert Bay industrial school, judged the results an outright failure, interpreted by the Indians "as a great victory over the government." Flushed with their defeat of the law, "these men had returned to Alert Bay and were potlatching worse than ever."[30]

Without admitting defeat, Halliday and the department took no further action. Halliday was told that, "for the time being," the department would not require him to institute proceedings against potlatch practitioners. He did nothing in 1915–16 to the six hundred Kwakiutl gathered in Alert Bay over the winter except to push them about sanitation. They were quiet and orderly, he reported, engaged largely in singing and dancing, though "a certain amount of property is given away." Friction between potlatching Indians and Alert Bay whites brought a decision by native people to meet at Gwayasdums the following winter. The potlatching there continued from the first week of January into April. Halliday ventured on no prosecutions in 1916, 1917 or 1918, despite the "usual winter dances and potlatches" and "a certain amount of feasting and potlatches."[31]

The relaxation of government policy is apparent from the decline in the number of letters and petitions that protesting Indians sent to the department. At least six, signed by over two hundred Indians, were received in the ten months after the Harris-Bagwany trial. After March 1915 the natives ceased their protests. Quiet had once more descended upon the issue.

The available documents do not clearly explain the department's more conciliatory mood, but several factors were at work. The war may have been an element. While nothing appears in the official record, Halliday apparently sought a tempering of the potlatch for the duration of hostilities. As one Kwakiutl reported, "Mr. Halliday told us during the war, not to enjoy ourselves while the war was on. We all agree to do as he told us. And had no Potlatch as long as the war was on."[32] Certainly, Halliday began to reappraise the policy, partly because of the "strained relations between the agent and the people he is trying to help," partly as a result of a meeting with a number of young men in his agency. He worried, apparently for the first time, at the consequences of breaking up the entire system. The potlatch was, he wrote, "not without its good points."[33]

The main reason for the lapse, however, remained the inability to secure penal convictions. Halliday feared that further prosecutions would be similarly inconclusive. He wanted no more suspended sentences, no more acquittals. "There seems," he wrote even before Kiskwagila's Nanaimo dismissal, "to be considerable difficulty in having any penalty imposed." Unable to secure success at court, the department decided to discontinue proceedings for the time being.[34]

Behind the signal failure to achieve the department's goal was the public belief that potlatching was simply not a crime.

The situation had been made apparent to Ottawa by R. R. Maitland, the department's counsel in the Harris-Bagwany case. Indicating clearly that he was himself an unwilling participant, Maitland reported "that public sentiment was very strong against a conviction in this case because the potlatch in question was a perfectly harmless affair" with no "detrimental effects other than the giving away of blankets." Judge McInnis, who heard the Cessahollis case, was blunt. He had given the guilty man a suspended sentence because a penalty for potlatching would not be at all popular. He told Halliday that "no crime had been committed even if there was a statute making it such," and that he "doubted very much if any judge in B.C. would do anything else than give a suspended sentence."[35]

Indications of public sentiment reached Ottawa through other channels. Halliday wrote that, though small potlatches were occurring in his agency, "it had not been deemed wise to prosecute as public sympathy would be absolutely opposed to any conviction under existing circumstances." H. S. Clements, the Conservative MP representing the Alert Bay area, wrote Scott about his sympathies over "the little festivals" of the Indians. From the government's own Victoria Memorial Museum came impressive testimonial in defence of the potlatch. Edward Sapir, who had noted a "good deal of trouble" among the Indians in his 1914 West Coast field trip, collected letters from every major Northwest Coast anthropologist in Canada and the United States: Franz Boas of Columbia University, John Swanton of the Bureau of American Ethnology, Harlan I. Smith of the Ottawa museum and British Columbia specialists J. A. Teit, Charles Hill-Tout and C. F. Newcombe. All advocated noninterference with the Indians' customs.[36]

The backlash was sobering to Scott. Responding to an Anglican demand that the law be put in force, he advised his minister, W. J. Roche, of the difficulties. The Indians were "very loath to give up" a practice so deeply ingrained in their social system. Suppression required "some diplomacy." More significantly, there was "considerable difficulty in having any penalty imposed." He recommended, in order to insure that future prosecutions "may be disposed of without delay and with some degree of success," that the offence be made summary rather than indictable. Scott's recommendation actually had its basis in a letter from Halliday in 1913 that suggested "it would very much simplify matters if the Indian agent would summarily deal with this indictable offense."[37] Further reports of renewed and increased activity elsewhere in British Columbia may have reinforced the decision.[38] In the 1918 parliamentary session the change was made almost without comment. According to the new minister of the interior, Arthur Meighen, it was a simple change "to avoid the expense of proceeding by indictment."[39]

The change was simple but not minor. Formerly, the agent, acting as a justice of the peace (technically as two, since two magistrates were required for summary cases), could only take evidence and lay information for a hearing before a British Columbia county court. Now he could try the case and, on conviction, lay sentence. This gave the agent a great deal of power. In effect he was prosecutor and judge. Convictions were now very likely. Grand jury refusals to indict (as for Kiskwagila at Nanaimo) or jury trials (as for Harris and Bagwany in Vancouver) were no longer possible.

More significantly, a suspended sentence following conviction was now unlikely. The alteration from indictable to summary proceedings meant that Judge McInnis's opinion that no judge would give anything stronger than a suspended sentence was largely irrelevant. Agents would be free to set sentence, up to six months' imprisonment, as they saw fit. As Scott put it, the change meant "greater control of cases being placed in the hands of the Indian Agents."[40]

Both conviction and sentence remained subject to appeal to the county courts, but getting a conviction, and especially a sentence, overturned would be more difficult than avoiding one in the first place. In this instance, a reversal by a superior court would have especially serious consequences because of the mingling, in the Indian agent, of administrative and judicial functions. Reversal of Justice Halliday's conviction or sentence would inevitably have an impact upon Agent Halliday's effectiveness. Judge Cayley noted the problem: a quashed conviction would lessen the authority of the agent.[41] Even more, the change was a clear indication of governmental intent. No judge would easily lay his own opinion about potlatching or his private assessment of public sentiment against this recent expression of Parliament's will. Judges could read signals as easily as they could read law.[42]

Scott's 1918 amendment thus gave Halliday a very strong

weapon, though left to his own devices it was one that he might not have used. He had been burned by appeal courts, had had some second thoughts about wiping out the value of blankets and coppers, and seemed to want to leave things alone. But neither the Kwakiutl nor Scott would permit it. Scott moved first.

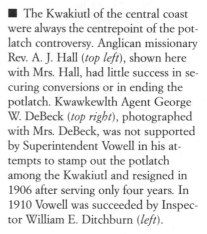

■ The Kwakiutl of the central coast were always the centrepoint of the potlatch controversy. Anglican missionary Rev. A. J. Hall (*top left*), shown here with Mrs. Hall, had little success in securing conversions or in ending the potlatch. Kwawkewlth Agent George W. DeBeck (*top right*), photographed with Mrs. DeBeck, was not supported by Superintendent Vowell in his attempts to stamp out the potlatch among the Kwakiutl and resigned in 1906 after serving only four years. In 1910 Vowell was succeeded by Inspector William E. Ditchburn (*left*).

Photo credits: BCARS, *No. 89312;* BCARS, *No. 96512;* RBCM, *No. 12472*

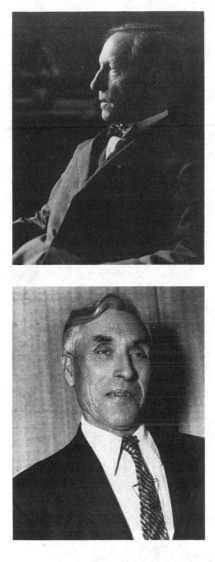

■ In 1913 Duncan Campbell Scott (*top left*) became deputy superintendent general of Indian affairs. Scott ordered Kwakiutl agent William H. Halliday (*top right*) to enforce the law. Initially unsuccessful, Halliday and Scott renewed their efforts after 1918. Prosecutions culminated in over fifty convictions for those participating in the 1922 Village Island potlatch hosted by Dan Cranmer (*left*).

Photo credits: *Thomas Fisher Rare Book Library, University of Toronto, photo by M. O. Hammond;* BCARS, *No. 95771; Courtesy U'mista Cultural Centre, Alert Bay*

■ Convicted Kwakiutl were allowed suspended sentences if they promised to stop potlatching and "voluntarily surrendered" their potlatch paraphernalia. The surrendered material, including masks (*top*) and coppers (*bottom*), were stored in the church hall before being sent to the National Museum in Ottawa and the Royal Ontario Museum in Toronto.

Photo credits: RBCM, *No. PN 11637, photo by Rev. V. S. Lord;* RBCM, *No. 12194, photo by W. H. Halliday*

7

"The Potlatch Is Killed"

SCOTT'S AMENDMENT WENT through Parliament in April 1918, at a time when the Great War in Europe was not going well. Germany's spring offensive had imperilled Paris for the first time since 1914. The Allied front eventually held, but the outlook was grim. With Russia out of the war, with troop morale low after four bloody years of attrition, and with the American effort yet slow and uncertain, the Allies expected the war might last another two years. Canada was hardly indifferent to the grave threat of defeat. She had entered the war in August 1914 of her own accord, professing a willingness to expend the last man and the last dollar for the vindication of her own honour and that of the empire of which she was a loyal partner. It is hard now to appreciate fully the dedication and determination of those Canadians who, after four years of unprecedented effort and sacrifice, of losses of family and friends, of reading column after column of casualty lists in the daily press, remained committed to winning the war at any cost.

Duncan Campbell Scott, too old to enlist, could do little to win the war. He wrote a few gracious elegies to fallen heroes, but his Booth Building offices were far from the central concerns of wartime Canada. He encouraged native enlistment, an initiative that Inspector Ditchburn, elevated to inspector of the entire province in 1917, accepted with enthusiasm. A number of British Columbia Indians served in the Mesopotamian campaign, with Oweekano David Bernardan commanding a vessel on the Euphrates. Four of seven volunteers from Metlakatla died in service. An Alert Bay man received the Distinguished Conduct Medal, a Metlakatlan the Military Medal. In all, several hundred British Columbia native men in khaki joined almost four thousand more from across the country. Indian affairs officials attributed the smaller proportion of Indian enlistments from the westernmost province to the fact that B.C. native people were less warlike in character than prairie or eastern Indians and had a natural disinclination to leave their homes for unfamiliar ventures.[1] The enlistments were entirely voluntary; men of Indian status were exempted by Order in Council from the 1917 Military Service Act.[2]

While Scott was proud of the Indians' response to the war, by 1917–18 his part in the nation's "greater production campaign" had come to overshadow all other considerations in his mind. The military drain on manpower had placed a very heavy burden on domestic production of food and material needed for the war effort. Here Scott could at least help in the country's crisis. Agents were sent urgent instructions to promote both conservation and production. Major efforts were made to maximize crops on reserves; land unworked by Indians was leased to whites. Halliday reported on his effort "to conserve food for our fighting men"; he had asked the Kwakiutl to do their bit by maximizing native food sources, by minimizing store purchases and by selling all the fish they could to the canneries.[3]

The problems of conservation and production became ever more pressing. The Canada Food Board restricted consumption of beef, pork and sugar; the 1918 "Anti-Loafing Law" demanded useful employment of all males between sixteen and sixty. Most of Canada was dry by 1918, partly as a consequence of the campaign to utilize grain efficiently. In February Scott circularized all agents on the food crisis. Food production, he wrote, was "literally fighting the Germans." In October, seized by the "urgent need for conservation in all directions" and especially in food supplies, Scott condemned any "wasteful practice or mode of life." More specifically, British Columbia agents were told of their new power to try Section 149 offences without reference to a higher court. Agents were to exercise these powers to the full in ending the wasteful practice of the potlatch. He left no doubt of his meaning: "This policy is now most essential; and it is expected that you will act accordingly."[4]

Whether the greater production campaign brought about the circular or merely served as the pretext for a renewed assault under the more favourable circumstances of summary procedure is a moot point. Once set in motion, Scott's revived campaign against the potlatch continued with its own momentum. The armistice, signed three weeks after his instructions, made no difference.

Halliday did not greet Scott's instructions as enthusiastically as he had met the deputy's 1913 push. He had been burned then—by courts that had not sustained his depositions or given the desired sentences, and more especially by the bad relations with the Indians under his jurisdiction. Kwakiutl hostility had evaporated once the prosecutions ceased. While investigating white complaints of Halliday's negligence of sanitation during five months of potlatches in the winter of 1916, Ditchburn found Halliday popular among the Indians. Charles Nowell even asked how it was that white people "could be saying such bad things about our good friend the Indian Agent."[5]

Halliday did not relish a renewal of the ordeal, but dutifully read Scott's circular to an Alert Bay feast, trying to ignore the potlatch that accompanied it. The Kwakiutl, firm in their belief that such an unjust law had to be based on misunderstanding, asked that he petition Scott to meet with them to learn the true story. Halliday agreed.

Just after Christmas, 1918, Halliday fulfilled his promise in a long letter to the deputy superintendent general. "I have given the matter of the potlatch," he began, "a good deal of consideration." The system, he now realized, was a mixture of good and evil. He had no doubt that as long as the potlatch prevailed there would be a lack of progress and he remained convinced that no allowance should be made for that "chief evil" of the system, the customary Kwakiutl marriage. That a woman could be married without her consent or that she might be given as a pledge for property was wrong. Yet the potlatch did have its good sides: the cultivated hospitality that was the chief characteristic of the coast natives and the sustenance that this gave to the poor and the destitute. "If the entire potlatch system were done away with in one swoop," Halliday concluded, "these poor people would either suffer from want or would become a heavy burden on the relief account."[6]

What bothered Halliday that festive season was less a balance sheet of good and bad than "the difficulties which confront an Indian Agent in the performance of his duties." The memories of the

1913–15 difficulties haunted him. He would do his duty and suffer the necessary, but he did want Scott to understand that many of the gatherings, though illegal, were perfectly harmless and that granting an agent some discretion would be advantageous both to the department and to the Indians. At the customary public mourning for the dead, for example, the singers were given "a consideration" that gave comfort to the friends of the deceased, and, lasting only a day, the ceremony itself did no particular harm. To suppress these because they fell within Section 149 "would be almost too drastic a proceeding." Similarly, distributions of the spring's oolachan catch were planned for the coming winter. The oil really belonged to all the people, with each individual knowing to the pint his or her entitlement, but the agent had no option but to refuse permission for its public, ceremonial distribution. He had suggested that the oil be given out privately, but that "did not quite suit the Indian Idea [sic]." In trying to convey his problem, Halliday fell back, again and again, on the "difficulty" of the agent's role. "If he conforms with the letter of the law he is doing what he knows to be an injustice," he told Scott, "but the difficulty is knowing where to draw the line." He found it "difficult to know just where to shut an eye and when to come down absolutely flat footed." More seriously, would the law work? Certainly progress required that the Indians' nature be changed, but it was a "very difficult matter by a single law to change the entire nature of the habits and customs of any people." It now appeared to Agent Halliday "that only by education and advice and that repeated year after year" would the Indians see for themselves that they would be better off by changing their old customs for new ways.[7] His request that Scott or someone else from headquarters investigate the situation first-hand therefore reflected his own wishes as well as those of the Kwakiutl.

Halliday's musings were considered and sincere. He did not relish the hostility that enforcement, prosecutions and trials would bring upon him. But he was caught between Scott's determination and Kwakiutl insistence. Neither gave him leeway and, when he learned of some "misunderstanding" about enforcement of the law, he toured his agency's villages to deliver "a last and final warning." Upon returning to Alert Bay he found that "a so-called marriage had taken place" and took immediate action.[8]

Likiosa (Johnnie Seaweed) had given Kwosteetsas (Japanese

Charlie) some $700 cash as a bridal payment for the latter's sister. This kind of "barter" was bad enough in Halliday's eyes, but the transaction was hardly ameliorated by Likiosa having two previous wives, both of whom were not only alive but now living with other men "under the potlatch law."[9] No better red flag could have been waved. Halliday's reflection turned to indignation and he came down "flat footed" by charging both men.

This prosecution, the first in almost five years, broke the fragile truce. Tried on 29 January 1919 before William Halliday, J.P., under the new summary procedures, the two defendants were convicted; receiving the minimum penalty, they were the first Indians to be sentenced to penal servitude under the potlatch law of 1884. The case was immediately appealed to Vancouver County Court where Judge H. S. Cayley released the two after bail bonds of $1000 each had been posted by B.C. Packers, owners of the Alert Bay cannery. The appeal was scheduled for a March hearing.

At almost the same time a deputation of three, Charles Nowell from Fort Rupert, Moses Alfred from Alert Bay and William Roberts from Campbell River, left to plead the case of the potlatch itself before Duncan Campbell Scott in Ottawa. The reception they received was as cool as the Rideau River in February. The department's evidence, they were brusquely told, gave no reason to change the statute in question.[10]

Back in Alert Bay, Halliday was more concerned about the Likiosa-Kwosteetsas appeal. "The Indians," he wrote, "are determined to make a test [of this] case." Were the convictions and penalties overturned, there would be "very little use in ever prosecuting another case."[11] Prior to the appeal's appearing before Judge Cayley's bench, however, another Alert Bay prosecution intervened.

Chief Harry Mountain, John McDougall, Isaac and Chief August of the Klawatala were charged in early March with potlatching. The details of their offence are lost, but this second summary process before Halliday promised to be yet another test. The defendants engaged their Vancouver counsel, Frank Lyons, the lawyer handling the Likiosa and Kwosteetsas appeal, to argue before Justice of the Peace Halliday.[12] The department responded with the distinguished J. H. Senkler, K.C., to conduct the prosecution.

Lyons's boat was late and the trial was rescheduled from 19 March to Saturday, 22 March. Halliday was uneasy. He understood that Lyons intended to challenge his right to occupy the bench by calling upon him, as Indian agent, to be a defence witness. Moreover, the Indians were making a determined effort to suppress evidence; it would be difficult to sift out the facts and determine who had been present at the potlatch. When Halliday's court opened on Saturday, however, Lyons spoke of the tremendous hardship that a jail sentence would place upon his clients at the beginning of the fishing season and asked for an adjournment to consider if the matter could not be negotiated. As justice, Halliday granted the delay, though as agent he made it clear that the department was determined to end potlatching and, unless some agreement was definitely made, the prosecution must proceed. The result was an unprecedented compromise that, while avoiding conviction and imprisonment, seemed to assure the end of Kwakiutl potlatching. At Lyons's suggestion, Senkler and Halliday agreed to adjourn the case against the four Mamalillikulla on their written promise—and the promise of the seventy-five other Kwakiutl who crowded the courtroom—to potlatch no more.[13]

"We will," promised the Indians, "obey the law and will not potlatch in any form" so long as the Indian Act stood unaltered. The seventy-nine promised to "use our influence in every way to uphold the law and to discourage any others from violating this section of the law,"[14] while at the same time reserving the right to make representation to have the law changed. Likiosa and Kwosteetsas, appellants to Halliday's January convictions, were among the signators. Crown and defence joined to ask that their appeal be withdrawn and the judge requested to reduce the penalty to a suspended sentence. Judge Cayley obliged a week later.

The case of the four Mamalillikulla was a watershed. Under threat of prison sentences and at the suggestion of their counsel, the Indians capitulated, not just the four men arraigned before Halliday's bench but appellants Likiosa and Kwosteetsas and seventy-three others. It was, on the face of it, an astonishing collapse. Previously the Kwakiutl had opposed the law in every way; now a significant number had committed themselves to obedience. Halliday was not exaggerating when he described it as "a great moral victory." "Now that the Indians have agreed of their own free will to uphold the law," he hoped "that the potlatch evil will be stamped out."[15]

Neither the seventy-nine Kwakiutl nor their counsel have left a record of the circumstances behind the remarkable rout. Most likely, Lyons realized that he was up against not just Senkler but Halliday. "Lyons saw," the agent later wrote, "that he could not possibly win in any of the cases."[16] Perhaps he felt he could not win the Likiosa-Kwosteetsas appeal either. He was an eccentric lawyer—legal folklore has him practising from the back of his car before joining a major law firm—but a good one. Though very much junior to Senkler, it is unlikely that Lyons feared the more experienced lawyer. In the end, confronted by a doubtful appeal and an even more doubtful case, in which failure meant jail terms just at the approach of the fishing season, he suggested a negotiated settlement.

The motives of the Indians who signed are only slightly more obscure. Certainly they had the idea that there would be, as a result of the agreement, an investigation of the potlatch law and, if the inquiry so concluded, a mitigating amendment. This was a course that the Kwakiutl had been seeking since at least February 1915, when a committee had requested that Halliday ask Scott or some other commissioner to come to Alert Bay to allow them to state their case. The Kwakiutl were so convinced that the law and its enforcement were based on a misunderstanding that they pinned their cause to the results of one or two commissioners coming from Ottawa to "look into the potlatch themselves, so that we may explain to them what they call a potlatch." They seemed to think that an unprejudiced commission of "honerable [*sic*] gentlemen" would arrive at "a definite opinion with regard to our method of trade and recreations" that would be in their favour. Scott's 1918 circular renewed the idea, which became the mainstay of Kwakiutl strategy. Chiefs of seven bands, confident that the government was neither fully nor correctly informed, asked Ottawa "to send a good straight man to come and see all the Indians so that you may know exactly what the potlatch is." Halliday had accepted the idea, recommending that Scott or someone else prominent hear the matter openly discussed from both sides. Scott refused. The department, he wrote a group of Kwakiutl chiefs, had reliable information both for and against the potlatch, and nothing would be gained by sending someone to inquire about it among the Indians.[17] Now, scarcely a month after Scott's terse rejection of an inquiry, the Kwakiutl took the Lyons agreement to mean that an investigation would, after all, be held.

The proceedings of the Likiosa-Kwosteetsas appeal seemed to

confirm their interpretation. Senkler, appearing with Lyons, asked that the penalties be remitted and emphasized that the Kwakiutl had accepted the agreement on the understanding not only that they reserved the right to apply to Ottawa to have the law amended, but also that they would be able to "get an investigation into the time-honoured customs of their tribe and to have an opportunity of putting before an independent investigator their troubles and difficulties in regard to Potlatching." At Lyons's insistence, Judge Cayley stated "in open court" that Senkler would support their request for an investigation. Cayley went further: he wrote the minister of the interior recommending that the Indians have an opportunity of putting their case before a dominion investigator. In short, the Kwakiutl had grounds to believe that the agreement, Halliday's "moral victory," represented a very major victory of their own. They even understood—or at least the idea grew—that the government intended a modification of the act that would allow potlatching. Little wonder that Senkler found them content with the arrangement.[18]

Halliday never acknowledged any such understanding, preferring his own triumph. He had his moral victory, but it had come at some personal cost. After the Likiosa-Kwosteetsas prosecution, he was again the object of Kwakiutl hostility. "All the Indians are up in arms over the matter," he wrote, "and are laying all the blame on the shoulders of the Indian Agent." The native reaction was understandable. Accumulated grievances and petty complaints against Halliday were presented to Scott by the delegation to Ottawa and Inspector Ditchburn carried out another investigation at Alert Bay. Ditchburn's report was lengthy, its conclusions predictable. All but one of the catalogue of charges against Halliday were unjustified; his suppression of the potlatch was the root cause of all complaints.[19]

Scott and Ditchburn were willing, now that they had secured the pledge of the Nimpkish and Mamalillikulla, to relax the pressure a little. Scott agreed with Halliday and Ditchburn that prosecutions for the simple mourning potlatches should not be sought, though no announcement of their toleration should be made. He was, moreover, willing to investigate concerns about the consequences of the potlatch's suppression upon Kwakiutl savings.[20]

No concessions on the main point, on the potlatch system itself, were possible. A request by Member of Parliament H. S. Clements on behalf of a delegation led by Chief Tom Johnson of Fort Rupert was rejected. Johnson had asked to be allowed to distribute $2000 and 700 five-gallon cans of oolachan oil to "about two hundred old deserving Indians" at a double marriage. There would be no dances, no liquor, no objectionable features of any kind. He had the support of lawyer Senkler and Judge Cayley, both of whom thought that the proposal did not necessarily break the law. Scott would have none of it: the Indians must stand by their agreement to potlatch no more.[21]

The Indians, however, were waiting for Scott to stand by what they understood to be his side of the bargain. As Clements wired, "the Indians signed agreement good faith but only understanding investigation would be granted by govt Senkler KC also Judge Cayley recommended investigation long ago but department has not moved." Faced with this reminder, Scott budged only a little. He would submit the whole question to the minister, but the Indians must keep to their agreement. To Minister of the Interior Arthur Meighen, Scott was frank. He did not recommend such an inquiry. The facts were already known; "indeed we probably know more about the aboriginal system of the potlatch than do the Indians themselves." Meighen agreed to Scott's suggested course: the department would ask the anthropological division of the National Museum for a report and allow the Indians to make whatever representations they wished in writing. This was not quite what the Kwakiutl had in mind. They wanted someone to whom they could talk, someone to whom they could show their dances, someone who would see them all.[22] Above all, they wanted a fair and full investigation with action to follow.

The March 1919 agreement thus fell by the wayside. It had been a compromise, a way of allowing six Kwakiutl to stay out of jail and continue to provide for their families. The undertakings on both sides were loosely constructed to secure this end. The Kwakiutl had signed with a caveat, understood by Senkler as well as Lyons, but one that Scott never accepted. For this reason, or merely because most had never put much stock in what had been promised anyway, the Kwakiutl went on in their customary way. The agreement did not survive the 1919–20 season.

Halliday approached that winter in a mood of tolerance and with a sense of strength. He ignored the customary Christmas feasts on the grounds that they resembled white holiday celebrations. The letter of the law was being broken, but not the spirit. There was tolerance, but within lay an iron hand: the presence of a detachment of mounted police at Alert Bay.

The Alert Bay provincial police had been cooperative with Halliday in recent years. Constable Robert Matthews had worked hard on the earlier prosecutions, but his time was taken up with the whole range of normal police duties in his large district. Between 1918 and 1920, law enforcement was greatly altered by a series of federal Orders in Council that extended the jurisdiction of the Royal Northwest Mounted Police across the entire country, integrated within it the former Dominion Police's 150 officers and men, and renamed the unified force the Royal Canadian Mounted Police. The new, enlarged force established "E" Division, comprising about 220 men, in British Columbia with headquarters in Vancouver. A sergeant and constable were posted to Alert Bay in December 1919. They would be concerned solely with enforcement of federal law, most particularly the Indian Act, and Halliday predicted that now "fear of the law will take possession of the Indians to a much greater extent."[23]

The Mounties may have been a deterrent, but they were not yet a very effective one. In January 1920 Halliday had before him eight summonses for potlatches, with all informations laid by RCMP Sergeant Donald Angermann. All eight men pleaded guilty. Halliday sentenced them all to two months at Oakalla, though he suspended one old man's sentence on compassionate grounds.[24] These were the first Indians to actually serve sentence for potlatching.[25] The convictions, Halliday felt safe in saying, had done "a lot towards its extermination."[26]

Things did seem to be better from the department's point of view. School attendance and applications to the residential school increased, church attendance was up, and more marriages were solemnized in Alert Bay's Christ Church in a few months than in the thirty previous years. The prosecutions, Halliday reported, had taught the Indians "the necessity of having their marriages performed legally instead of under the potlatch law."[27]

But the potlatch was not dead yet. The winter of 1920–21 brought reports from a missionary that "things have been going very badly among the Indians again" with potlatching "as bad as ever."

Alert Bay was "thrown into a pig stye" and potlatching was carried on freely at Blunden Harbour. The descriptions were exaggerated. Provincial Constable Matthews attested to the relative cleanliness of the Alert Bay reserve; though there was a little potlatching going on, Sgt. Angermann had it under control and doubtless would soon stamp it out altogether.[28]

Indeed, Angermann had already laid informations against two Kwakiutl in another marriage case. An old man named Munday had arranged to pay Mrs. John McDougall $2000 to marry her young daughter. Jennie McDougall, raised in the residential school, resisted. "She did not want to go," said an Indian friend later, "she was heartbroken," but her parents insisted and the marriage went ahead. Mrs. Jane Cook of Christ Church, a vigilant native opponent of the potlatch, helped bring the matter to light and Munday and Mrs. McDougall were arrested. At the trial before Halliday, both pleaded not guilty and Angermann's witnesses, including Jennie McDougall, denied all knowledge of the events. The case had to be dismissed, but Angermann, frustrated by his witnesses, dedicated himself to securing evidence for perjury.[29]

In March 1921, after a long investigation similarly frustrated by uncooperative natives, Angermann secured witnesses for the prosecution of Charles Nowell for a January potlatch. Nowell was a high-born Fort Rupert Kueka whose status had been increased by an arranged marriage to the daughter of Nimpkish chief Lagius. After a decent education from Rev. Hall, he had found employment in a variety of usual Kwakiutl occupations, but, like George Hunt, had worked part-time as an anthropological assistant. Dr. Charles F. Newcombe, the Victoria physician occupied largely as an ethnological field collector, had begun employing Nowell in 1899. Five years later Nowell and his friend Bob Harris had gone with Newcombe to the St. Louis World's Fair where, with several Nootka, they performed dances and a mock hamatsa. Now just over fifty, Nowell succeeded, at his brother Tom's death, to the senior Kueka name of Owadi.

Nowell dispatched gas boats to bring all the tribes to the Alert Bay funeral, since "we Fort Ruperts and Nimkis are not able to bury him by ourselves. A big chief is too heavy for two tribes to lift the coffin." After the church ceremony and cemetary pole raising, Nowell and his witness gave speeches at the village community house and the new Owadi passed out seven or eight hundred dollars as compensation to those who had dug the grave, carried the coffin, put up the pole and offered the boats that brought people to Alert Bay. The ceremony had been held under the noses of Halliday and the RCMP, but it was only because Nowell had made a few local enemies that Angermann could secure evidence for an information. Nowell did not contradict the facts it contained; he was sentenced to three months imprisonment.[30] Nowell's conviction brought to eight the number of Kwakiutl made guests of His Majesty's Government at Burnaby's Oakalla prison farm.

The next winter, 1921–22, was not much different, excepting an obvious effort by the Kwakiutl to carry their ceremonies further afield. Five men were prosecuted for purchasing a copper at Kingcome Inlet, an innocent act that now brought legal action.[31] Halliday laid sentence of two months, but was forced to suspend it pending appeal. The defendants' counsel, Edwin K. DeBeck—partner in the Vancouver firm Dickey & DeBeck and son of Halliday's predecessor—argued that the copper purchase could not be classed as a ceremony since there were neither dances nor gifts involved and asked that the question be submitted to a higher court. DeBeck also protested in principle that the Indian agent could hear offences against the Indian Act. The point worried Halliday a little; he intended in the next case to invite other Alert Bay justices of the peace to sit with him "so that the Indians may not say that the court is in any way biased."[32] The appeal was heard in January before Chief Justice Gordon Hunter of the British Columbia Supreme Court. Conviction was upheld.

The series of arrests and sentences were already having an effect, but the Kwakiutl were thrown into "a state of fright" by Angermann's pursuit of evidence in yet another case, one that possibly involved twenty or thirty charges. The RCMP constable was intent on prosecuting "anyone and everyone who took an active part in it." His task was made easier by information from two informants, identified by Herbert Martin as Kenneth Hunt and Dave Shaughnessy, who had attended the December potlatch.[33] By February, Sgt. Angermann had his evidence and laid his information. It was a blockbuster: thirty-four Kwakiutl, six of whom were women, were charged, including Chief Billy Assu of Cape Mudge and Indians from tribes stretching up to Blunden Harbour.

On 16 February 1922 thirty-two people (two were ill) appeared in Halliday's schoolhouse courtroom for the beginning of the most decisive legal action against the potlatch. The charges stemmed from Dan Cranmer's potlatch, the largest ever recorded on the central coast. Held at Village Island partly because "that was away from the agent" and partly because that was where Cranmer's wife's relatives lived, it lasted most of a week. The potlatch was actually Emma Cranmer's "repurchase," followed by Cranmer's distribution of the goods received from his wife and her family as well as more of his own. To avoid detection, the potlatch gifts were shipped to Village Island at night.[34] Cranmer issued invitations "to all the chiefs of all the tribes." Three hundred or more guests appeared at the house of Harry Hanuse, though only a few of Cranmer's own Nimpkish people attended, since most were afraid of Agent Halliday.

The first two days of the potlatch were taken up with repaying Cranmer's earlier loans and with the transfer of property to Cranmer from his wife's side. Billy Assu paid $2000 in blankets as well as giving Cranmer a *xwéxwe* dance and names. Hanuse, acting for Emma Cranmer, gave Dan canoes, furniture and other goods. Meanwhile a copper changed hands several times; in the end, Cranmer received $3000 and the copper. Others gave over to him sewing machines, bracelets and money. With the paying back completed, Herbert Martin danced the hamatsa and James Knox the q'ominoqa.

Now began Cranmer's giving away. "I started giving out the property," he recalled. "First the canoes," twenty-four of them, "some big ones." He gave pool tables to two chiefs. Such large gifts cast high honour upon Cranmer and incurred a deep obligation upon the recipients to match the gesture in future. "It really hurt them," commented Cranmer; "They said it was the same as breaking a copper," another display of unsparing wealth. Assu received a gas boat and $50 cash. Three more gas boats were given away and another pool table. Dresses, shawls and bracelets went to the women, sweaters and shirts to the young people. For the children, small change: "I threw it away for the kids to get," Cranmer remembered. Then came blankets, gas lights, violins, guitars, basins, glasses, washtubs, teapots, boxes, three hundred oak trunks, sewing machines, gramophones, bedsteads, bureaus and more cash. Finally, on Christmas Day, the fifth and last day of the ceremony, came the sacks of flour. (Angermann recorded "about 400" sacks, Cranmer recalled 1000 at three dollars each.) Moses Alfred handed them down to carriers Kenneth Hunt, Johnson Cook, and Peter and James Knox while Sam Scow called out the recipients. "Everyone admits," said Cranmer, "that this was the biggest yet." So were the trials.

After several adjournments caused by storms that prevented first the witnesses, then Angermann, from getting to Alert Bay, proceedings finally commenced on 27 February. Halliday shared the bench with A. M. Wastell. Angermann handled the prosecution himself; the Indians were defended by W. Murray of former premier Joseph Martin's Vancouver firm, acting also on behalf of clients of the ill J. N. Ellis of McTaggart & Ellis. First to appear were second offenders Moses Alfred, Nahok and Johnny Drabble. The testimony of four Crown witnesses, along with that of Alfred and Drabble, quickly established the strength of the prosecution's case. Murray, prepared for this, abruptly altered all pleas to "guilty." He asked for the leniency of the court on the basis of an agreement, already signed by all defendants and some fifty others, to potlatch no more.

Once again, the offer to sign an agreement seems to have been motivated by the desire to avoid imprisonment. "Jail sentence would be a severe matter to heads of families at beginning of fishing season," one of the Indians' lawyers had earlier wired Scott.[35] Halliday was willing to give the Kwakiutl another chance, but Angermann was pressing for severe sentences. He refused to accept the proposal, a virtual duplicate of Lyons's 1919 agreement. Within months of that, Angermann claimed, a number of the covenanters had ignored their promises and several of them were now sitting in the docket as admitted participants in the Cranmer potlatch. The sergeant insisted upon more than another piece of paper; he wanted "some tangible evidence of good faith." His suggestion that the whole Kwakiutl agency make a voluntary surrender of all potlatch property was accepted by the court. The case was remanded for a month pending acceptance of the terms by the defendants.

A new agreement was drawn up. It contained an acknowledgement not only of the law but of the fact that it was to be strictly enforced, with no expectation of amendment or repeal. Signatories agreed to obey the law, to do all in their power to see that others kept it, and even to assist authorities in its observation. Furthermore, they agreed, as a "token of our good faith," voluntarily to surrender to the department "all our potlatch paraphernalia" by 25 March. Halliday and Wastell agreed that those signing the agreement and surrendering their property would receive suspended sentences and that the minister of justice would be asked to pardon the three second offenders.

The decision now rested with the Kwakiutl: to sign and surrender their material or go to prison. That choice rested not just with the thirty-four offenders but also upon the three hundred or so others who had attended Cranmer's potlatch. Angermann stood ready to pounce on a good number more against whom he had evidence.

Halliday did his best to persuade all to sign and surrender. He read the letter from Scott that stated the department's intention of retaining Section 149 unaltered. The Indians, he felt, "realized themselves the hopelessness of a fight against the law." Having spent in the vicinity of $10,000 on legal fees and deputations, they now felt that they had thrown it all away. Most did not object to signing—they had themselves suggested the agreement—but did object to losing the coppers and the great value behind them. "I tried to show to them," Halliday wrote, "that as they could not use these coppers anymore in the potlatch that [they] were useless property" and should be viewed as any person would see "a foolish or unsound investment."[36]

On the morning of 31 March, the answer was clear. Virtually all Cape Mudge Lekwiltok, Village Island Mamalillikulla and Alert Bay Nimpkish accepted the agreement and turned in their coppers and dancing gear.[37] Condemned prisoners from the three complying groups were given, as agreed, suspended sentences; second offenders were granted a stay pending an appeal for parole to the Department of Justice. The appeal was granted six months later.[38]

Other groups, notably the Fort Ruperts, refused to sign. Seven offenders—Jim Hall of Karlakwees and six Fort Ruperts, including the alleged police informant Kenneth Hunt—received two-month sentences. Angermann executed his threat of further prosecutions, summoning seventeen more Cranmer potlatch participants as well as issuing summonses against three others for offences in January and February on Harbledown Island. On 7 and 8 April all were found guilty. Five were given suspended sentences because they had played minor roles or because they signed the agreement, but fifteen others were given sentences of two months. Nimpkish Charlie Hunt, a second offender who refused to sign, received a sentence of six months.[39] Angermann escorted the twenty-two prisoners to Vancouver aboard the CPR steamer *Beatrice* on 10 April.

The twenty-two had already spent several nights in the residential day school at Alert Bay, sleeping under blankets but without mattresses on the wood floor. Emma Cranmer provided food. Once in Vancouver, they were trucked to Oakalla. Emma Cranmer, as a member by marriage of the Nimpkish band, which had surrendered its potlatching materials, had not been imprisoned for her part in the potlatch. However, she was "in a prison of her own for she blamed herself for what happened and continually wept over it." She followed the sentenced Indians to Vancouver, where she supplied their needs and waited for their release. She paid their streetcar fares, their restaurant and hotel bills, and their steamship ticket back to Alert Bay.[40] They brought back from prison stories of the humiliation felt by women who were forced to strip naked for medical inspections, of breakfasts of mush without milk or sugar, of fire hoses turned against them, and of John Whonnock and Bill McDuff feeding the farm pigs ("Imagine! the great Chieftains of the Kwakiutl degraded to feeding pigs.").[41] Herbert Martin went on from Alert Bay to the oolachan fishery at Knights Inlet where he gave a grease potlatch to "cleanse those that were put in prison with me." Afterward, he distributed almost four thousand gallons of oolachan oil to Kwakiutl from Blunden Harbour to Alert Bay to Newitti.[42]

The surrendered potlatch regalia and coppers from those accepting the agreement were gathered in Halliday's woodshed, then moved to the parish hall and put on exhibition.[43] They numbered over 450 items, including twenty coppers, scores of hamatsa whistles and dozens of masks. Halliday was directed to ship the material to the National Museum in Ottawa for evaluation, but a lack of time and the summer shortage of labour delayed crating for several months. In the meantime, George Heye, founder of New York's Museum of the American Indian, called in and wanted to buy "a considerable amount of the stuff." Halliday, feeling that Heye's prices were exceptionally good, sold him thirty-five pieces for $291. The agent, certain that "no one but a very enthusiastic collector would have given as much," viewed his action as consistent with the object of securing as much money as possible for the Indians. The department, however, was angered at this "unwarranted action."[44]

The remaining material, seventeen cases, went to Ottawa where museum anthropologist Edward Sapir appraised it at a value of $1456, without the coppers. Cheques were sent to Halliday in April to be given to the former owners. Some Kwakiutl do not remember receiving payment, and there were accusations of omissions, but there can be no question that the cheques were issued and sent, since the matter was the point of an auditor general's inquiry. Halliday did record that the Indians considered the compensation "entirely inadequate." No compensation was ever paid for the coppers.[45] (The bulk of the collection was kept by the National Museum with a portion donated to the Royal Ontario Museum in Toronto. Both have since returned their portions to native museums in Alert Bay and Cape Mudge where they are displayed with stunning appropriateness.[46])

The loss of masks and coppers hurt, but the crackdown on the potlatch hurt more. In all, during April 1922, fifty-eight Kwakiutl had appeared before Halliday's makeshift bench. Nine cases were dismissed, twenty-three received two-month suspended sentences, and four were given six-month sentences, although three were later paroled. But twenty-two people served two-month sentences. Four of those imprisoned were women, and at least one was a grandmother. Halliday regretted this, but felt that the women had been very influential and that punishment for their misdeeds would have a salutary effect. He felt he had been lenient in giving the minimum sentence to all but Charlie Hunt. Sentences should have been six months, but that, he told Scott, "would have left me with a very small agency to look after and a big burden of expense in the case of the families." The salmon season was approaching and he did not want the offenders and their families to be deprived of a livelihood or to be dependent upon the department for relief.[47]

Halliday felt he could be lenient because the potlatch had now been killed. The Indians were "inspired by a wholesome fear of the law." There might occasionally be minor affairs, but there was "absolutely no danger of any great potlatches ever taking place again." His legal triumph was confirmed when Judge David Grant upheld the convictions. A week later Amos Dawson and Bob Harris were convicted of perjury for their testimony in the Munday-McDougall marriage case of January 1921. The potlatch prosecutions had, Halliday wrote, created such divisions among the Indians that the facts came out and Harris made a full confession. He pleaded guilty and was sentenced by Judge Cayley to three months' hard labour; Dawson, pleading his innocence, was found guilty and sentenced to four. The penalties, again, were tempered by leniency: both Halliday and Cayley wanted the men out in time to put up the winter food supply. Despite a setback the next year, when Justice Denis Murphy released ten Nakwakto of Blunden Harbour on a technicality, the Kwakiutl potlatch as Halliday understood it had been dealt a heavy blow.[48] Agent Halliday considered it dead.

Halliday's agency had been the major battlefield in Scott's war on the potlatch, but all agents had been instructed by circular to put an end to the "wasteful practice." In January 1921 Agent Cox and Provincial Constable J. Bartlett charged forty-three Nootka Indians with dancing off their reserve, a lesser charge deliberately chosen to allow fines rather than imprisonment in the first prosecution on the west coast of Vancouver Island. All pleaded guilty and were fined a nominal dollar or, in the cases of a few who failed to appear at their first trial, five dollars. Across the island, Cowichan Agent W. R. Robertson wired that he was "unable to cope with situation" presented by four hundred Indians gathered at the Hallalt reserve near Westholme. This was no repetition of the showdown between the Cowichan and Powell at Comeaken in 1885. The gathering turned out to be orderly, the Indians so well-behaved that Robertson sent Sergeant N. D. McLaren back to Nanaimo. Charges were laid against Jimmie Albert and four others. All received suspended sentences.[49]

The Skeena Valley had its own confrontations in this period. Agent Loring's notice threatening RCMP enforcement, posted in late 1920, curbed that winter's potlatches at Kispiox, Glen Vowell and Hazelton. When potlatching continued the next winter, the new agent, Edgar Hyde, brought charges against Edward Saxsmith, Robert Wilson and John M. Morrison. All were convicted and received suspended sentences from Agent/Justice of the Peace Loring. The prosecutions seemed to have an effect. While the annual summer ceremonies at the neighbouring Hagwilget village were held in 1922, "they were not able to get away with much of the old stuff."[50]

Hyde renewed his attempts to repress the continuing potlatches. He brought charges against Silas Johnson and Sam Disk in 1927, but the two received only a severe lecture and warning. By 1929, enforcement was again looser. "Small affairs" grew in number and underground activities developed into full-scale, overt ceremonies. A week-long Christmas celebration on the occasion of the opening of a new Kispiox hall was followed by the installation of a new chief at Kitwancool and a pole raising there. The United Church minister assisted in the Kitwancool investiture, which was also attended by the agent. Speeches, dancing (which "imitated the old time dance"), seating by rank, and gifts of beef, sugar and cash were reported. While these seem to have been held almost with official sanction, three Indians were soon prosecuted for offences at Kispiox and Hazelton. Moses Stevens had received Agent G. C. Mortimer's permission for a feast before a Kispiox pole raising in January 1931, but violated his promise by giving away money. Because of Stevens's advanced age and because, thought Mortimer, it was "the first prosecution of its kind in this district," the offender was given a one-month suspended sentence. Offences by Tom Campbell and John Smith brought more severe action. Agent Mortimer regarded Smith as naive, led down the path by the troublesome Campbell, a man of "the i.w.w. type" (the reference is to the Industrial Workers of the World, a radical industrial union). Smith's case was dismissed, but Campbell received a three-month sentence, suspended on condition he keep away from all future ceremonies.[51] The Smith-Campbell cases were the last invocation of the potlatch law on the Skeena.

These seem the only actions taken. Agent Ivor Fougner in Bella Coola pleaded for discretion if no wastefulness, intemperance or immorality was present. The Indians under his charge differentiated their gatherings from those of the neighbouring Kwakiutl and he wanted to deal with them "in a just and fair manner, whenever possible avoiding the wounding of inherited feelings that seem sacred to them, though they are strange to us." He was told that presents must not be given, but that an agent "may and should use his discretion."[52]

Fougner did. An old Norwegian-American who had lived in the

valley for over twenty years, he never went near the village unless there was trouble. Thomas McIlwraith, a Cambridge-educated anthropologist, lived in Bella Coola while researching for the National Museum. In October 1923 he feared that the law would prevent any dances that winter, though he was supposed to take part in one himself: "It would be very funny if it should land me in jail." He need not have feared either. The Bella Coola danced for six weeks, each dance followed by a potlatch. The young anthropologist joined in as prompter when not performing as a supernatural mosquito, a role which, he recalled, "seemed simple, except that I could not find the mouth of the mask, however I hummed nobly, and jabbed at four or five people."[53]

8

"All We Want Is Justice"

THE INDIAN DEFENCE against Scott's offensives of 1913-15 and 1918-23 took various forms. The Kwakiutl fought back mostly through petitions, but also through lawyers in the courts, suppression of evidence, appeals to Scott, including the 1919 delegation to Ottawa, and attempts to mobilize white friends like C. F. Newcombe and their Member of Parliament H. F. Clements. The first round of courtroom tactics worked well: the department called off its offensive. Scott's change of the courtroom rules frustrated a legal defence in the second round; there were successful prosecutions and prison terms. The Kwakiutl concentrated on securing a repeal or modification of the law by appealing for an investigation. When stonewalled on this, they fell back on underground resistance.

Scott's initial enforcement had prompted anger and protest all along the southern coast. Agent Charles Cox reported from Alberni on the indignation caused by the Alert Bay convictions, but distinguished the ceremonies of his Nootka from the extremes of the Kwakiutl. Anthropologist Edward Sapir, researching in Alberni, found the Nootka "very much disturbed by the renewed rigour with which the old more or less dead letter potlatch law was being applied." When Cowichan Agent W. R. Robertson read the deputy superintendent's letter to the Corpus Christi potlatch at Somenos, Indians protested "about the Department interfering in their harmless festivals and dances." Farther north, at Hazelton, a number of Gitksan chiefs met to protest against the ban.[1]

The most visible response, however, was a flood of petitions sent to Ottawa from all along the south coast. Eighty chiefs and sub-chiefs of the Squamish, Nanaimo, Musqueam and Kwakiutl sent an eloquent one in September 1914; in December of that year came petitions from fourteen Nootka chiefs and thirty-three Sechelt chiefs. In March 1915 twenty Kwakiutl asked for a commission of investigation. More petitions followed in 1919, 1920 and 1921. They had little effect, but do embody an articulation of the native position.

The arguments put forward by native people had changed little since the passage of the act thirty years before. Their weight fell on the injustice of the law and how it suppressed an institution that was "one of our oldest and best customs." The native petitioners insisted that their potlatch was quite harmless. It hurt no one and interfered with no one's rights; it contained nothing criminal or degraded, and "no mishap or sin of any kind." "We don't see any fault in it," one petition said. In addition, the potlatch was "a good thing for us all." The system helped "every Indian," especially those who could not get work and those too old to work. The potlatch spread the wealth by periodic distribution. Everyone received a share and the poor and the old were looked after. There was a pension principle at work: "When we give a potlatch we insures for our lives & our children when we get old & unable to work for our selves."[2]

The Indians still argued that potlatches were their "chief sources of pleasure and amusement." Songs, dances, games, puzzles—"all these things are the best, as regards native amusements, that the indian [*sic*] has been able to create in the course of generations." Without them, "life is made gloomy."[3]

The Indians simply refused to consider that the law could stand if the government were correctly informed about the potlatch. As the Kwakiutl and Salish insisted, "Peoples dont [*sic*] understand our Costume [*sic*]," "the white man don't understand our fashion." "We think the law is not right and that you have been mistaken," the Kwakiutl chiefs wrote Scott. "The Government has not been fully and correctly informed and we would respectfull [*sic*] ask you to send a good straight man to come and see all the Indians so that you may know exactly what a potlatch is."[4]

To native people, the most irritating misunderstanding was the idea that a potlatcher became impoverished. The charge that potlatches rendered an Indian poor was "entirely unfounded." People who did not understand the custom claimed "that we spend all our earnings, and waste our money away for nothing. But this is not so. What we spend is to be returned back sometimes [*sic*] in the future." Every Indian person knew that custom required a return. "In this way," wrote the Nootka, "the fruits of work, while they may seem at first sight to be squandered at a potlatch, are really not lost at all." Lawyer DeBeck, on behalf of the Indians, pointed out that what was given was only personal property and never hunting or fishing rights, land or other real property.[5]

The most insistent refrain of the petitioners was that the law was unjust, and that the injustice was based on intolerance as well as misunderstanding. "We maintain," wrote the articulate Nootka chiefs, "that this law is quite uncalled for, that it works needless hard ships on our people, and that it is diametrically opposed to the principles of tolerance and Justice which we have been taught to believe are the laws of this country."[6] No law prevented whites from hosting dinners, giving gifts or attending dances. "We see our white friends give presents to one another. Why cannot we do the same. They give feasts why should we be persecuted for giving a feast. They have dances. Why should we not be allowed to dance also." Cox's 1920 Christmas arrests brought a similar response: "We were doing no more than is costumary [*sic*] with the white people during this Season." The inconsistency was aggravating. The government did not prohibit different kinds of customs among the Scots, French and Irish; it allowed Catholics, Presbyterians and Anglicans to follow their own beliefs. "Why then," the Nootka asked, "should the Indian be selected for Intolerant treatment?"[7]

Indian customs were not bad, merely different. "The Whiteman's ways are not Red-man's ways and the Red-man's ways are not White-man's ways," wrote one Indian elder. To stop the Indian custom was "intolerance pure and simple." "God created us here and it was the Almighty that put us here, and it is our fashion," the Indian chiefs insisted. "Each nation has dance of their own, and no one stops them." Understanding, tolerance, justice: these formed the bedrock of the Indian appeal. "All we want is justice," they stated, "and therefore we are not afraid to tell you that the law about the potlach is not just."[8]

These arguments, strained occasionally through an especially literate amanuensis, displayed the Indians' own concerns. Arguments

from white supporters presented many of the same points, but, because these supporters shared more assumptions with white policy-
makers, they added ideas not often used by the natives. Unlike Vancouver Island merchants, lawyer DeBeck and several anthropologists, few Indian petitioners argued that the potlatch was "the greatest stimulus to ambition" and that its suppression would deprive native people of incentive and encourage shiftlessness.[9]

The Indians' white allies put their own emphasis upon understanding, tolerance and justice. Archaeologist Harlan I. Smith of the
National Museum decried the government's inability "to even try to
understand the other fellow's point of view and the real working of
his customs," while John Swanton of the Smithsonian voiced his
concern at the denial of "social rights." These sentiments were
echoed by Edward Sapir and C. F. Newcombe. The dances, dramatic performances, songs and games were "perhaps the chief
source of genuine pleasure" among the Indians, wrote Sapir. Newcombe, who knew the coast Indians as well as did any white, judged
that nothing else existed "to supply life and colour during the long,
dark, winter nights." This was an old but valid argument shared
with the Indian petitioners. DeBeck wrote at length on the absence
of theatres, lectures, concerts, organized sports and libraries among
the coastal Indians. The government denied them civic or political
activities, thus the Indians' "whole scheme of life is comprised in
the Potlatch."[10]

The economic implications of an end to the potlatch most exercised the anthropologists. Viewing the custom, as Franz Boas had
done in his letter to the *Province* in 1897, partly as a credit and in-
surance scheme, Sapir, Smith, Newcombe and Boas all warned of
the great hardship its abolition would bring. The Indians would be
paralyzed by the sudden valuelessness of blankets and coppers. The
result would be the "same sort of havoc" as would be created by the
destruction of a white man's cheques, drafts and other forms of
credit money—a "complete demoralization of their business system." Boas, in Victoria for further research in 1922, took several occasions to reiterate his view that the prohibition of the potlatch signified the destruction of the native credit system, a matter "of the
greatest difficulty for the Indians." If the whole system of property
were really understood, he told a Victoria audience, "we should not
have the effect of the whole economic system of the Indians broken

up by the annulment of all debts." The point had already been emphasized by Newcombe. He had been in Alert Bay in the spring of 1913 when Halliday announced Scott's new enforcement push. Many older Indians had turned to him for help, stressing that they had since childhood contributed directly or through relations to the general potlatch funds with an expectation of repayment when they could no longer maintain themselves. They now foresaw their reduction "from moderate affluence to comparative poverty."[11]

But economic demoralization was only part of the general demoralization that the anthropologists foresaw if the potlatch law was enforced. The old Indian life, Sapir believed, was being broken up quickly enough. Enforcement would bring it to "a rapid finish." "With all their customs connected with birth, marriage, family life and death" suddenly destroyed, Newcombe foresaw the Indians becoming "more listless and indifferent." Sapir was the most outspoken: "It seems to me high time that white men realized that they are not doing the Indians much of a favour by converting them into inferior replicas of themselves." However one might view the Indians' customs, "the fact remains that they have a completely different outlook on life, and that their more immediate motives of action are necessarily rather different from ours." Attempts to force Indians onto a different path meant "maladjustment and unhappiness for the worthier members, degeneration for the less worthy."[12] These were voices of cultural relativists, anthropologists who sympathized with their subjects and sought the protection of native social institutions from the steamroller of thoughtless uniformity.

Not all views supported the potlatch. Antipotlatchers among the Sechelt and Fraser Valley Salish as well as a few Christian Kwakiutl submitted letters and petitions of their own. The Salish petitions insisted that the potlatches and dances

are absolutely opposed to civilization, religion, prayer, etc., that at the time of the Indian dances two or three months are passed by the pagan Indians in mere wild enjoyment, laziness and very often drunkenness; that a great deal of money and other resources are spent uselessly, for nothing or worse.[13]

Mrs. Jane Cook, at the centrepoint of Kwakiutl agitation against the potlatch, was the most articulate and outspoken of the pro-law natives. Born in Seattle of a Kwakiutl mother and a white father, she had been brought up by Rev. Hall's wife. In 1891 she had married Stephen Cook, another half blood, who had been educated in Victoria, Metlakatla and at Alert Bay by Hall. Cook ran the CMS sawmill and store, then his own store and wharf in the village. Both remained very active in the church, Stephen as vicar's warden and Jane on the vestry committee. One of their sixteen children, Edwin, had received the Distinguished Conduct Medal before being killed in action.

The potlatch, wrote Mrs. Cook in 1919, governed all Indian life, binding every man, woman and child to the system. "They are slaves to it," she declared, "all their time is devoted to it thier [sic] mind and money has to be used for it, therefore there is no expansion of mind, or Progress of any thing worthwhile." The law should be enforced because allegiance to the potlatch challenged loyalty to government and king (no potlatchers, she noted, had volunteered for overseas service), because it subverted marriage (in all the agency, only five couples had married within the church), and because it hindered education. "This system keeps them from progress, every cent they have must be used to keep them in caste. There is nothing new done or allowed them. all [sic] must be done as their ancestors did." Finally, there was no liberty, no choice, within the potlatch. "They are all bound and have to pratice [sic] all the different features of this system or they will lose their caste. Those who have left the Potlatch are looked upon as not Indians, or Have [sic] no standing or voice in any matters affecting their tribe or band. They are practically Outcasts."[14] No missionary could have expressed the view with more sincerity or personal feeling.

Few missionaries joined in the letter and petition campaign. Probably they felt no need to. Those who did emphasized, as had their predecessors in the 1880s, sanitation, health and the problems of marriage, promiscuity and drunkenness. The 1922 Methodist Conference of Workers rejoiced at the movement among Indians to abandon the old practices, supported Halliday in his prosecutions and looked forward to a fair and wise enforcement of the law.[15]

D. C. Scott, the recipient of all these letters, resolutions and petitions, maintained his own views. The potlatch was "highly objectionable" and its economics were on "a false basis." He admitted that the Indians had "quite an amount of capital locked up in trade blankets and coppers, and it would be a hardship to cancel their value." His concern with the coppers and blankets issue had come from a letter of Charles Nowell's passed to him by Clements. Nowell had written that "our coppers is our safty [*sic*] bank" and that their value "is the main thing that troubles our mind." Halliday also raised the issue of the value, perhaps over $40,000, of coppers and blankets, which would be totally lost. Scott gave some thought to compensation, going so far as asking Ditchburn for an estimate of the cost. There, however, the matter ended.[16] Scott's only other concession was his order to allow simple mourning ceremonies to go unpunished. Otherwise, the petitions, delegations and letters of support made little impression upon him.

Scott preferred his own viewpoint. His files contained all the information he needed on the issue. "Whatever the purpose or principal [*sic*] of the potlatch may be," he replied, "the fact remains that potlatches are attended by prolonged idleness and waste of time, by ill-advised and wanton giving away of property and by immorality." These were its usual and undeniable features. Potlatching was "most harmful to the Indians," and its continuance "cannot be justified." Moreover, the great majority of Indians, convinced the custom was harmful, had voluntarily given it up. "The efforts of the Department," Scott reported, "have been directed to the promotion among the Indians of industry, progress and morality, all of which are greatly hindered by indulgence in the potlatch." This was Scott's view, this his policy. "One can hardly be sympathetic," he wrote of the potlatch some years later, "when one knows that the original spirit has departed and that they are largely the opportunities for debauchery by low white men."[17] The law would remain the law and it would be enforced.

The Kwakiutl, however, had pinned their hopes on an impartial investigation which they confidently expected would vindicate the custom and bring a revision of the law. They assumed that the March 1919 agreement between Lyons, Senkler and Halliday had carried a promise of an inquiry. When none appeared by the fall of 1920, they retained E. K. DeBeck to seek repeal of the agreement. His brief, some twenty persuasively argued pages, was given to the department in May 1921.[18] However, the nearest thing to an inquiry was a report, prepared by National Museum ethnologist Marius Barbeau, that was compiled largely from Department of Indian Affairs files. Barbeau interviewed no Kwakiutl. DeBeck had to travel to Hazelton, where Barbeau was doing field work among the Gitksan, to give his clients' side of the issue. The report, while sympathetic to the native custom, made no recommendation. More important, it was never released to the Indians or their counsel.

Scott was obdurate. "The question of amending Section 149," he told DeBeck in June 1921, "cannot be considered." Barbeau's report was unavailable for distribution, and the establishment of a royal commission, as the Kwakiutl requested, was not an advisable course. "The Department," wrote Scott's secretary, "has fully looked into the question of the potlatch, and at present there is no change in its attitude in dealing with the same." Little wonder that Charles Nowell, writing on behalf of a meeting of chiefs at Fort Rupert, expressed the utter hopelessness of all their attempts at a remedy of their grievances. They had spent money for lawyers to defend men put in jail, "but they have never done any good"; they had spent money to send a delegation to Ottawa, "but it was no use"; they had asked the government to send an investigator to come and listen to both sides, "for we all said that we will never be satisfied until the investigator be sent," but no one had come.[19]

The news that Minister of Mines Charles Stewart, in whose department Indian affairs now fell, would be on the coast in July 1922, and Stewart's promise that he would take this opportunity to go into the potlatch question from all angles, raised hopes once more. The Kwakiutl prepared their arguments and unpacked their regalia to give an illustration of their dances. When they learned that Stewart would spend only a few hours in Vancouver, they were "greatly incensed." Their outrage was expressed by DeBeck: the Kwakiutl felt "absolutely in the right," and yet were prevented not only from carrying on their customs, but were "not even given a hearing as to the merits of their case."[20] DeBeck met briefly with the minister, but all he could do was reaffirm his clients' request: Stewart should order an extensive investigation of the whole potlatch on the understanding that, if the findings were favourable, the law would be repealed. The interview produced no result.

That same month the Kwakiutl tried another route. They sent a large delegation to a Vancouver meeting of the Allied Tribes of British Columbia and other Indians. The Kwakiutl had earlier shown little interest in the Allied Tribes organization; now Billy Assu,

Charles Nowell, Johnny Drabble, Harry Mountain, Bob Harris and five others made up a sizable portion of the forty-five delegates at the 1922 meeting. The main agenda of the assembly was the land question, particularly the implementation of the McKenna-McBride "cut-offs" of "surplus" reserve land. The Kwakiutl, largely unaffected by that issue, were doubtless there to air their potlatch grievances. According to DeBeck, almost all the delegates supported a potlatch resolution, but Rev. Peter Kelly, a Haida, and others "connected with missionary work" blocked the motion by threatening to withdraw should it carry. The attempt to turn the meeting against the potlatch law failed.[21]

The move was probably doomed in advance. Organizationally amorphous, the Allied Tribes was largely its executive, dominated by Andrew Paull, a devout Squamish Catholic, and Peter Kelly, an ordained Methodist. Devoted mainly to recognition of aboriginal land title, the group's other concerns—improved medical care, better education and greater control over Indian funds—were intended to modernize the Indians. The Allied Tribes and its leadership were not keen on taking the organization in a quite different direction.[22]

The Kwakiutl had tried almost everything, and had even toyed with the idea of enfranchisement to evade the Indian Act.[23] "All these things that we have done has not done us any good," wrote Nowell. Yet they decided to try the political and parliamentary process once more. Perhaps H. S. Clements would use his parliamentary position "to speak to the government for us"; "there is no other friend to help us but you."[24]

Clements had long been the beneficiary of Kwakiutl appeals. Dan Cranmer, writing on behalf of the Nimpkish, had earlier asked that the law be changed. "We all obey the other laws of the white man[.] we never steal we never do no murder only this sec 149 gets us all the time and we have been wasting lots of money on it too." Similarly the Mamalillikulla, through Nowell, had pleaded with Clements. "We know that the law is not all right," they said; "we therefore earnestly ask you to help us helpless Indains [*sic*] to have the law ammended [*sic*]." The Kwakiutl, wrote Spruce Martin and Frank Walker after canvassing most of the tribes, thought that "if anyone can do anything for them, it will be Mr. Clements."[25]

Clements met with the Kwakiutl, listened to their case and passed their letters on to the department. He was sympathetic, but did no more. Scott remained immovable. There may have been a glimmer of hope in late 1921 when federal agricultural minister S. F. Tolmie of Victoria and Kamloops MP F. J. Fulton promised support. The December election, however, put both on the opposition benches and Clements, the champion of Indian complaints, was defeated. In 1922 Leon J. Ladner, the Conservative member for South Vancouver, who was in touch with lawyer DeBeck, defended the potlatch in the House, but received little satisfaction from Superintendent General of Indian Affairs Charles Stewart.[26] Ladner, briefed by DeBeck, pressed the matter personally on Stewart. The MP urged a change in the law, certainly an end to all prosecutions pending an investigation. Stewart responded with an expression of his personal regret at the drastic nature of the law, but pleaded that he had no control over the penalties assigned. Ladner was convinced of Stewart's sympathy, but felt that the minister required "proper public support" before he could move. DeBeck's connections with the Vancouver press resulted in several favourable articles and a sympathetic editorial. But public opinion, while no doubt still opposed to the law and its enforcement, had little effect. Non-native people remained, as DeBeck noted, "apathetic and listless" on all Indian matters.[27]

Against the determined opinion of the deputy superintendent general, the Kwakiutl and other potlatchers were powerless. Their allies—retained legal counsel, a handful of anthropologists, a sympathetic fisheries inspector, some local merchants, one or two backbench MPS and a vague but entirely unmobilized public opinion—were impotent.

The law had been passed because of an Indian petition and at the urging of the most knowledgeable people involved with Indian affairs. By 1914 the position that the potlatch was harmful was still held by missionaries and many departmental officials, but outside experts, notably anthropologists with considerable experience on the coast and in the interior, were in strong disagreement. Cracks soon appeared even in missionary ranks, but this changing climate of knowledgeable opinion carried little weight with Scott. Departmental views were solid and intractable; contrary opinions were ignored, even suppressed. Native opinion meant even less.

Indian protests made no impact because they carried no threat. Although the Nootka and the Gitksan may have retained a numerical superiority within their own localities, no one feared that their disaffection would result in any armed threat to white neighbours.

The Kwakiutl were no danger to anyone's peace of mind, Halliday possibly excepted. With the native population now reduced to a miniscule proportion of the white one, with communications and transportation transformed, with a federal police force established on the coast, the Department of Indian Affairs' policy could be enforced without concern.

At the same time, Scott operated with almost total freedom within his sphere. Ministers responsible had other things on their minds and they came and went—nine in the years between 1913 and Scott's retirement in 1932—but he remained. Department policy, government policy, was almost entirely his policy. Administering a minor department that seldom made headlines and even less often exercised the attention of Parliament or cabinet, he was free to set policy and effect its implementation. Such was a fact of Canadian government. H. G. Blair, deputy minister for immigration, had much the same latitude in retaining an almost personal policy of excluding Jews, even Jewish refugees from the terror of Nazism, from Canada.[28] In an area where few cared very deeply, an entrenched bureaucrat had the liberty to do as he pleased. Indian affairs concerned few people, most of whom were not even voters.[29]

And yet, as the following years were to show, the Indians were not supine victims of Scott, nor of Parliament, courts, agents or mounted police. When their petitions secured neither a modification of the law nor a commission of investigation, the Kwakiutl gave up on the process. Their last such supplication was in May 1925 on the occasion of the opening of the new St. George's Hospital in Alert Bay. Chief Ohwalagaleese took the opportunity to implore the lieutenant governor's representative to restore the potlatch to the Kwakiutl and delivered yet another petition on behalf of seven Southern Kwakiutl tribes. "We feel that the law in sec. 149 Indian Act is not just for the people that made the law has never come to see what the Potlatch is, although we have asked for a commission to come," read the petition. They asked that the provincial viceroy do all in his power to get the government in Ottawa to listen: "All we want is justice." Chief Ohwalagaleese's speech elicited a favourable editorial in the Vancouver press and provoked a few letters to the editor, but his plea, like all previous ones, was buried in Scott's overstuffed files.[30] Petitions and appeals having had no effect, the Kwakiutl fell back upon their own resourcefulness.

9

"Acts of Christian Charity"

HALLIDAY HAD PRONOUNCED the Kwakiutl potlatch dead. Nine years later, a year before his retirement in 1932, he had to admit that "although the prosecutions which took place some time ago killed it for the time being, I am sorry to say that I have reason to believe that it has broken out again." In 1934 C. C. Perry, Ditchburn's successor as inspector of agencies, complained that "we are about as far away from doing anything really effective towards the suppression of the potlatch system as we were when actions against the Indians were started years ago." Scott's triumph of 1922-23 had crumbled into ashes. The Indians, feeling persecuted, found ways around the law. By the 1930s it was the Kwawkewlth agents, not their wards, who felt frustrated and thwarted. "My position in relation to the Potlatch," wrote Agent Murray S. Todd in 1936, "is becoming intolerable." Duncan Campbell Scott had already confessed that "we are quite powerless." The feeble clause in the Indian Act had proven "inoperative."[1]

The prosecutions of 1922 had created bitter feelings in the Kwawkewlth agency. Halliday again complained that he "bore the burden in the heat of the day" and was "extremely unpopular" with the Indians. Franz Boas, returning to Kwakiutl country some years later, reported that Indians were still paying debts for the uncompensated coppers surrendered to Halliday. The enforcement of the law caused general confusion and resentment. C. F. Newcombe found that his Kwakiutl informants felt "demoralized by their treatment and think they have been cheated by the whites." The prosecutions nonetheless subdued the Indians. "Practice of the custom quieted down for the time being," Jane and Stephen Cook later testified.[2]

Indeed, there were no official reports of potlatches until March 1927, when Halliday learned of "a real old time potlatch" at King-come Inlet. Determined to quash the resurgence at the outset, he arrested ten of the participants and brought them to Alert Bay for trial. The potlatchers pleaded guilty, claiming they were under the impression that the law had been amended "as there had been little violations of the Act going on in various parts." Halliday allowed suspended sentence "under the circumstances." Later that same year, when Jimmy Sewid married Flora Alfred in Christ Church, Sewid's grandfather "gave a big potlatch" for all the people who had come to Alert Bay. "He didn't call the people together," recalled Sewid, "because it was against the law to give a potlatch, but he just went around to the houses and gave money and other things to the people in honor of me." Sewid's mother called the ladies together in the Alfred home and gave them dishes, pails and other utensils.[3]

By 1927, then, the Kwakiutl had established a pattern of evasion. No open potlatching was done at Alert Bay. With agent and police in the village, the ceremony went underground—secretly or from house to house. "Real old time potlatches," however, continued at distant or inaccessible locations, notably at Kingcome Inlet and, to a lesser extent, at Village Island, Turnour Island, Fort Rupert and Cape Mudge.

Kingcome Inlet was the chief seat of relatively unimpeded potlatching. The four Gilford Island bands, who previously had wintered at Gwayasdums, began wintering at Kingcome, perhaps as early as 1922, "for no other purpose than to carry on the potlatch." According to one Gilford Islander, "Chief Phillip" was the host who initially chose Kingcome to escape "official discovery." Halliday's brother, who farmed in the area, "was pleased that the potlatch was going to be given there because he was able to sell a number of cows for the event." Gwayi village was two miles up a shallow, snag-infested river that froze over in winter. It had been abandoned because of the difficulty of obtaining food and wood for fuel, but the Tsawataineuk discovered that they "could survive up Kingcome without any major hardship."[4] Gwayi had no regular access from Alert Bay, some sixty miles away; only by Union Steamship from Vancouver could police approach the place, and then only by landing at Charles Creek, there to meet Ernest Halliday's mail boat for travel upriver. Surprise was impossible. As Agent Todd informed his Victoria superior, the village was so situated that "no one can approach without being observed, by night or day."[5] Although Halliday had made his arrests there in 1927, as a rule the village was safe.

Within the security of Kingcome's Gwayi, the potlatch went on much as before. Willie Seaweed of Blunden Harbour, one of the great Kwakiutl artists of the twentieth century, made dance masks for Hector Webb, Sam Webber and Tom Patch for Kingcome potlatches in the 1930s and 1940s. Indeed, the thirties and forties were prolific decades for the carver, his "time of greatest Hamatsa mask production."[6] In 1939 Charles Nowell sold two coppers for thousands of blankets and goods so that Arthur Shaughnessy, his son-in-law, could potlatch in Kingcome, Shaughnessy's home village. Shaughnessy's potlatch must have rivaled the size of any ceremony at any time.[7] Kingcome's advantage led others to claim a relationship, no matter how remote, to its villagers so that they could have the benefit of its security.

The impregnability of Kingcome's defences was aggravating to the Alert Bay agents and they sought ways to overcome it. E. G. Newnham, interim successor to Halliday, asked that RCMP officers be sent to Kingcome disguised as fur buyers, but the police realized that the role could not long be maintained and the assistant commissioner in Victoria wanted to avoid any "expensive or experimental enterprises." Halliday's successor, Murray S. Todd, asked for a mounted policeman to be permanently stationed at the village. Even the possibility of using an airplane was proposed. No such measures were ever adopted. The 1930s were a time of retrenchment and *Festung.* Kingcome remained unbreached: "There in their frosty isolation they potlatched as much as they pleased."[8]

Kingcome was the safest spot, but other villages, sheltered by the stormy winter season, were also very suitable. Village Island, only some twenty kilometres from Alert Bay, was enough removed that "there were a lot of potlatches" there in the early 1930s, though, as Jimmy Sewid remembered, "We had to be very careful because of the law." People, as many as fifty, would come to the island to invite its villagers to potlatches; their immediate hosts would take them "up to have a big feast and give a small potlatch." Jim Bell gave "a big do" there in about 1932 for his grandson Jimmy Sewid. The youngster, only about eighteen but already a father, was reluctant— "I guess I was afraid of the law." He gave in to family pressure. "It was the time," he recalled,

> to open that big chest which had all the regalia and different dances in it that had been given to me by the Fort Rupert Kwakiutl when I got married. My grandfather had been holding all those things for me and it was up to us to take them out of that box and perform those dances. It was time for me to become a hamatsa.

Jimmy was given a house that had been moved from Alert Bay as part of the bridal repayment. Two seine boats carted in the other potlatch goods. "We bought out the wholesale," his mother-in-law remembered.[9]

Turnour Island, Fort Rupert and Cape Mudge were also scenes of such potlatches. "If there is nobody to watch," wrote Franz Boas about his Fort Rupert friends, "they do whatever they like." Ed Whonnock's granddaughter, born in 1928, remembers dancing in potlatches from the time she was a child. "They used to hide in places and do their Potlatches," she recalled. In 1939 Charles Nowell shared in a large potlatch at Bella Bella, the aftermath of a Bella Coola wedding.[10]

But open potlatches, while they seem to have increased after 1927 in the absence of new prosecutions, were not the usual means of potlatching. Fear of the law remained and most Indians sought nearer and more convenient ways to continue their interest in the system. Most potlatches were held "on the quiet." When Jane Nowell married Arthur Shaughnessy in 1921, the groom's payment of $1000 was given privately with only the Tsawataineuk chiefs present. A church wedding was followed by a feast and dance "in the white man's way" at the day school. Nowell, however, announced that everyone could go to the movie show free on Saturday night and bought boxes of apples and oranges, candy, cakes, soda pop and chewing gum to distribute there. To the old people who did not attend the cinema, he had Arthur and Jane distribute the fifty-cent admission in cash. When one of the couple's daughters died,

Nowell sent three men around Alert Bay with $300 to give some to everyone. "If the Indian Act hadn't been enforced," he later stated, "I would have called all the people here for a potlatch, and we would have gone through all the ceremonies. As it was, she was buried in the white man's way."[11]

Such house-to-house visitations satisfied obligations but little more. As the Cooks wrote, "Part of the glory was taken away." They also introduced a drastic modification in potlatch procedure: the abandonment of gift distribution according to the order of rank. Theoretically, it would have been possible to have made the rounds of the houses observing the sequence of rank, but it was simpler to begin at one end of the village and go to the other.[12]

Nor did these distributions satisfy the spiritual demands of the potlatch. The dances and songs, the vital intangibles of the ceremony, could not be properly conferred on a doorstep. Consequently, the Indians separated the dancing and ceremonies from the giving away. The "disjointed potlatch" (as Ditchburn dubbed it) was a new dodge, resulting partly from the advice of Vancouver lawyer W. R. Vaughan. The first ones that came to the attention of the Department of Indian Affairs were at Village and Turnour islands. At the former there was "no doubt whatever that approximately fifteen hundred sacks of flour were given away," but no dance or ceremony took place. At Karlakwees village Henry Speck gave a large dance with "all the old time ceremony" but "absolutely nothing was given away."[13] Speck had all the names recorded in a book and the guests were told that he would give things away after six months.

Two loopholes were involved. First, the Indian Act was specific that the giving away must form a part of an Indian festival, dance or ceremony in order for the event to be illegal and, second, the statute of limitations provided by the Criminal Code allowed only six months to prosecute. While the Ministry of Justice had no doubt that the limitation did not apply until all the actions constituting the offence had been committed, it remained very difficult to prove that a giving away formed a part of a dance held half a year earlier. Halliday could secure proof that the Village Island flour was given, but he saw major difficulty in connecting it with an earlier dance or ceremony.[14]

Similar dances in March 1932 at Fort Rupert and at Village Island carried no potlatches. Halliday saw the dance at Fort Rupert, but had no evidence "that even a five cent piece had been given away." At Village Island there were dances, but he and the police "got absolutely not one tittle of evidence to show that anything illegal had taken place." The flour distributions were particularly aggravating. The man delivering the fifteen hundred sacks to Village Island left it there with the remark, "Here is some flour I have brought to help you out over the hard winter." When Nowell landed nine hundred sacks at Fort Rupert two years later, he told police that it was nothing more than "an act of Christian charity for the benefit of poor people who were hard up."[15]

There were other expedients. Moses Alfred built a "gymnasium" in the upper storey of his house. The large room did have some athletic equipment, but its "true purpose" was for secret potlatches. Alfred, an elderly man who had been arrested in 1920 and was among those second offenders of the Cranmer potlatch pardoned for signing the agreement, had an enormous amount of goods stored and ready to give away in 1934. In December he simply tagged each article with the name of the person for whom it was intended ("I must say it certainly looked like a Christmas tree to me," the agent commented) and walked away. Alert Bay potlatching was planned to coincide with the Christmas season and the gifts were wrapped as presents. Most couples married at that time too. "The variations that grew out of the possible loopholes were as numerous as the people who kept the tradition strong," stated a later Indian leader.[16]

Such stratagems, however they may have modified aspects of the customary potlatch, worked. Remote Kingcome was impossible to patrol. Elsewhere patrols were ineffective because everything would be delayed until the police left. After the invention of the disjointed potlatch, such patrols were useless. They could see only half of the whole. The single Kwakiutl prosecution after 1927 was under the little-used provision against dancing off one's own reserve. Todd used it successfully in 1935 against several Indians, including Henry Bell. Bell's option was ten dollars or fifteen days in jail.[17]

Such evasions of the law depended upon the solidarity of the Kwakiutl. Should anyone have turned witness, as two men had for Angermann in 1922, circumvention would have been defeated. No one did. The rivalries and factions of the small Kwakiutl community did not cease, but all ranks closed after the trauma of 1922. Not even the Christian Indians would cooperate. The authorities' greatest problem, never overcome, was securing evidence.

Provincial Constable George H. Clark complained of the problem in 1931: "Obtaining evidence that would convict is a very difficult matter; naturally the Indians who take part will not divulge the proceedings, and those who dont [sic] take part (who are few) have their own reasons for not wishing to become implicated in any prosecution proceedings." He knew Indians who could tell him what was going on, "but everywhere I find myself up against a stone wall." Halliday fully realized the situation. The Indians "have all made up their minds that they will lie systematically before any of them will give evidence against any of the others." A young man at Cape Mudge, who did not support the potlatch but had watched a recent one, told him frankly:

> Mr. Halliday, if I were to go into court and say there what I have told you, I would be an outcast amongst all the Indians. There is no Indian in the whole countryside who would not think that I deserved to be turned out from amongst them altogether.[18]

Agents virtually gave up on securing evidence from Indians themselves. They pinned their hopes on surprise raids, constant patrols, the use of plainclothes constables, and constant changes of police personnel. But there was no longer an RCMP detachment at Alert Bay and such plans never received the support of the Victoria office: Newnham was temporary and too inexperienced to take responsibility for activities that might plunge the department into great expense and possible embarrassment;[19] the RCMP were preoccupied with other duties, including labour demonstrations; the possibility of success was too remote to justify the extraordinary costs. Blocked in such efforts at enforcement, Kwawkewlth agency officials sought scapegoats. Public opinion, lenient judges and, after 1929, missionaries were seen to bear some responsibility for the Kwakiutl remaining outside the law.

The department had good reason to be concerned with the attitude of the church. Views there were becoming wobbly to an alarming extent. Christ Church parishioners, though they might complain of the lack of enforcement, were not prepared to supply evidence to the police. A more serious concern was the Anglican clergy. Rev. John A. Antle, founder and superintendent of the Columbia Coast Mission, a medical service primarily concerned with loggers and settlers, had assumed responsibility for the Kingcome and Village Island missions in 1927. Soon Antle began advising Indians that he would try to have the act amended to permit some festivities. "The Indians 'bootleg' the potlatch," Antle wrote, by doing it secretly, thus bringing back its worst features and fostering a habit of law-breaking. He announced himself "wholly in accord" with the Indians' demand for "such modifications of the law which will enable them to retain certain parts of the potlatch which enter into their social life and without which life in their villages would be absolutely without amusement or recreation." To the department, this was bad enough, but Antle also wrote that "the ruthless tragedy upon the ancient customs comes not too well from a Christian nation."[20]

Antle's remarks, which continued in this vein over the next several years, were most annoying to the department. Enforcement, he told the minister of the interior, "had disrupted and upset" the whole social life of the Indian. The natives should be allowed their orderly dances and feasts and be allowed to give away "to *a limited amount.*" Antle's comments, recorded in the mission's *Log of the Columbia*, irritated Scott enormously. "It does not seem to me to be 'Cricket' to make public his views on this vexed question," the deputy wrote. Scott felt that if Antle expected department support (the mission's medical and educational services received government funding), he should be loyal to its policies, even if opposed to them.[21]

Even more troublesome from the department's point of view was the newly called vicar of Christ Church, Rev. C. K. K. Prosser. Ministers at Alert Bay, from A. J. Hall through A. W. Corker and F. W. Comley, had all been supporters of departmental efforts to suppress the potlatch. Prosser changed the pattern. On his Lenten visit to Village Island he found the Indians holding dances and, assured by Chief Harry Mountain that the law was not being broken, Prosser accepted an invitation to attend. He was, he told Bishop Schofield, "most impressed with what I saw." Instead of objectionable things, he found himself witness to "a finished work of art." He emerged from the experience convinced "that the Indians who are living at the moment have no more right to alter the main outlines of the custom than one generation of Christians has to alter the creeds." Seeing nothing wrong in the ceremony that could not be met by ways other than an outright ban, he concluded his letter to the bishop with strong statements. "We have done the Indians a great injustice," he wrote; enforcement "would be a disaster."

> We cannot afford to deprive our descendants & theirs of the contribution the present generation of Indians can make to the common stock, the witness to the reality of the spiritual, the witness to a God who has revealed Himself to them through His attributes of beauty and ordered ceremonial.[22]

Prosser's impassioned and poetic views, communicated privately to his bishop, could not bother the department, but his attendance at dances did. Agent Newnham was outraged "that these evil practices continue to flourish under missionary encouragement." Prosser made a practice, the agent claimed, of attending as many as possible "and actually dons Indian regalia while present." That was legal, of course, but it gave the Indians the impression that they had the support of the church. The agent's complaints to his superiors brought a letter from Ottawa asking the bishop for continued cooperation in dealing with the potlatch.[23]

The bishop's synod, which had already taken up the issue for investigation and reevaluation, came out in 1935 against the potlatch. Opinions had been divided between the new line pursued by Antle and Prosser and that of the older missionaries, including Comley and the retired Corker. The final resolutions were a compromise. There was a hint of regret that "the time is too late, and the complications too many, to attempt to save the potlatch," but converts should renounce it and the church should make every effort to find substitutes for the loss.[24] The conclusions were welcomed by Indian affairs officials, but the church's waffling had been trying. Agent Newnham was convinced "that the encouragement which has been given in the past is largely responsible for these pernicious habits being continued in this Agency long after they have been abandoned elsewhere."[25]

Missionaries were easy scapegoats for the frustrations of Kwawkewlth agents. Newnham left Alert Bay feeling very ill-used by the department. A government report stated that the agent, initially "zealous and well-intentioned according to his lights and not lacking ability," had turned into an "awkward, obstructive and insubordinate" official. Murray S. Todd's Kwakiutl experience was little better; he earned the irritation of his Victoria superior by constantly harping on the subject of the potlatch, for which conviction seemed impossible.[26] They could not get the Indians to talk, Todd said. The government would not supply police to patrol the whole agency, the courts were lenient, the clergy unsympathetic. Obviously, the law itself was defective. There were just too many ways to evade it.

"I am not a person to get excited over anything," Todd wrote in November 1934, "but unless this thing is dealt with and smashed, we are going to have lots of trouble on our hands." The Indians had been kept down by the potlatch; they remained "the most backward Indians of this whole province, and so long as we permit them to carry on this old custom we will always have them in the same position." Assistant Commissioner Perry had to admit that the situation was no better than when the prosecutions had taken place a decade earlier. The time had come, he concluded, to approach the matter "from a different angle," by an amendment strengthening and augmenting the law's provisions.[27]

Perry proposed that the department, either under the existing section of the act which gave the superintendent general control of Indian property or by a new amendment, authorize an agent or the RCMP to seize and detain any goods and supplies, in excess of immediate family needs, accumulated by an Indian and reasonably believed to be intended for potlatch purposes. "A few seizures of this nature," Perry stated, "would have a most salutory effect, and would result in the Indians abandoning the practice of accumulating such immense stores in preparation for the potlatch." Stipulation should be added that no appeal would be possible. Agent Todd pursued this strategy. A man of conservative propriety, he was extremely conscientious in his duties. In Ottawa in December 1934, he discussed his proposals for a solution to the potlatch problem with the department's legal officer, A. S. Williams, and Secretary T. R. L. McInnis. The three agreed that the act required amendment providing penalties and seizures for the accumulation of large quantities of potlatch goods.[28] Back home in Alert Bay, the Kwawkewlth agent sat down to make his own recommendations, coming up with three. He accepted the idea of confiscation, but wanted also to enlarge the prohibition against participating in dances to include attendance, since he had a case against several Kwakiutl on just this point and feared appeal. Todd went even further by suggesting the addition of a clause penalizing anyone possessing "any Indian masks, coppers or paraphernalia" and allowing confiscation of such articles. The Indians, he explained, had not surrendered all their material in the Halliday prosecutions and were secretly making more masks. He too suggested that all judgements be final, with no appeal allowed.[29]

Ottawa officials judged Todd's suggestions "too drastic," and the abolition-of-appeal provision was deemed impossible to get through Parliament. They accepted, however, the idea of a seizure of property and six months' imprisonment of the guilty party.[30]

This then became the department's solution to almost a decade of inactivity. Tightening the Indian Act was a tried and true method of overcoming obstacles to enforcement of antipotlatch legislation. The department had used it to remedy the drafting defects Justice Begbie had exposed in the original enactment, and Scott had modified it again after the 1913-15 enforcement had failed to secure convictions.

The initiators of the seizure amendment were a new group. Halliday, Ditchburn and Scott were all gone by 1934. Ontario-born M. S. Todd, Halliday's successor, had worked in prairie lumberyards, served in the Great War, then worked in the lumber business on the British Columbia coast before securing the Indian affairs post at Alert Bay. Ditchburn had not been immediately replaced. Charles C. Perry, an agent before becoming assistant commissioner, had assumed Ditchburn's duties on the commissioner's death. Born in Devonshire, Perry had come to Canada in 1908 as a Methodist teacher, working with Rev. G. H. Raley on the Skeena before joining the department. Twenty years of service in the Nass, Skeena and Vancouver agencies had preceded his 1929 appointment as Ditchburn's assistant. Even more significant than the changes at the local level was Scott's retirement as deputy superintendent general after fifty-two years in the department, eighteen of them as its head. Major H. W. McGill, the new deputy, was a patronage appointment. A physician, McGill had served as surgeon with the Canadian Expeditionary Force, then returned to Calgary for private practice. Elected an alderman, then to the provincial legislature, he resigned his seat to accept appointment by Prime Minister R. B. Bennett, a fellow

Calgary Conservative, as deputy superintendent general of Indian affairs.

The draft amendment, made on the advice of Todd, Perry, and McGill and his Ottawa staff, was introduced in the House of Commons by an even newer face. T. A. Crerar had become superintendent general of Indian affairs only with the return of the Mackenzie King Liberals to office the previous October.[31] Tabled in February 1936, with a dozen other changes to the act, few of them controversial, the amendment reached second reading on 20 March. Almost immediately Crerar ran into trouble. Raising objection to the potlatch amendment, partly at the instigation of Indians who had written him, was Clements's successor, the Independent member for Comox-Alberni, A. W. Neill.

The Scottish-born Neill had been elected to the House of Commons in 1921 and had survived four subsequent general elections (indeed, he would serve until he declined renomination in 1945). Previously he had been a member of the B. C. Legislative Assembly and mayor of Alberni. More relevant, he had served as West Coast agent for about ten years under Vowell. There he had been one of the most tolerant of agents on the question of dances and potlatches. He had discouraged "excesses," but granted Indians the right to "amusements" which, he felt, were no sillier or more wasteful than masked balls, Christmas pageants or holiday dinners. Enforcement of the law would create resentment, dissatisfaction and even bloodshed. A law "repugnant to the traditions & wishes of *all* the people," he had written, was almost impossible to enforce; attempts to stop the custom would make it "at once ten times as dear as it is now."[32]

Neill launched an attack on the department's confiscation amendment. The Indians were very upset, he told the House, especially by press reports that they were going to great excess, even so far as to give away their women. Four chiefs in his riding had written in protest, asking him to put the matter in its true light. He did so, expressing both their and his own objections to the proposed amendment. "The Act is stringent enough and it has been effective," said the thin, bespectacled member, "and the necessity for its enforcement is becoming less and less." The difficulty with the tabled amendment was that it rested upon intention, and who could read into a man's mind? "That a man shall be put in peril of his liberty for six months because someone in office thinks the Indian has it in his mind to do something" was unreasonable, unjust and un-British. The law was already stern; the new proposal merely sought to save the local agent from hunting up evidence.

Though Neill was far the most informed, vocal and persuasive, others joined in opposition, including J. S. Woodsworth, the Cooperative Commonwealth Federation MP from Winnipeg, and British Columbia members from Nanaimo, Victoria and Yale. Crerar, new to his office and badly briefed, could answer few of their concerns. The potlatch, he said, put a hardship on Indian families; the law was beneficial to the Indians and no injustice to any Indian would result. He had to admit, however, that potlatching was dying out in all but one agency and, even there, he could not say that it was any worse than before. The proposed amendment, he said, sought only to draw a little tighter the provision that had been law for fifty years, having been put in the books, so he had been informed, "originally at the request of the Indians themselves." All this was not very persuasive and, when other members expressed doubts, Crerar dropped his defence of the proposed change.[33]

The reversal of the seizure amendment was in one sense a fluke. It was fortuitous that Neill, a former agent who reflected Vowell's policy of discretion, was a member of the House and able to rouse other members against a hapless Crerar, unfamiliar with the Indian affairs responsibilities of his portfolio. The minister could well have pointed out, from recent departmental correspondence, his officials' views that the Kwakiutl potlatch had "reached the greatest height of many years," that "the Indians have got bolder and quite open in carrying it on."[34] That would have answered at least some members' concerns. On the other hand, the debate reflected a move away from the old paternalism, a movement already apparent in the conversion of some Anglican missionaries to sympathy with the native viewpoint.

Failure of the amendment was another blow to the frustrated Kwawkewlth agent. Todd had been writing of the increase of potlatching and of the thousands of dollars in goods and money recently potlatched. Anticipating the amendment, he had expected many prosecutions to take place, but the tide was running against him.

A delegation of Kwakiutl visited Neill at his Port Alberni home and came back with the report that he had told them there was no harm in potlatching. Agent Todd wrote the member of Parliament stating that, since the delegation's return, one Indian had distributed goods reportedly running into thousands of dollars in value and "the impression is general that you are sympathetic toward them with the potlatch and that no action will be taken." Neill's tart reply was that he had made clear that the law forbade potlatching, but his own opinion was that, if not carried to extremes, "there was no harm in carrying it on." Moreover, when he had been West Coast agent, he had never prosecuted and yet the ceremony "has fallen into greater disuse in that district than it has in the Alert Bay one where they prosecuted."[35]

Todd went on cursing the potlatch as "degrading and interfering with the progress of the Indians," reporting that it was "rampant" and getting stronger, and threatening to "prosecute them regardless of public opinion." Now, however, his continuing complaints wore down the patience of Major Donald M. MacKay, distinguished war veteran and former member of the provincial legislature, appointed Indian commissioner for British Columbia on Perry's retirement. Todd had been instructed, MacKay wrote Ottawa, "not to bring up the matter of potlatches unless he has definite and willing evidence that will bring a conviction." Yet MacKay was convinced that convictions were impossible under the present statute. Under these circumstances, MacKay stated, Todd should be informed not to report in useless generalities.[36]

Todd did not get the point immediately. His monthly reports about bolder, more open and more extensive potlatching continued, but his only action (against which there was no appeal) was to cut off an old man from relief because he reportedly had given away several hundred dollars, though "I have no proof of this."[37] Eventually Todd seems to have grown tired of his own complaints. Few reports enter the files after 1939.

Todd in 1943 again described the practice as growing. Rev. E. W. Christmas, stationed at Kingcome, also reported retrogression. The new wartime demand for labour had given rise to greater prosperity and, in turn, greater potlatches. The Kingcome Kwakiutl had shifted to the more accessible Gwayasdums on Gilford Island where, in 1944, dances were celebrated with "all the old evils." War or no war, Christmas said, nothing hindered the annual potlatch. The Kingcome-Gilford Island missionary was new to the coast, with little perspective on the ceremony about which he complained. F. Earl Anfield took things more in stride. Formerly principal at the Alert Bay school and now agent at Bella Coola, he toured the inland waters in the summer of 1944. In an almost jocular, even mischievous, style, he wrote to his old friend Todd of a Saturday night dance he had chanced upon at Kildala cannery. "They were slightly embarrassed when I appeared on the scene," he stated, "and I had a pleasant time going around and renewing old acquaintances." He asked their names ("they were not quite sure what I wanted the names for"), but "a good time was had by all." There was no drinking and everyone was well behaved. He suggested that a Red Cross collection be taken and the charity's war fund was thus increased by $61.56. Otherwise the potlatch was a small summer affair, only $1000 changing hands, and, according to Anfield's "Gestapo," the gifts ran from thirty cents to three dollars—"so no one got very rich." At midnight he "chased them all off to their boats" and admonished them to get a permit for dances off the reserve next time. They promised to do so.[38] Todd's reply is lost.

Even Todd had come, by February 1939, to hope that "the Indians themselves will see the wisdom of giving up this practice before very long." Major MacKay also wrote with resigned hope. His own "considered opinion," in February 1938, was "that it is better to leave the matter to the final good sense of the Indians themselves[,] encouraged by education to drop the custom as they have done elsewhere." A year later, in words that echoed those of Vowell four decades earlier, he judged that "the influence of Church and school should in time do more to eliminate these pagan practices than any prohibitory measures would accomplish."[39] And there the matter rested.

Things were somewhat similar among the Gitksan on the Skeena. They too had felt the force of Scott's 1918 policy and the presence of the RCMP, with convictions in 1921, 1927 and 1931, although all received suspended sentences. Most often, it appears, the ceremonies were restricted to feasts, with little or no giving away. Enforcement, which waxed and waned, certainly had its effect, but with nothing approaching the Alert Bay cases of the early 1920s. By the end of the 1930s renewed potlatching was apparent among the Gitksan.

From late December 1938 to the end of the following month, major ceremonies were held almost continuously at Kitsegukla and Kitwanga, with guests from Kitwancool, Hazelton, Glen Vowell, Kispiox and Morricetown—all the major Gitksan groups—and many from Hagwilget villages as well. Like most Tsimshian ceremonies, they were memorial or succession occasions. David Williams raised a new pole at Kitsegukla (carved by "Wobblie" Tom Campbell). At Kitwanga, Robert Harris's elevation as chief was similarly celebrated with dancing, feasts, speeches and the dedication of the tombstone of his predecessor. A nontraditional element was included: the Sunday blessing of the new chief in the Kitwanga church. The Kitsegukla pole raising invoked a protest from missionary teacher Bishop Black about the potlatch, "involving large sums of money," that accompanied it. Agent Mortimer, after investigating the complaint, reported that, while there were a large number of visitors at the evening's feast and ample provisions for them, the only payments had been to the carver and those helping to raise the pole.[40]

Later that year the Kitsegukla funeral for Dan Cookson reached such a scale that it provoked official concern. Agent S. Mallinson assured the department, however, that nothing illegal had occurred: all the money contributed was used for funeral expenses and the expensive radio, apparently a gift, was actually only the repayment of "an old debt."[41]

A feature of at least some of these Gitksan occasions was the awarding of "prizes." "After the expenses being settled and goods placed in the hand as prizes to those with authorized Indian names, speeches were made by well known chiefs." Prizes might be given for "the best speeches by chiefs," an ingenious, if transparent, circumvention of the giving ban.[42]

Old poles, some fallen from age, others rescued from the Skeena River flood of 1937, were ceremonially erected, as were newly carved ones. The federal government's restoration of a number of decayed or fallen totem poles along the railway line during the mid-1920s and again in 1939 may have played a part in the renewed interest in traditions and poles. Three old poles were put up at the Hazelton baseball park, with ceremonies as much adapted as traditional. In 1942 Kitwanga re-erected three old poles and in 1944 Kitwancool restored some of their fallen ones. In both villages, the ceremonies were patterned after the old procedures.[43] The 1942 Kitwanga pole raisings were kept under RCMP scrutiny, but again the constables found no indication of potlatching.[44] The 1942 surveillance is the last recorded police report.

The Kitwanga and Kitwancool raisings were followed in 1945 by a much larger ceremony at Kitsegukla. A five-day series of potlatches and *halait* dance performances culminated in the main business, the erecting of five memorial poles. Among the guests was Nishga William Beynon, anthropologist Marius Barbeau's ethnological informant, who made almost two hundred pages of notes.

"One might suspect," commented a later anthropologist after reading Beynon's account of the 1945 ceremonies, "that they would represent only an attenuated and watered-down version of earlier potlatching." This was true in a few respects, but "one is amazed at the clear picture of old Tsimshian practise that emerges." For one thing, the old people were making a deliberate effort to revive the old forms.[45] The conservative aspect came out clearly in discussions preliminary to the ceremonies. Some of the younger people were opposed to spending money on the poles; a majority of the young men wanted the ceremonies shortened and modernized; but the older people wanted the old procedures followed. They prevailed. Tom Campbell, the "troublemaker" who in 1931 had received a suspended sentence from Agent G. C. Mortimer on condition that he stay away from all such ceremonies, not only carved one of the new poles but served as song leader for the whole affair. George Woodcock visited the area in 1950 and found a store outside Morricetown with almost nothing to sell. The Indians, explained the proprietor, had held a potlatch over the weekend and had bought almost everything in his shop. Nor could he make change: the Indians had broken their twenty-dollar bills into smaller notes to give away. Woodcock's companion noted that potlatches were illegal. "They don't seem to be illegal here," the shopkeeper responded. "Everybody knows they go on." A young Indian who entered the store only smiled. "Maybe somebody had a party. I don't know."[46]

In all of Beynon's notes, which include accounts of controversies between old and young, arguments over procedures and a major confrontation over the use of a crest, there is no word about the law or a fear of its enforcement. The ceremony was not secret or underground. A number of spectators, both native and white, were present.

Departmental officials ignored, even suppressed, reports of potlatching. Commissioner MacKay wanted "to leave the matter" to the Kwakiutl themselves and was easily convinced by Agent Mortimer "that the potlatch has disappeared in the Babine Agency." When Rev. Black carried his complaint about the Kitsegukla potlatch to a Vancouver newspaper, MacKay's officials suggested to the editors that no good purpose could be served by its publication. The department's school inspector took the occasion to suggest that Black be transferred elsewhere.[47]

By the end of the 1930s the government had resigned itself to letting things alone, not only the potlatch, but, in a general sense, the entire mission of civilization. "Government attempts to civilize the Indian," writes Dan McCaskill, "began to dissipate in many parts of the country." "Protection" and "civilization" remained as ideals; actual policy, however, might well be characterized as "protect and forget."[48]

■ The Kwakiutl sought, by petitions, delegations, lawyers' briefs and official inquiry, a repeal of the potlatch law. Among their spokespersons was the twice-imprisoned Charles Nowell (*top*), shown here in happier days as host of a potlatch. After 1927 the Kwakiutl gave up on the legal processes and simply evaded the law in various ways. Pictographs (*bottom*) on remote Kingcome Inlet depict potlatch coppers and eleven cattle sold to potlatching Kwakiutl in 1927 by farmer Ernest Halliday, brother of agent William Halliday.

Photo credits: RBCM, *No. 1071, Cadwallder Collection;* RBCM, *No. 2197, photo by Wilson Duff, 1955*

■ Kwakiutl ingenuity frustrated Halliday's successor, Murray S. Todd (*top left*), pictured here with his wife Myrtle at Alert Bay in 1941. Todd drafted sweeping amendments to the law that would have allowed confiscation of goods believed to be for potlatch purposes. Comox-Alberni Independent A. W. Neill (*top right*), photographed here earlier as a member of the Alberni city council, had been a West Coast agent during the time of Vowell's policy of tolerance. Led by Neill, Members of Parliament spoke so strongly against the proposal that the government withdrew the amendment. Even the church had become more sympathetic, with Rev. John Antle (*left*) of the Columbia Coast Mission writing publicly in favour of the potlatch.

Photo credits: *Courtesy of Patterson Todd; Alberni Valley Museum, Photographic Archives, No. PN102;* BCARS, *No. 59743*

158

■ Attempts to enforce the law among the Kwakiutl halted. Ceremonies continued, as seen in these 1946 photographs of a "public dance" at Johnny Scow's Gilford Island house. The dance was probably part of a "disjointed potlatch" that evaded the law by separating the giving-away from the ceremonial dances.

Photo credits: RBCM, *No. 15250-32;* RBCM, *No. 15250-41*

■ On the Skeena River, potlatching continued in spite of occasional arrests. Anthropologist C. M. Barbeau took this 1924 photograph of participants during the third day of the Hagwilget Laxsel'yu ceremony.

Photo credit: *National Museums of Canada, National Museum of Civilization, No. 62324, photo by C. M. Barbeau, 1924*

■ The 1960s witnessed a cultural revival among the native peoples of British Columbia. This, with the dropping of the antipotlatch law from the statutes, prompted a renewal of potlatch ceremonies all along the northwest coast. Witnesses to a 1970s potlatch of Douglas Cranmer (son of Dan Cranmer) look at some of the gifts to be distributed (*top*), and dancers perform at Peter Smith's October 1981 Gilford Island potlatch (*bottom*).

Photo credits: *Courtesy of Douglas Cranmer, photo by Peter Macnair; Courtesy of Mrs. Alice Smith, photo by Peter Macnair*

10

"Advancing in a Civilized World"

SINCE AT LEAST 1882, missionaries and officials had placed their hope in time, Christianity and the younger Indians to bring an end to the potlatch. Generations had passed, but among the Gitksan, Kwakiutl and others, the young had taken the ranks of the elders and continued the system. Now, however, the younger people were less and less interested in maintaining the customs. White man's ways, even without enforcement of the law, were changing Kwakiutl attitudes. Rev. Christmas thought the process too slow, but he recognized the change: "The young men will not memorise the ceremonial chants and harangues as their fathers have." Anfield, while in Alert Bay, had commented that "the young men are not interested"; they "do not understand all the implications of the custom." At the 1945 Gitksan potlatch, a Kitwankool speaker noted sadly that "there are really only a few of us left who really know." A Kitsegukla man regretted that many young people had neglected even to assume their own names. Potlatching, Neill noted in a 1938 Commons exchange, "is wearing itself out. It only needs time and moderation." When Nanaimo MP James Taylor made his own investigation of the Kwawkewlth agency situation, older chiefs complained that he talked only to young people and asked his questions only in Alert Bay, where the Apostolic Mission, a Pentecostal group, had had great success in the interwar period.[1]

Altered attitudes affected not just the young. The Apostolic Mission was very strict in imposing among its adherents a renunciation of the potlatch. The Anglicans too had finally begun to take deeper roots in the community. After the death of his first wife, Charles Nowell married a Christian. "I didn't go through any ceremony," he said. "We just went to the church." Church marriages continued to increase throughout the 1920s and even more in the 1930s. These included a mass marriage of twenty older Kwakiutl couples, including high-ranking men such as Dan Cranmer, Moses Alfred, Sam Scow, Isaak Abraham, Henry Speck, and Ed and Johnny Whonnock, on 26 December 1933. By the 1930s young people seem largely to have been choosing their own partners. Nowell's daughter Agnes married in church. "Herbert Cook didn't pay me anything; it was all done in the white man's way," Nowell said later. Harry Mountain, chief at Village Island, declared that there had been no Indian-custom marriages there since the early 1930s, the parents consenting instead to the young people's choices.[2]

When Franz Boas revisited his Southern Kwakiutl friends in 1930, almost fifty years after his first field research among them, he noted that the feasts were nothing compared with former times. The people clung to the form though the content was almost gone.[3]

"It was somewhere around that time," Jimmy Sewid wrote about the mid-1930s, "that I began to feel that it wasn't right to have these potlatches." He had helped to start a native logging operation on the Village Island reserve.

> I thought a lot about why I should give up the logging operation and go to a potlatch. We wouldn't be producing any logs during that time so I began staying right in the village even though the other people went. A few of the younger people would stay with me but about 80 percent of our people would go to the potlatch. The way I looked at it, it was more important to be on the job. I thought it was all right if it was a free time but not when there was a job to be done.[4]

Sewid was hardly typical, but he was not alone. Bill Scow, believing the potlatch to be an obstacle to Indian advancement, renounced the potlatch and refused to participate in any of the ceremonies. Indicative of change, too, were the young Gitksan who protested the money spent on the 1945 Kitsegukla potlatch; the same money spent on sawmills, they said, would have kept the entire village employed.[5]

The decline of the potlatch's hold on the Kwakiutl was partly the

result of quite another factor. The system was dependent upon surplus wealth derived from the European economy, even on its continued expansion. Interest on potlatch loans could run to 100 per
cent and the price of coppers, though unsystematic, was expected to
rise with each transaction. Some were so valuable that they could
hardly find a buyer. By the 1920s there were signs of strain in the
system, "signs that the expansion in earnings was not quite keeping
up with the constant increases demanded by the potlatch," especially those connected with copper purchases. A preliminary payment, the "pillow," came to be accepted as a kind of down payment, with the purchaser taking the copper on agreement to complete the purchase later. The vender might have to carry the credit
for years, might never see the balance repaid. In the 1920s defaults
and entrenched indebtedness became so serious, either because of
the law's threatened enforcement or, more likely, because of the discrepancy between cost and ability to pay, that Kwakiutl chiefs
agreed to stop the payment as well as loans and credit sales for coppers. As a result, copper transfers came nearly to an end.[6]

Part of the money shortage came from structural changes in the
fishing industry, the Indians' main source of income. The advance
from sail and oar to gasoline boats was difficult. The Kwakiutl had
usually rented boats and nets from canneries; now there was pressure to buy the vessel and its gear, but financing was a major problem. Indians, because they could not be sued, were dependent upon
the fishing companies for credit, and the canneries regarded white
and Japanese fishermen as more dependable debtors. Equally difficult for native fishermen was the increased competition from the
Japanese, despite limitations on the number of licences issued them.

The Kingcome Inlet cheque episode was another indication of the
difficulty. A cash shortage caused George Scow to use paper, rather
like cheques, in a Kingcome copper sale and purchase. This paper
money circulated as real and the practice was copied by others.
Within a short time "fantastic amounts of worthless paper were cir-
culating among the Kingcome Inlet group in purchases of coppers,
in potlatches, and in private transactions as well." Soon bickering
over the fictitious money threatened the potlatch itself. The chiefs
stopped the use of paper and directed a return to hard money.[7] The
bitter, endless squabbles over potlatch canoe shares among the Lekwiltok were a factor in Chief Billy Assu's decision, pivotal among

that Kwakiutl group, to abandon the potlatch completely. Prosperity, not poverty, was instrumental. The Lekwiltok had made a considerable sum from logging their Drew Harbour reserve, and Assu called the people together and suggested they use the money to modernize their village, building new homes that would have electricity and running water. The villagers, even the older generation, went along. In April 1920, two donkey engines were brought down from the Drew Harbour operation to level the land and to demolish all the old-style potlatch houses. "It wasn't easy," recalled Assu's son Harry, "for my father to lead his people into a new way of life," but "the most important people supported my father, and, finally, when a real chance came to take advantage of changing times, people were all for it."[8]

The Indian cash economy, already strained in the twenties, was pushed to the limit by the Great Depression. The salmon packs of the decade declined only a little, but the same was not true for prices and wages. Much of the record 1930 pack could not be sold and over twenty canneries were idle the next season, some permanently. The Alert Bay cannery, in production since 1881, closed its doors in 1930. The value of output declined by almost two-thirds at the bottom of the depression. At the end of the decade the number of B.C. canneries had sunk from seventy-six to forty-four. Possessing older equipment and operating at lower efficiency than their competitors, the Indians generally lost out in an industry that was already suffering a severe decline. Provincial native income from fishing fell from $539,472 in 1929 to less than half, $233,540, before rising to $449,809 in 1936.[9]

The potlatch's dependence upon an expanding European economy threw the institution into a severe crisis. The shortage of money made it difficult to potlatch. Even when a Kwakiutl had sufficient wealth, guests were often unable to raise funds for a return. Helen Codere notes that "those few who stubbornly potlatched became self-righteously embittered at the failure of the debtors to repay them and refused to continue to 'just give away property for nothing.'" Those unable to potlatch were also embittered by reminders of their debts and obligations. Younger people, not yet part of the structure, saw the system as the source of trouble and unhappiness.[10]

Prosperity returned in the wartime 1940s. Canneries on the coast, including the Alert Bay plant, reopened. The removal of the Japanese helped other coastal fishermen, and prices improved immensely. "Since the Japs were taken away the Indians have had a greater scope," testified the Native Brotherhood leader, Haida Rev. Peter Kelly, "and the price of fish is much higher than it used to be."[11] The potlatch, however, did not recover to the same extent. As a system, it was crippled—by acculturation, by the end of arranged marriages, by disuse, by the younger generation, even (though probably not much) by the threat of Section 149 of the Indian Act.

The Kwakiutl social system was changing; among most Kwakiutl people, it had already changed. No longer was it so based on ranking of individuals, of lineages or of tribes. Few people any longer knew the protocol of winter ceremonials or of potlatch seating, many did not care, and some disapproved. An elderly informant told Ronald Rohner early in the 1960s that many of his age had taken little interest in potlatching or any other custom when they had been younger. This was due, in part, "to the fact that such activities were illegal," he said, and he now regretted that his generation had not given more attention to social and ceremonial activities. Yet the Kwakiutl were an extraordinarily tenacious people. A remarkable series of photographs, reportedly taken by a provincial policeman at Gilford Island in 1946, show an elaborate, well-attended "public" ceremony, doubtless one-half of a disjointed potlatch. As late as November 1950, the Kwawkewlth agent (now termed "superintendent") wrote a Kingcome Inlet man about a rumour that the man was planning "on practicing the Indian Custom in a large way this coming winter." Superintendent Todd hoped the report was incorrect. He pointed out that the Indian Act had not changed and it was his duty "to inform you that [potlatching] is against the law."[12]

The Gitksan potlatch probably survived the strains more easily. It was less dependent upon the economy; it required enough money to feast and to raise a pole or a tombstone, never inconsiderable sums but manageable with the assistance of kinsmen. Moreover, in the long run the accounts evened out.[13]

Among the Nootka, the 1930s and 1940s also witnessed "a real diminution of interest in traditional forms." While potlatching never died out, the ceremonies became smaller, quieter, less well attended and less elaborate. Even as potlatching began to fall into abeyance, feasting remained strong. Families who did not potlatch still gave "dinners" to mark major rites of passage or to transmit traditional names. In assessing the reasons for the decline of the Nootkan potlatch, reduction to a minority population, exposure to decades of boarding-school education and the struggle to live in a depressed economy "were undoubtedly weightier forces for change than the existence of any statute on the books."[14]

By war's end the potlatch and, even more, the law against it, had ceased to be live issues. The postwar concerns of British Columbia's natives were predominantly about modern social justice: equality in old age pensions, veterans' benefits and child allowances; more hospitals and better health care; adequate housing; equality in liquor laws; the right to vote without sacrifice of native status; better education, especially through access to provincial public schools; an end to the imposition of the federal income tax on earnings off the reserves, especially in the fishing industry.

Similarly, *The Native Voice*, a new native monthly newspaper closely associated with the Native Brotherhood, concerned itself with equality, education, the franchise, an end to discrimination, and welfare matters. The few references to the potlatch in the paper's columns were largely negative. Chief Councillor Jonathan Brown of Glen Vowell, a Gitksan village on the Skeena, wrote of the need for better education of Indian children. "The Glen Vowell people are hard-working and one thing I want to get off my chest. The Potlatch business of spending money is the foolish way. If the Potlatch is stopped in the Skeena, it would be a lot better for the children, they would learn at school in the full season, and this would advance their education." Brown's letter brought a "hats off" from "One Who Knows" in the next issue. The potlatch was a source of "uncalled-for poverty"; by carrying it on, "we are making ourselves poor and our children are the big losers." Consistent with the postwar preoccupation with social and material advancement, the anonymous correspondent condemned the dual life the potlatch meant for the 1948 Indian: "He is trying desperately to advance in a civilized world, and at the same time, he is forced to fulfill his obligations to his clan, in a system that definitely belongs to a DEAD PAST." The same issue quoted Andrew Paull, the Coast Salish Native Brotherhood leader, who upheld the "good features" of the potlatch, which should have been retained by the government, but condemned the "bad features," which should have been eradicated.[15] Alongside condemnations of the potlatch were both a desire for equality in modern life and a growing—and not inconsistent—pride in being Indian. "Take From No Man His Song," a January 1949 editorial, dealt with retaining Indian dignity and self-respect. "Today Indians must sing their Songs. They must paint their pictures, tell their legends, speak their language, dance their dances." Nootkan artist George Clutesi told the Massey Royal Commission that native children should be in regular schools with whites, but condemned the dance prohibition: "It's against the law for the Indian to go out and show the world his own dances." That, however, was almost all that was said of the potlatch or related issues by the official organ of the Native Brotherhood, presided over during most of the period by a leading Kwakiutl. The potlatch and the law had lost both salience and significance. As one writer stated, "The whole potlatch issue just disappeared."[16]

In the voluminous hearings of the parliamentary joint committee on the Indian Act, held over three years from 1946 to 1948, neither potlatch nor antipotlatch law received mention. A few Indians spoke of wanting to keep their customs, but even this sentiment was buried beneath the issues of land, veterans' benefits, resource rights, income tax, welfare measures and education. The Native Brotherhood's eleven-page submission to the committee, drafted in April 1947, highlighted these concerns. It made no mention of the potlatch law.[17]

The joint committee concluded that there were so many "anachronisms, anomalies, contradictions and divergencies" in the act that virtually every section should be repealed or amended. It recommended that the act's offence and penalty section be brought into conformity with the Criminal Code and other statutes.[18]

The government's proposed revision was tabled late in the 1950 parliamentary session as Bill 267. It kept the ban on potlatches untouched except for renumbering the section. But it was other matters in the bill—or, more accurately, matters that were not in the bill—that led to the avalanche of criticism that overwhelmed the government. Indians across the country, the Conservative and Co-operative Commonwealth Federation parties, civil liberties groups, provincial officials and virtually the entire press condemned the bill. Within the House, former members of the 1946–1948 committee spoke of their disappointment, and the committee chairman said that he was not quite certain he recognized the bill as the child of its recommendations. The tabled legislation did not remedy old injustices, did not advance away from wardship and perpetuated the power of the bureaucracy over the Indian.[19] With little time remaining in the session for detailed consideration or for the promised consultation with native people, the St. Laurent government bowed to the storm and withdrew the offending bill.

British Columbia's Indians had rejected the bill as a mere repetition of the existing act that failed to deal with the recommendations of the joint parliamentary committee. Criticism focussed on taxation, reserve lands, the right to vote, old age pensions and especially education. A Prince Rupert meeting, attended by two hundred Indians from the Skeena, Nass and Queen Charlotte regions, disapproved of every part of Bill 267. The Native Brotherhood convention at Alert Bay demanded more schools and hospitals, nondenominational education, the right to vote in federal elections, an end to alienation of Indian land without negotiation, and the reduction of agents' powers to a minimum. The potlatch section received no recorded mention.[20]

Early in the next session, the government introduced a revised proposal, Bill 79, which met some of the criticisms of the previous bill. The new draft omitted any provision touching on dances, giving away, or mutilating flesh. The specific omission seems to have come as part of an attempt to bring the revision into line with the committee's recommendations rather than from any specific native protests. Chief Bill Scow and Rev. Peter Kelly of the Native Brotherhood and Andrew Paull of the North American Indian Brotherhood conferred with the government during the bill's drafting, but there is no record to indicate what influence, if any, they had on the dropping of the potlatch section. With the passage of Bill 79, the potlatch law quietly disappeared as of 4 September 1951.[21]

The preceding June, Jimmy Sewid, as chief councillor at Alert Bay and chairman of the St. George's Hospital Week committee, had proposed that the Kwakiutl "put on a big do" for the hospital's benefit. "It just came to me that it would be a good idea to bring the potlatch custom and the dancing out to the surface again and let the public see it because it had been outlawed and lost," he later remembered. Instead of giving things away, the process would be reversed: people would pay money to get in. Sewid and Bill Scow, president of the Native Brotherhood and "one of the leading men of the people," wrote to all the chiefs, inviting them to a meeting at Alert Bay to hear the idea. Sewid's proposal did not command immediate enthusiasm, but his relatives and friends rallied behind him. His uncle Ed Whonnock spoke: "Well, Jimmy, put me on your list. I've got quite a few masks and I'm going to perform tomorrow night. I've got nothing to be ashamed of." That did it. "He really hit those chiefs when he said, 'I've got nothing to be ashamed of.'" One by one, the leading members of the Kwakiutl nation fell into line. There was trouble over precedent, but everything was put in order. The community hall was crowded. Agnes Cranmer acted as convenor and Bill Scow, master of ceremonies, interpreted each dance and mask to the white community. Nine hundred and eighty-eight dollars and thirty-one cents was raised for St. George's Hospital.[22]

11

"What Is Best for the Indians"

THE LAW WAS dropped from the statutes in 1951. By then the potlatch had become a "non-issue," a matter of no concern—or very minor concern—to most Indians, church officials and government agents. The potlatch, at least the potlatch that Sproat, Dawson, Boas, Blenkinsop, Pidcock, DeBeck and Halliday had known, seemed pretty much dead. It survived, largely unseen, on the west coast of Vancouver Island, along the Skeena River, in remote Kwakiutl villages and elsewhere, and in subtle forms in feasts, sports days and Christmas celebrations all along the coast.

In 1951 the Indians of coastal British Columbia, after three decades of rapid change, were subject to conflicting tendencies. For many the postwar forties had been a time of reassessment, with younger progressives seeking equality, an end to discrimination and even integration into Canadian society. The old ways seemed doomed to inevitable demise. Few worked to retain them, and native spokespersons, especially the Native Brotherhood, were more concerned with gaining equality and opportunity in the postwar white world than in preserving customary usage and practice. Most younger Indians were apathetic, even antagonistic, towards rituals, dances and songs in languages fewer and fewer knew well. Integration, long a goal of Euro-Canadian society, seemed now a native goal as well.

Old people like Billy Assu among the Lekwiltok and Mungo Martin of Alert Bay recognized the tendency. They sought to preserve Kwakiutl culture, if not as a living continuity among the Kwakiutl people, at least as a memory in anthropological literature, in museums and on recording disks. Martin came to the University of British Columbia in 1950, at the age of seventy-one, to supervise the restoration and replication of poles for the campus' Totem Park. Working with curators at the university museum, he "was influential in directing to the museum many of the Kwakiutl people who were at a point of culture change where they wished to abandon their places in the potlatch system and had no wish to hold onto the materials of the potlatch which had lost its importance." At the same time Martin and his wife Abaya recorded for ethnomusicologist Ida Halpern 124 native songs. Halpern had already recorded eighty-eight from Chief Assu. She found that the younger people at Assu's Cape Mudge village were not interested in the music, that "they wanted to be westernized" and "didn't want to know anything about Indian songs." None of Assu's sons, she reported, knew their hereditary songs. Chief Assu, however, was anxious to record the songs for Halpern's machine. Otherwise, he said, "They die with me."[1] The dropping of the potlatch law coincided with this nadir of native peoples' interest in their own culture.

However, a dramatic reversal of the trend soon occurred. In one of the most remarkable shifts in Indian and Indian-white history, a renewed sense of pride and consciousness of "Indian-ness" set in, a development that has yet fully to define itself and to clarify its significance. Most notably, within the Indian communities of coastal British Columbia, there was a rebirth of artistic endeavours, a resurgence of potlatching and an increase in political activity centring on land and self-government. The resurgence of the potlatch seems to have first taken place in areas where the ceremony had never ceased or where it remained freshest: among the Nootka, Gitksan and Kwakiutl.

On Vancouver Island's west coast the Nootka potlatch ceremonies had continued, especially at out-of-the-way places such as Nrumakimyiis, Tlehuu-a and Dodger Cove. While generally more infrequent, smaller, quieter and less elaborate than earlier potlatches, some rivalled in length and complexity those at the turn of the century. Even before the change to the Indian Act, a revival of public ceremonialism was underway. George Clutesi and others founded the Alberni Dancers in 1948, part of a conscious effort among middle-aged and older people to "bring back" the old songs and dances. Though unrelated directly to potlatching, such public dance troupes symbolized renewed Indian self-consciousness and contributed to its growth. The potlatch was also experiencing a resurgence within Nootka society, and by the 1970s it was in "full flower," expanding in frequency, scale and complexity. The contemporary potlatch might have well over a thousand guests.

Among the Kwakiutl, Jimmy Sewid, in 1962, gave his first real potlatch in over twenty years. The previous year his uncle, Chief Tom Dawson of Kingcome, had put on a potlatch at which he gave Sewid a talking stick that bore crests from Sewid's mother's and father's sides. Sewid decided to put on his own "do" to announce the gift publicly at Alert Bay and to give his grandchildren names. People were invited from Gilford and Turnour islands, from New Vancouver, Fort Rupert and Kingcome. Although the potlatch lasted only one night, almost all the protocol was traditional. The value of the gifts was less than $1000, "just small presents." He had not borrowed money or relied on his family for help. "It was," he confessed, "not like the ones in the past, the real big potlatches"; "it was just a small token and I just wanted to do it." When his youngest son married a Saskatchewan Cree woman, Sewid arranged "a big do" on their return to Alert Bay. Previously, for his other childrens' marriages, he had sponsored a reception and a dance "in the white man's way"; now, with a new chest containing dances from Moses Alfred, he gave "this Indian do."[2] In 1978 his daughter Daisy remarried her husband, this time in the Indian way. On that occasion, Chief Harry Assu of Cape Mudge announced his own potlatch to celebrate the raising of a memorial pole to his father, Chief Billy Assu. The ceremony, held in the new Kwagiulth Museum, cost Assu "around fifteen thousand dollars." Assu's biggest potlatch, a memorial to his wife, Ida, was five years later. Participants came from almost all Kwakiutl groups, even from the Nootka people. Jimmy Sewid gave Assu a copper; other coppers came from Willie Cranmer of Alert Bay and from Paul Willie and Adam Dick of Kingcome. The red cedar bark ceremony was performed, then the *klassila* dance, and speeches were made. Finally "the big gift-giving" started. "You know," recalled Assu, "some of our people used to wonder whether the potlatch was a good thing or not. When I think about that potlatch now, I know it was good."[3]

The potlatches of Sewid and Assu were just part of the renewal of the ceremony among the Kwakiutl people. Dozens, perhaps hundreds, of "dos" have occurred since 1951, growing ever larger, more elaborate and more costly. Bill Holm, the Seattle artist, connoisseur and curator, was first a guest at a Kwakiutl potlatch in 1953. He received fifty cents as payment. In 1987, he received over one hundred dollars at each of the three potlatches he attended.[4] New community houses at Alert Bay and Cape Mudge helped to accommodate the resurgence. Museums were also built in both communities, in part to house the seized potlatch paraphernalia of 1922, returned in 1979 and 1980 by the National Museum of Canada (now the Canadian Museum of Civilization) after prolonged negotiations. The Royal Ontario Museum's portion of the material followed. The presence of these potlatch masks, rattles and coppers within the two major Kwakiutl centres has been yet another element in the renewal not only of the potlatch but of other aspects of native culture. Even before the founding of these community museums, the growing interest in potlatches meant that the flow of artifacts from the Kwakiutl to the University of British Columbia's Museum of Anthropology had dried up.[5]

Behind the resurgence lay various factors. Increased mobility, contacts and prosperity have played a role, writes Susan Golla about the Nootka, but "the overwhelming consideration would seem to be that the act of potlatching in and of itself has become a primary symbol of Indian identity."[6] Reinforced by a new consciousness concerned with heritage, rights and land, the resurgence of the potlatch can easily be seen as largely a product of renewed pride and identity. It is important to recognize, however, the strength of social and cultural continuities within native societies. Titles, status and family pride retain meaning. At an individual, day-to-day level, Nootkans potlatch, as they always have, because "it is good for the family," it gives them reputation and fame within their community, and it is just plain fun.[7]

While contemporary potlatches are undoubtedly different from those of the nineteenth century, many alterations are superficial. The occasions on which a potlatch is held do not depart significantly from tradition. The same phases of the life cycle—births, namings, female puberty, marriages, deaths—are marked. There is the same sense of rank and descent, the same concern for recognition of guests according to station and the same spirit of free and unconcerned generosity. The Gitksan potlatch continues to rest upon a society in which every person "has his place," a place affirmed and constrained by feasts, potlatches and a shared knowledge of status and protocol. Coastal Tsimshian have kept their feasts as "knots holding together the Tsimshian fabric." As elsewhere, the feasts are "fun," supportive of crest lines and community. "These are feasts of solidarity, of community, of shared experience," with "all the key factors of the pre-Christian potlatch still visible." Much the same can be said of the Haida potlatch. Traditional precepts, "old Indian ways," still suffuse their world view. Obligations in life-cycle rituals, property as a means of defining relationships and the high value placed on prestige, status and honour are now once again asserted in the potlatch.[8]

Blankets, now store-bought (for real honour, Pendleton rather than Hudson's Bay Company blankets), remain a staple potlatch gift. Bedding, well-decorated afghans, homemade quilts, china, glassware, T-shirts, Indian sweaters and various smaller articles— shotgun shells, fish knives, shellfish and coins—are among the payments distributed. Native art has reappeared as a potlatch item, including the engraved silver bracelets that were prominent at turn-of-the-century potlatches.

In some areas where the potlatch had disappeared as a recognizable phenomenon, native people have made a conscious effort to revive and reinvent it by going to the ethnological literature, emulating other groups and drawing on their own creativity. Even among the Kwakiutl, where potlatching continued despite all the pressures brought to bear upon them, there has been study of turn-of-the-century ethnological descriptions and of museum collections. However done, whether as a "revival" or "resurgence" or something of both, today the potlatch is a meaningful part of the life of many Indians.

It is tempting, in considering the history of the potlatch, to argue that the law, for all its symbolism, had little to do with what actually happened between 1885 and 1951. After all, there was only one successful prosecution (and that a minor one) before 1914, and almost all convictions came in eight years from one agency. A good case could be made that the law really had little effect. It was left unenforced for most of its time in existence and attempts at enforcement were more often futile than not. The potlatch, in any easily recogniz-able form, disappeared from sight in most of the province without the law being a demonstrable cause in its demise. Moreover, in American sections of the Northwest Coast, where no statutory pro-visions against the potlatch existed, the ceremony withered and died at least as soon as in Canada.

Comparisons between Canada and the United States are difficult. While no law against the potlatch existed south of the border, agents and their extralegal courts often acted as if one did, and American missionaries, who had a quasi-official authority, exercised the same zeal as their Canadian counterparts.[9] It seems true, how-ever, that among the Coast Salish, the last potlatch on the American side of the border was held about 1905 and on the Canadian side about 1915.[10] The Makah of Cape Flattery retained theirs less than did their Nootka kinsmen on Vancouver Island.[11] More instructive, in Alaska, where American Indian legislation did not apply and where there were, therefore, no Bureau of Indian Affairs agents, the potlatch died away soon after the turn of the century. In Canada, on the other hand, the potlatch, despite the law, continued among the Gitksan and expanded among the Kwakiutl. One could even argue (as Drucker and Heizer have) that the law created among some In-dians a kind of rebellious backlash that promoted the potlatch's per-petuation.

Some perspective on the law can be drawn from the similar pro-scription of the thirst and sun dances among the Canadian prairie Indians. Their ceremonies, which also involved mutilation of the flesh and gift-giving, could take up to six summer weeks and were seen by missionaries and Indian administrators as incompatible with civilized and settled life. Various means, from the requirement of passes to leave reserves to outright imprisonments, were attempted between 1890 and 1927 to control the dances. The 1895 revision to the Indian Act was applicable to the prairie ceremonies, but en-forcement was tempered by a fear of "evoking a mutinous spirit" and by a lack of enthusiasm by the mounted police. The threat of the law, occasional arrests, and doubtless other factors brought modifications, including the virtual disappearance of self-mutilation by the turn of the century. The dancing went on, however, despite the efforts of school officials, agents and police. Department agents might announce that suasion had brought the end of the sun dance, but the ceremonies continued, even went through "a certain recrudescence."[12] Scott's accession to power was followed by the adoption of measures similar to those aimed at the British Columbia potlatch. In 1914 he secured an amendment that prohibited Indians from participating in dances outside their own reserves.[13] A number of convictions followed, but the desire to secure Indian cooperation and enlistments in the war effort brought a temporary relaxation. The Cree, Blood and Blackfoot, however, were recipients of Scott's 1918 zeal and of the new summary procedures. With RCMP cooperation, 1921 and 1922 were, as in British Columbia, the peak years of prosecution. Soon, however, even these measures were seen as futile. As one writer notes, "The sun and the thirst dance gatherings were as elaborate and well attended as ever." The law was openly defied and went unenforced. While the ceremonies changed in many ways, "the transformation was as much the product of conscious adaptation as it was the result of the department's designs." Prairie Indian experience was an almost exact duplication of that of coastal natives. Ceremonial life was interrupted by the legislation, but forms of the ritual complex persisted widely. Surprisingly, there were many more arrests and imprisonments on the prairies for dancing and giving-away than in British Columbia.[14]

While an argument could be made that the law had, on balance, no real effect upon the potlatch, the story is much too complicated to accept such easy generalization. The law was there and it made some difference to Indian conduct. Missionaries, as Vowell reported, used it "as a lever of no inconsiderable force" in their efforts to eradicate the potlatch. Even Agent Neill, who avoided any prosecutions under the law, urged that it be retained. Even unenforced, "its moral influence is considerable," he wrote; "The teachings of Missionaries & the warning of the Indian officials backed up by the Knowledge that sec. 114 could be called on, have had a good effect."[15] The law, ineffective as it may ultimately have been, did affect the Indians, their feasts and their dances, and did fester among many as both a real and a symbolic grievance. However, it does seem that the potlatch law has been given a symbolic importance far exceeding its actual impact. "The relative effects of the potlatch law," concludes Rolf Knight, "seem often overexaggerated."[16]

The law was probably considerably less significant than writers and others, white or Indian, have tended to think. That may well have been the consequences of timing. Scott's enforcement of antipotlatch legislation in the early 1920s came at a time when the potlatch, as a system interrelated with traditional marriage, customary rank and increasing wealth, may have already been breaking down. That the enforcement coincided with accelerating acculturation and the decline of the Kwakiutl economy may well have excessively highlighted the role of the potlatch law in the unquestionable decline of the potlatch itself. Focussing on the potlatch ban, writes Knight, misdirects attention from more fundamental legislative restrictions, disregards the differing interests within Indian society by the 1920s and "glosses over the fact that by that late date, much more drastic changes had occurred."[17]

Whether or not the law was unjust is quite another question. The great difficulty in answering that question is the lack of an accepted standard upon which a judgement can be based. Elvin Hatch, an anthropologist concerned with ethical relativism, suggests applying the humanistic standard of avoiding coercion. "We may judge it to be wrong," he writes, "when some member of society deliberately and forcefully interferes in the affairs of other people." While Hatch finds it reasonable to argue that "the *point* of morality. . . is to promote the well-being of others," that promotion need not descend to coercive interference. The law, then, at least by this standard, was wrong: the lawmakers' motives could be seen as ethically proper, but not their use of coercion. Adopting this position would dispose of the moral difficulties: even if the potlatch was inappropriate, even if it was damaging to the natives themselves, white society, even with the best intentions, had no right to interfere forcibly. The imposition of unwanted changes upon native society was intolerant and denied freedom of choice.[18]

And yet, it could be argued, the situation was somewhat more complicated. Using the standard described above, the law could be justified to the extent that it sought to assist those victimized by a system that was itself sometimes coercive. A significant number of those upholding the law made just such arguments: that families were impoverished by the hoarding required for a potlatch; that the health of Indians, especially children, was impaired by the long, crowded winter ceremonials; that Kwakiutl women were maltreated by the marriage system. To the extent that humans—children, the old and women—may have been victimized by a system that, some-

times from hygienic innocence, sometimes from the tyranny of male
domination, sometimes from avarice, placed status and prestige
above humanistic principles, the potlatch itself was morally wrong.
If these arguments are accepted, a case for coercive interference can
be made.

Moreover, it could be argued that the potlatch system itself was
coercively intolerant of dissent. Agents noted again and again that
some, especially younger natives, did not wish to participate but
could find no escape. Kwakiutl children were involved long before
they had reached any age of conscious decision and marriage was arranged without choice. Even those who made no protest, such as
the Kwakiutl woman who was suddenly told that she had a new husband, made none because the system gave no alternative. Jane
Cook's boys, because she had never been "paid for," were seen as illegal and "boycotted from any work in this district for years by their
own tribe." Jennie McDougall was taken from the mission school in
1920 to be married, against her wishes, to Munday. Younger
Gitksan were intimidated into participation by ridicule, insults and
other means. "If we do not participate," said one young man, "you
know there are still *nadowigets* (witchcrafters) and there are yet
many ways of making you embarrassed among our people. So we
have to subscribe to their views." Another said that "we have to do
this or our lives will be miserable amongst our people." The potlatch, as a "*total* social phenomenon," precluded the alternatives
necessary to real choice.[19]

Here was the tyranny of tradition, as interfering and as coercive as
legislation—and usually more effective. A foreign practice ought to
receive approval, writes Hatch, unless it involves illegitimate coercion. "People ought to be free to live as they choose,"[20] and surely
that freedom extends beyond the group to the individuals who com-
prise it. The slave, by any humanistic principle, must be free to live
as he or she chooses, even if his or her society approves of slavery.

The ethics of legislative action against the potlatch are not clear-
cut. Like all questions of social action, it is filled with ambiguities of
conflicting rights and principles. Issues of our own age, such as
abortion and blood transfusions for Jehovah's Witnesses, raise similar problems of disputed rights. On one side of the potlatch issue
were natives, such as the petitioning Nass River chiefs, asking to be
let alone to continue a harmless, time-honoured, even eleemosynary

institution. On the other side were Christians, both white and native, deploring the tyranny and human degradation allegedly implicit in the same institution. "No issue," comments John Webster Grant about directed acculturation of Indians, "has raised more clearly the difficulty of seeking to improve a society without becoming in effect its destroyer."[21]

From an ethical viewpoint, however, one cannot defend the massive paternalism that lay behind Canadian Indian policy generally and the potlatch law in particular. No one else expressed it with quite the nakedness of Agent DeBeck, who wanted to be in a position "to make them do what I know is best for themselves." The power invested by the Indian Act in the administration of Indian affairs was very, very great. Power inevitably corrupts, and it no doubt corrupted agents; even more, it corrupted that embodiment of power over Indians, the deputy superintendent general. "Viewing the matter entirely from the standpoint of what is best in the interests of the Indians," Scott wrote in 1922, there was no reason to alter the department's policy of emancipating the natives from an ancient practice that seriously hindered their advance towards civilization.[22] What was evil, perhaps, was not so much the law itself as the massive, unreflective power and paternalism of which it was merely one exemplification.

In that respect at least, it is consoling to come back to historical reality and to realize that most administrators—one has in mind agents such as Guillod, Neill and Fougner—avoided coercive interference in the potlatch. They did not, at least in this instance, exercise the corrupting power of massive paternalism. Again, it is somewhat consoling to realize that the law was "a baby" for much longer and among many more Indians than ever it was enforced. When a Catholic priest told some Hagwilgit Indians that they should not potlatch because of the threat of the law, they merely giggled.[23]

One point often overlooked is that no native consensus existed on the issue. Native petitioners were instrumental in the original adoption of the law and a number of similar appeals for enforcement are dotted through the record. Indeed, one could argue that by 1900 or so, a majority of Indians might well have favoured the law. Neither the Allied Tribes of British Columbia nor the Native Brotherhood backed repeal. The Allied Tribes' leadership turned back the 1922 pro-potlatch motion and the Native Brotherhood deliberately avoided any stance, even when led by Kwakiutl Bill Scow. Certainly after 1945 and probably before, the brotherhood's leadership—and doubtless its membership—were deeply Christian, concerned with political, economic and social justice, not with the perpetuation of old customs that some at least felt retarded the progress of the province's Indians. On the Skeena, younger Gitksan would join the brotherhood only if the organization opposed feasts and the formal assumption of names and titles, while older ones would have nothing to do with it if it did. At Hazelton, fifty-five younger Gitksan met in January 1940 to petition the department to allow them authority to elect their own village council because "the older generation, namely our chiefs and elders of this village seem to prefer to practise the old customs and ceremonies" instead of endeavouring "to lead us into a mode of life which would tend to improve our living conditions." When, three years later, the group elected one of its own as chief, Agent Mallinson suspended the election at the insistence of older Indians.[24] The progressive and Christian leadership of the Alaskan Native Brotherhood was strongly against the potlatch. Native differences merely underscore the ambiguities of the issue. The potlatch was not simply an issue that placed whites against Indians; it more often pitted Indians against Indians. Even now muted opposition may continue.

The Indians of British Columbia, in general, exercised considerable autonomy on the issue. They did with their potlatches pretty much what they wanted to do, the Kwakiutl, between 1919 and 1927, always excepted. In many areas natives opted, largely of their own volition, to alter or abandon the ceremony. The Coast Salish, the Haida, the Coast Tsimshian and the Nishga fall generally into this category. Others, such as the Gitksan and the Nootka, continued to potlatch, according to the altered circumstances of their lives, with little heed for the law or any other external agency. Pressure to discontinue, as elsewhere, came largely from within. Only among the Kwakiutl (and to a much lesser extent among the Gitksan, and then only for a brief period), was the exercise of native autonomy severely compromised by legal sanctions.

British Columbia's natives were not objects acted upon by an all-powerful government or by authoritarian missionaries who could bend a passive native will. The Indians too were actors in the historical drama over the potlatch. At some times and under some circumstances, government and missionaries had little effective power and almost no influence over them. In a few instances, on the other hand, the natives could do little to resist the intrusion of a government department intent on imposing its will upon them.

The divergent history of the potlatch among Northwest Coast groups raises a question that can only be tentatively answered here. The Kwakiutl and the Gitksan persisted with their potlatch to a greater extent than did many of their neighbours. This seems clear, though it must be qualified by the incompleteness of easily available documentation and by the paucity of historical studies among other groups. Available evidence indicates that the Nootka too went on more or less as before; the Bella Coola probably continued within the measure of their resources. Nevertheless, there were clear divergencies, certainly between the Haida at one pole and the Kwakiutl at the other.

In the absence of detailed studies, Kwakiutl and Gitksan exceptionalism is not easily explained. Both groups were considered more conservative than their neighbours, but this only begs the question. Kwakiutl exceptionalism on the potlatch probably rested in part on the importance of inheritance of status and privilege through marriage. Among the Gitksan, a probable factor was the close connection between status and ownership of resource territories. The potlatch, as a validation of territorial rights, may have received extra reinforcement as a means of furthering land claims against the government. If these suggestions are true, the persistence among the Kwakiutl and the Gitksan came for quite different reasons, relating to the different nature of the two potlatch systems. Among both groups, however, the potlatch seems to have become "a touchstone of Indian identity in a world increasingly dominated by Whiteman's values," "at once a symbol of defiance and a reminder of the good old days."[25]

The conflict over the potlatch was a conflict over values, and judgement upon clashes of value requires a serene certainty of standpoint that has not been bestowed upon the authors. We have, of course, a sympathy with tradition, an appreciation of cultural relativism and a distrust of governmental intrusion into the lives of people, especially a disenfranchised minority. On the other hand, we have to recognize a role for government, a right to intervene to secure some measure of conformity to its own customs and values and in pursuit of its goals. No one would grant government or the majority society that it represents a blank cheque to interfere in aboriginal life, but almost as few would challenge the justice of the government's suppression of slavery among Northwest Coast Indians or its condemnation of female infanticide elsewhere. Some aspects of some Northwest Coast ceremonies were so morally repugnant that, as with slavery, infanticide, cockfighting and suttee, there were defensible grounds for their legal abolition. Other aspects of dancing and potlatching were condemned not from a moral point of view but as undesirable on grounds of social policy. The customary marriage system fell into both categories, but potlatching, as an economic system and as a native preoccupation, was judged an obstacle to Indian health, progress and assimilation.

Again there are ambiguities. Few would question the need for effective western-style schooling for twentieth-century Kwakiutl children. Did the government have the right, even the duty, to suppress the potlatch when it disrupted the school year? The law, however, was unselective in what it aimed at eradicating. It sought not only to end mutilation of the flesh and truency, but also to stop the natives from "wasting their time" and to alter their patterns of consumption and investment. Even if there were defensible reasons for the law in 1885, questions remain of its continued appropriateness as conditions changed.

If the authors may be allowed some quite subjective judgements, we conclude that the legislation might have been justifiable on the basis of what the government knew and the advice it was receiving in 1885, and that its lack of enforcement, pursued as a conscious policy by Vowell after Powell's retreat at Comeaken, was probably the right course. Scott's policy of enforcement was probably not only unnecessary but harsh and ill-advised. By that time British Columbia's Indians, even the Kwakiutl, had modified the potlatch's most offensive features and most of the arguments against the institution had lost their original validity. Moreover, the advice that the government received was overwhelmingly against rigid enforcement. Scott, for his own reasons, decided to proceed otherwise. Though largely unenforceable after 1927, the law probably continued as a threat that disturbed and debilitated much that was vital to what remained of the Southern Kwakiutl and Gitksan traditions.

Yet it must be remembered that the Indians were not supine victims of white legislation. That the law went largely unenforced was in great measure a result of native resistance, even defiance. In this resistance, local sympathies lay largely with the Indians. The federal government had to overcome these sympathies, especially as evinced by judges and juries. And, once enforcement measures seemed perfected, the natives, certainly both the Kwakiutl and the Gitksan, devised stratagems that defeated further attempts at enforcement. In the contests over the law—at Comeaken, before Begbie's bench, in the suspended sentences and dismissals following Scott's 1913 enforcement attempts, in the native inventiveness that led to the frustration of agents and superintendents after 1927, and, ultimately, in the dropping of the law in 1951—the Indians won at least as often as they lost.

Notes

AADBC Archives of the Anglican Diocese of British Columbia, Victoria

AAEPBC Anglican Archives of the Ecclesiastical Province of British Columbia, Vancouver

AGP Attorney General Papers, British Columbia Archives and Records Service, Victoria

BCARS British Columbia Archives and Records Service (formerly Provincial Archives of British Columbia), Victoria

DIA Department of Indian Affairs Papers (RG10), Western (Black) Series, National Archives of Canada, Ottawa

NAC National Archives of Canada, Ottawa

NOTES

Introduction

1. Peter Macnair, "From Kwakiutl to Kwakwa̱ ka'wakw," 514-15.
2. Daisy Sewid-Smith, *Prosecution or Persecution,* passim.

Chapter 1   "A Very Complex Institution"

1. H. G. Barnett, "The Nature and Function of the Potlatch," 1.
2. See Abraham Rosman and Paula G. Rubel, *Feasting with Mine Enemy.*
3. Useful, however, are articles by Steve Langdon, "The Development of

the Nootkan Cultural System"; Vernon Kobrinsky, "Dynamics of the Fort Rupert Class Struggle," 32-54, and Eugene E. Ruyle, "Slavery, Surplus, and Stratification on the Northwest Coast," 603-31.

4. John R. Jewitt, *A Journal Kept at Nootka Sound...*, 12, and often reprinted subsequently. See also [Bernard Magee], "Log of the *Jefferson*," and José Marino Moziño, *Noticias de Nutka,* 33. We are indebted to Robin Fisher for some of these references.

5. Wayne Suttles pioneered this idea in his "Affinal Ties, Subsistence, and Prestige among the Coast Salish." This and other relevant contributions are in Suttles, *Coast Salish Essays.*

6. Ruyle, "Slavery, Surplus, and Stratification on the Northwest Coast," 615-17; Kobrinsky, "Dynamics of the Fort Rupert Class Struggle," 38.

7. Ronald L. Olson, "The Quinault Indians," 124; Yvonne P. Hajda, "Regional Social Organization in the Greater Lower Columbia," 214.

8. Robert Steven Grumet, "Changes in Coast Tsimshian Redistributive Activities," 301; Helen Codere, "Kwakiutl," 445; Codere, *Fighting with Property,* 95; Suttles, "Post-Contact Culture Changes among the Lummi Indians," 46.

9. Verne F. Ray, "Lower Chinook Ethnographic Notes," 89; Wilson Duff, "Contributions of Marius Barbeau to West Coast Ethnology," 81; John Swanton, "Social Conditions, Beliefs and Linguistic Relationship of the Tlingit Indians," 436.

10. George Gibbs, "Tribes of Western Washington and Northwestern Oregon," 205.

11. Philip Drucker, "Rank, Wealth, and Kinship in Northwest Coast Society," 137.

12. Edward Sapir, "The Social Organization of the West Coast Tribes," 30, 33; Ruyle, "Slavery, Surplus, and Stratification on the Northwest Coast," 609; Drucker, "Rank, Wealth, and Kinship in Northwest Coast Society," 141; Sapir, "The Social Organization of the West Coast Tribes," 30.

13. Sapir, "The Social Organization of the West Coast Tribes," 35.

14. Ronald L. Olson, "The Social Life of the Owikeno Kwakiutl," 237; Barnett, "The Nature and Function of the Potlatch," 77; Macnair, "From Kwakiutl to Kwakwa̲ ka̲ 'wakw," 514.

15. Drucker, *Cultures of the North Pacific Coast,* 46, 53.

16. Franz Boas, "Tamanos," 681.

Chapter 2   "A Worse Than Useless Custom"

1. Privy Council Office, Minutes, no. 1, v. 260, 7 July 1883, 5-12.

2. *Sessional Papers,* 1878, no. 23:8.

3. DIA, v. 3614, f. 4105, Blenkinsop to Powell, "Report on the West Coast of Vancouver Island and Barclay Sound," 23 Sept. 1874.

4. DIA, v. 3669, f. 10,691, Sproat to Superintendent General, 27 Oct. 1879.

5. DIA, v. 3701, f. 17, 914-1, Deputy Superintendent General to Powell, 30 Dec. 1879; v. 1329, Powell to W. H. Lomas, 13 June and 28 Sept. 1881; v. 1330, Powell to Lomas, 16 Oct. 1882.

6. The 1883 Nass River petition that, in a sense, touched off the legislative process has not been located. Its contents can be guessed at from references to it in the DIA correspondence. The DIA register records the petition as being dated 2 April 1883 and having been received in Ottawa on 11 April. It describes the petition as "asking that an order in Council may be passed prohibiting Potlatching as practiced by the Indians in British Columbia." It was sent to Powell on 13 April and apparently disappeared with the bulk of the Victoria superintendency papers.

7. DIA, v. 3628, f. 6244-1, Powell to Superintendent General, 19 May 1883.

8. Ibid., Deputy Superintendent General to Superintendent General, 11 June 1883 and Macdonald's minute, 12 June 1883.

9. *Canada Gazette* 17 (4 Aug. 1883): 228, proclamation dated 7 July 1883. Forrest E. LaViolette, *The Struggle for Survival,* 38-39, mistakenly quotes the council minute rather than the proclamation.

10. DIA, v. 3628, f. 6244-1, Powell to Superintendent General, 15 Aug. 1883.

11. DIA, v. 1353, Lomas to Powell, 25 Jan. 1884; v. 3628, f. 6244-1, Lomas to Powell, 5 Feb. 1884, with enclosures from Bryant to Superintendent General, 30 Jan. 1884, and Donckele to Lomas, 2 Feb. 1884.

12. House of Commons, *Debates,* 24 Mar. 1884, 1063.

13. House of Commons, *Debates,* 7 Apr. 1884, 1399. Blake's amendment was accepted by Macdonald but never found its way into the legislation.

14. Senate, *Debates,* 15 Apr. 1884, 620-625, 655.

15. *Sessional Papers,* 1882, no. 6:170; DIA, v. 3628, f. 6244-1, Lomas to Powell, 5 Feb. 1884; ibid., Donckele to Lomas, 2 Feb. 1883; v. 1353, Lomas to Powell, 25 Jan. 1884; *Sessional Papers,* 1882, no. 6:170; DIA, v. 1353, Lomas to Powell, 25 Jan. 1884; v. 3628, f. 6244-1, Bryant to Superintendent General, 30 Jan. 1884.

16. DIA, v. 3669, f. 10,691, Sproat to Superintendent General, 27 Oct. 1879.

17. DIA, v. 3737, f. 27,590, Powell to Superintendent General, 25 Apr. 1881; *Sessional Papers,* 1883, no. 5:66.

18. *Sessional Papers,* 1882, no. 6:164; DIA, v. 1329, Lomas to Powell, 25 Oct. 1881; v. 3628, f. 6244-1, Bryant to Superintendent General, 30

Jan. 1884; *Sessional Papers*, 1883, no. 5:xxiii, Deputy Superintendent General's Report; DIA, v. 3669, f. 10,691, Sproat to Superintendent General, 27 Oct. 1879.

19. DIA, v. 3628, f. 6244-1, Bryant to Superintendent General, 30 Jan. 1884; ibid., Donckele to Lomas, 2 Feb. 1884.

20. DIA, v. 3669, f. 10,691, Powell to Superintendent General, 19 Dec. 1879; *Sessional Papers*, 1882, no. 6:164; DIA, v. 3628, f. 6244-1, Deputy Superintendent General to Privy Council, 19 June 1883.

21. McGill University Archives, George M. Dawson Papers, Dawson, "Nature and the effects of the so called Potlatch System among the Indians," 7 Sept. 1885. Dawson's information came, it should be mentioned, not only from his own observations, which were made in the summer seasons, but from information supplied by Rev. A. J. Hall and Blenkinsop. His views are echoed in his article, "Notes and Observations on the Kwakiool People," 79-80.

22. DIA, v. 1353, Lomas to Bryant, 24 Jan. 1884; v. 3628, f. 6244-1, Bryant to Superintendant General, 30 Jan. 1884; ibid., Donckele to Lomas, 2 Feb. 1884; *Sessional Papers*, 1882, no. 6:171, Blenkinsop's report; DIA, v. 3628, f. 6244-1, Lomas to Powell, 5 Feb. 1884.

23. John Webster Grant, *Moon of Wintertime*, 185.

Chapter 3   *"The Law Is as Weak as a Baby"*

1. *Sessional Papers*, 1882, no. 6:171; 1883, no. 5:66; DIA, v. 1329, Lomas to Powell, 25 Oct. 1881; v. 1353, Lomas to Powell, 25 Jan. 1884.

2. Canada, 1881 Census, Manuscript, District 187D, 12.

3. *Sessional Papers*, 1882, no. 6:164, Guillod's report; ibid., 171, Blenkinsop's report; 1885, no. 3:98, Lomas's report.

4. *Sessional Papers*, 1885, no. 3:101.

5. DIA, v. 3628, f. 6244-1, Chiefs of the Nass River Indians to Vowell, 30 Aug. 1895; ibid., Chiefs of Cowichan Agency to Superintendent General, 26 Feb. 1887; ibid., Charles Todd to H. Moffat, 22 Jan. 1889; ibid., C. W. D. Clifford to Capt. Napoleon Fitzstubbs, n.d. [March 1890].

6. Ibid., Fitzstubbs to Attorney General, 13 Mar. 1890; *Sessional Papers*, 1882, no. 6:164; DIA, v. 3628, f. 6244-1, Guillod to Powell, 7 July 1886.

7. DIA, v. 3628, f. 6244-1, Comeaken "Doctor" and Lohah, quoted in Cowichan Chiefs in regard to the Potlatch Act to Lomas, 8 Apr. 1885; v. 3831, f. 63,210, Lomas to Moffat, 15 Nov. 1889, with Statement of Ken-a-wult of Qualicum, 14 Nov. 1889; v. 3628, f. 6244-1, Fitzstubbs to Attorney General, 13 Mar. 1890.

8. DIA, v. 3628, f. 6244-1, Chiefs of Cowichan Agency to Superintendent General, 26 Feb. 1887; ibid., Vowell to Deputy Superintendent Gen-

eral, 6 Sept. 1895; ibid., Powell to Deputy Superintendent General, 23 July 1886; v. 3631, f. 6244-G, Todd to Vowell, Monthly report, Sept. 1895; v. 3628, f. 6244-1, Clifford to Fitzstubbs, n.d. [March 1890].

9. DIA, v. 3628, f. 6244-1, Fitzstubbs to Attorney General, 13 Mar. 1890; ibid., Mamalillikulla petition to Governor Nelson, 10 Aug. 1889; ibid., Clifford to Fitzstubbs, n.d. [March 1890].

10. Ibid., Chiefs of Cowichan Agency to Superintendent General, 26 Feb. 1887.

11. *Sessional Papers*, 1886, no. 4:82, Guillod's report.

12. DIA, v. 3831, f. 62,977, R. E. Loring to Moffat, 12 Oct. 1889; v. 3631, f. 6244-G, Todd to Vowell, Monthly report, Sept. 1895.

13. DIA, v. 3628, f. 6244-1, Vowell to Deputy Superintendent General, 6 Sept. 1895; v. 3737, f. 27,590, Vowell to Superintendent General, 18 Apr. 1895; v. 3628, f. 6244-1, Chiefs of the Nass River Indians to Vowell, 30 Aug. 1895.

14. DIA, v. 3628, f. 6244-1, Mamalillikulla petition to Governor Nelson, 10 Aug. 1889; ibid., Chiefs of the Nass River Indians to Vowell, 30 Aug. 1895; ibid., Chiefs of the Cowichan Agency to Superintendent General, 26 Feb. 1887.

15. BCARS, Cowichan Indian Agent (Lomas) Correspondence (F5 C84), Lorne Good to Lomas, 20 June 1880; DIA, v. 3628, f. 6244-1, R. H. Pidcock to Powell, 19 Mar. 1887; ibid., Vowell to Deputy Superintendent General, 6 Sept. 1895; ibid., Fitzstubbs to Attorney General, 13 Mar. 1890.

16. DIA, v. 3628, f. 6244-1, Cehawitawet, quoted in Cowichan Chiefs in regard to the Potlatch Act to Lomas, 8 Apr. 1885; ibid., Vowell to Deputy Superintendent General, 6 Sept. 1895.

17. DIA, v. 3696, f. 15,316, Sproat to Superintendent General, 17 July 1879; *Sessional Papers*, 1880, no. 4:124, Powell's report.

18. DIA, v. 1329, Powell to Lomas, 13 June 1881; v. 3821, f. 63,210, Lomas to Vowell, 9 Jan. 1890; *Sessional Papers*, 1883, no. 5:66; 1886, no. 4:80; DIA, v. 3737, f. 27,590, Vowell to Superintendent General, 18 Apr. 1895.

19. *Sessional Papers*, 1883, no. 5:55; DIA, v. 3628, f. 6244-1, Lomas to Powell, 27 Dec. 1884.

20. DIA, v. 3628, f. 6244-1, Powell to Superintendent General, 7 Jan. 1885; ibid., marginal notation on Powell to Superintendent General, 7 Jan. 1885; v. 1331, Powell to Lomas, 5 Feb. 1885.

21. DIA, v. 1353, Lomas to Powell, 17 Jan. 1885.

22. DIA, v. 3628, f. 6244-1, Cowichan Chiefs in regard to the Potlatch Act to Lomas, 8 Apr. 1885.

23. Ibid., Powell to Superintendent General, 20 Apr. 1885.

24. Ibid.; *Sessional Papers*, 1886, no. 4:120; DIA, v. 3628, f. 6244-1, Deputy Superintendent General to Powell, 12 May 1885. Lohah seems to have kept his agreement. After the chief's death on 15 March 1897, Lomas wrote: "He was the first Chief to announce at a Potlach of his own that it was to be his last, as he was convinced that the White mens [*sic*] way of saving money or improving land was better. This made him very unpopular for a time." DIA, v. 1359, Lomas to Vowell, Monthly report, Mar. 1897.
25. DIA, v. 3628, f. 6244-1, Powell to Secretary, 7 May 1886.
26. Ibid., extract of letter from Green, 3 Apr. 1885, in Secretary to Powell, 9 June 1885.
27. Ibid., Powell to Secretary, 22 May 1885.
28. Ibid., Guillod to Powell, 7 July 1886; ibid., Pidcock to Powell, 13 Sept. 1886; ibid., Pidcock to Powell, 19 Mar. 1887.
29. Ibid., Todd to Moffat, 22 Jan. 1889.
30. Boas, "The Indians of British Columbia," 636; Boas, "The Houses of the Kwakiutl Indians, British Columbia," 206.
31. DIA, v. 3628, f. 6244-1, Powell to Superintendent General, 20 Apr. 1885; ibid., Powell to Secretary, 1 Nov. 1886.
32. Ibid., Powell to Secretary, 1 Nov. 1886; ibid., Powell to Provincial Secretary, 23 Mar. 1887; ibid., Powell to Secretary, 5 Apr. 1888.
33. Ibid., Secretary to Powell, 3 Oct. 1888; Privy Council no. 408, 12 Mar. 1888 and no. 2535, 11 Dec. 1890, copies of which are in DIA, v. 3780, f. 39,675-1.
34. DIA, v. 3628, f. 6244-1, Secretary to Powell, 3 Oct. 1888.
35. Ibid., Pidcock to Secretary, 2 Oct. 1889; ibid., Mamalillikulla petition to Governor Nelson, 10 Aug. 1889; *Daily Colonist,* 23 Aug. 1889; DIA, v. 3628, f. 6244-1, Moffat to Secretary, 12 Aug. 1889; ibid., Moffat to Deputy Superintendent General, 30 Aug. 1889, with copy of Begbie's judgement. See also David R. Williams, *". . . The Man for a New Country,"* 102-03, 118.
36. *Sessional Papers*, 1890, no. 12:102; DIA, v. 3628, f. 6244-1, Pidcock to Secretary, 2 Oct. 1889; ibid., Deputy Superintendent General to Deputy Minister of Justice, 2 Nov. 1889; ibid., Deputy Minister of Justice to Deputy Superintendent General, 13 Dec. 1889.
37. DIA, v. 1648, Pidcock to Vowell, 16 Mar. 1893; v. 3831, f. 63,210, Lomas to Vowell, 9 Jan. 1890; ibid., Deputy Superintendent General to Superintendent General, 29 Jan. 1890.
38. DIA, v. 3628, f. 6244-1, Deputy Superintendent General to Deputy Minister of Justice, 7 June 1890; ibid., Deputy Minister of Justice to Deputy Superintendent General, 8 July 1890; ibid., Deputy Superintendent General to Privy Council, 12 July 1890.

39. Ibid., Fitzstubbs to Attorney General, 13 Mar. 1890; Clifford to Fitzstubbs, n.d. [March 1890].

40. DIA, v. 3792, f. 45,094.

41. DIA, v. 3737, f. 27,590, Guillod to Vowell, 18 May 1895; v. 3631, f. 6244-G, Todd to Vowell, Monthly report, Oct. 1895; v. 1648, Pidcock to Vowell, 5 Jan. 1895; v. 3831, f. 63,210, Lomas to Vowell, 9 Jan. 1890; v. 3737, f. 27,590, Lomas to Vowell, 11 June 1895.

42. DIA, v. 3737, f. 27,590, Vowell to Superintendent General, 1 June 1895; ibid., Superintendent General to Vowell, 18 Apr. 1895.

43. DIA, v. 3628, f. 6244-1, Deputy Superintendent General to Vowell, 7 Sept. 1895; ibid., Kitwanga Council to Fitzstubbs, quoted in H. K. A. Pocock to Fitzstubbs, 12 Mar. 1890.

Chapter 4 "The Very Best Discretion"

1. DIA, v. 3737, f. 27,590, Vowell to Deputy Superintendent General, 1 June 1895.

2. DIA, v. 2497, f. 102,950, "Proposed Amendments to the Indian Act... with Explanatory Notes," 9 Jan. 1890.

3. DIA, v. 1350, Vowell to all Indian agents, 4 Sept. 1895.

4. DIA, v. 3628, f. 6244-1, Vowell to Devlin, 22 Jan. 1896; ibid., Devlin to Vowell, 3 Feb. and 18 Jan. 1896; ibid., Deputy Superintendent General to Vowell, 31 Jan. 1896; *Daily Columbian,* 3 Feb. 1896; DIA, v. 1358, Lomas to Guillod, 7 May 1896.

5. See Jean Usher, *William Duncan of Metlakatla,* 124-30; Peter Murray, *The Devil and Mr. Duncan,* 161-86; E. Palmer Patterson II, "A Decade of Change," 40-54.

6. British Columbia, *Papers Relating to the Commission Appointed to Enquire into the Condition of the Indians of the North-West Coast,* 419.

7. AGP, Box 2, f. 1-663/88, Fitzstubbs to Attorney General, 27 July 1888; NAC, R. E. Loring Papers, Fitzstubbs to Attorney General, 5 Jan. 1889, copy; DIA, v. 3628, f. 6244-1, McCullagh to Vowell, 1 Feb. 1896.

8. The following account is from DIA, v. 3628, f. 6244-1, McCullagh to Vowell, 1 Feb. 1896.

9. Ibid., Chiefs of the Nass River Indians to Vowell, 30 Aug. 1895; v. 3631, f. 6244-G, Todd to Vowell, Monthly report, Oct. 1895; v. 3628, f. 6244-1, McCullagh to Vowell, 1 Feb. 1896.

10. *Daily Colonist,* 20 Feb. and 23 Feb. 1896.

11. AGP, Box 3, f. 4, Chiefs of the Nass River to Attorney General, 20 July 1896; DIA, v. 3628, f. 6244-1, Indians of the Nass River to Lieutenant Governor and Attorney General, n.d. [1890].

12. AGP, Box 3, f. 4, Chiefs of the Nass River to Attorney General, 20 July 1896; Box 4, f. 2, David McKay, George Eli and Fredrick Allen to At-

torney General, 30 Mar. 1898; Box 5, f. 2, Osterhout to Attorney General, 6 Sept. 1899.

13. DIA, v. 3629, f. 6244-2, Todd to Vowell, 27 June 1899; ibid., Chiefs of the Kiweslith, Lakkalzap, Aiyansh and other Nishga Bands to Superintendent General, 1 July 1899.

14. AGP, Box 4, f. 5. Letter, not addressed, dated or signed, enclosed with President of Kincolith Council to Attorney General, 9 Mar. 1899; ibid., Oxican to Attorney General, 14 Apr. 1899.

15. DIA, v. 3629, f. 6244-2, Wes-les Yan and Sle-Ya-Wa to Vowell, 13 Sept. 1899; ibid., Vowell to Deputy Superintendent General, 14 Sept. 1899; ibid., Deputy Superintendent General to Vowell, 19 July 1899.

16. DIA, v. 3628, f. 6244-1, Vowell to all Indian agents, 16 Jan. 1897.

17. Ibid., Pidcock to Vowell, 15 Jan. 1897; ibid., Vowell to Deputy Superintendent General, 16 Jan. 1897; ibid., Pidcock to Vowell, Monthly report, Jan. 1897; v. 1648, Pidcock to Vowell, 4 Feb. 1897; *Daily Columbian*, 18 Jan. 1897; *Daily Colonist,* 20 Jan. 1897; DIA, v. 3628, f. 6244-1, Walker to A. Sutherland, 11 Feb. 1897 gives a different version that blames Vowell for the difficulty.

18. DIA, v. 3628, f. 6244-1, Vowell to Deputy Superintendent General, 16 Jan. 1897.

19. *Daily Colonist*, 13 Apr. 1897; *News Advertiser,* 14 Apr. 1897.

20. Grant, *Moon of Wintertime*, 186.

21. DIA, v. 3628, f. 6244-1, Powell to Superintendent General, 20 Apr. 1885.

22. DIA, v. 3628, f. 6244-1, Bryant to Superintendent General, 30 Jan. 1884; ibid., Donckele to Lomas, 2 Feb. 1884.

23. DIA, v. 3629, f. 6244-2, G. W. DeBeck to Vowell, 30 Oct. 1903. Lobbying exceptions are C. W. D Clifford, the Hudson's Bay Company manager at Hazelton, and merchants from Rock Bay, near Fort Rupert, who defended the contemporary potlatch and asked for an end to its prohibition. DIA, v. 3638, f. 6244-1, Clifford to Fitzstubbs, n.d. [March 1890]; v. 3629, f. 6244-2, Arthur Hanson and William Milne to H. S. C. Clements, 14 Feb. 1914.

24. DIA, v. 3831, f. 63,210, Lomas to Vowell, 9 Jan. 1890; *Province,* 21 Mar. 1896, William Dwyer to the editor; DIA, v. 3628, f. 6244-1, Lomas to Vowell, 18 Mar. 1896; *Province,* 8 Jan. 1902; *Daily Colonist*, 24 Jan. 1903 and 20 Jan. 1901.

25. *Province,* 21 Mar. 1896, Dwyer to the editor; DIA, v. 3628, f. 6244-1, Chiefs of the Nass River Indians to Vowell, 30 Aug. 1895; ibid., Lomas to Vowell, 18 Mar. 1896.

26. *Province,* 29 Feb. 1896, C. M. Tate to the editor; *Province,* 21 Mar. 1896, Dwyer and R. G. Ridley to the editor; *Daily Colonist*, 1 Apr.

1896, Maquinna to the editor; *Colonist,* 15 Mar. 1896, Rev. A. J. Hall to the editor. Tate's only support came from Rev. Hall.

27. DIA, v. 3628, f. 6244-1, Lomas to Vowell, 18 Mar. 1896.

28. Ibid., Deputy Superintendent General to General Secretary, Methodist Mission Board, 20 Mar. 1897; ibid., Deputy Superintendent General to Vowell, 31 May 1897.

29. Ibid., Vowell to Deputy Superintendent General, 22 May 1897; ibid., Vowell to Deputy Superintendent General, 1 June 1897.

30. DIA, v. 3628, f. 6244-1, Assistant Secretary to Secretary, 11 Jan. 1898; ibid., Superintendent General to Governor General in Council, 16 Jan. 1898; D. J. Hall, "Clifford Sifton and Canadian Indian Administration," 132; DIA, v. 3628, f. 6244-2, Superintendent General to Attorney General, 10 May 1899.

31. DIA, v. 1343, Vowell to W. R. Robertson, 1 Apr. 1903 and 7 Nov. 1900; v. 1342, Vowell to William McLaughlin, 24 Feb. 1900; v. 1340, Vowell to Lomas, 10 Feb. 1897; v. 3629, f. 6244-2, Vowell to Secretary, 6 June 1900.

32. DIA, v. 3628, f. 6244-1, Vowell to McCullagh, 16 Mar. 1896.

33. Paul Tennant, "Native Indian Political Organization in British Columbia," 16.

34. Patterson, *Mission on the Nass,* 134, 143; Rolf Knight, *Indians at Work,* 245-56; Stephen A. McNeary, "Where Fire Came Down," 32-35.

35. The following is based in large part upon Margaret B. Blackman, "Ethnohistoric Changes in the Haida Potlatch Complex," 39-53; Blackman, "Totems to Tombstones," 47-56; Blackman, "Creativity in Acculturation," 387-413, and J. H. Van den Brink, *The Haida Indians,* 56-91.

36. Blackman, "Creativity in Acculturation," 401; Mary Lee Stearns, *Haida Culture in Custody,* 177; Blackman, *During My Time,* 86-87, 92.

37. The *walal,* by conferring rank and validating it, was essential to elevation to chieftainship. The *walal* had been occasioned by the completion of a new house, the accession of a new house owner to the position of house chief, the raising of a pole or the adoption of a child.

38. Blackman, "Ethnohistoric Changes in the Haida Potlatch Complex," 48.

39. See DIA, v. 3864, f. 84,502. Todd, for example, was in Masset in 1899, his first visit to the islands in four years.

40. See Jan K. Krueger, "Masset, Aiyansh, Tahl Tan," 19-26.

41. Charles Harrison, *Ancient Warriors of the North Pacific,* 165.

42. Stearns, *Haida Culture in Custody,* 217; Blackman, "Ethnohistoric Changes in the Haida Potlatch Complex," passim; Blackman, "Totems

to Tombstones," 51. For a discussion of the continuity of feasting and exchange among the Masset Haida, see Stearns, *Haida Culture in Custody*, 346-82, 289-90.

43. Blackman, "Totems to Tombstones," 409; Drucker, "Comment," 90.
44. DIA, v. 3629, f. 6244-2, Morrow to Vowell, 13 Apr. 1904.
45. Ted C. Hinckley, *Alaskan John G. Brady*, 249-53. See also Victoria Wyatt, "Alaskan Indian Wage Earners in the 19th Century," 43-49. Frederica De Laguna, in *Under Mount Saint Elias*, discusses Yakutat potlatches between 1905 and 1916. Yakutat was the most northerly of Tlingit villages.
46. DIA, v. 3629, f. 6244-2, Neill to Vowell, 12 Feb. 1904; *Daily Colonist*, 1, 13 and 17 June 1902, 16 June 1903, 12 June 1906; DIA, v. 1358, Lomas to Guillod, 7 May 1896; BCARS, Tate Diary, 27 June 1901; ibid., 14, 15 and 19 June 1903.
47. Suttles, "Spirit Dancing and the Persistence of Native Culture among the Coast Salish," in Suttles, *Coast Salish Essays*, 207-08. Another reason, Suttles suspects, was the decline of the native economic system within which, according to his redistributive model of the potlatch, the custom "played its key regulatory mechanism." Ibid.
48. DIA, v. 3629, f. 6244-2, Deputy Superintendent General to Vowell, 6 Dec. 1904.

Chapter 5   *"The Incorrigible Kwakiutl"*

1. *Sessional Papers*, 1883, no. 5:xxiv, Superintendent General's Report; 1882, no. 6:140, Powell's report; 1884, no. 6:108, Powell's report; W. H. Collison, *In the Wake of the War Canoe*, 43; Hall to Wright, 30 Mar. 1878, cited in Barry M. Gough, "A Priest Versus the Potlatch," 78; *Sessional Papers*, 1880, no. 4:112.
2. *Sessional Papers*, 1910, no. 27:246, Blenkinsop's report.
3. Ibid., 1884, no. 5:48, Blenkinsop's report; 1907-08, no. 27:235, W. H. Halliday's report.
4. Boas, "Reisen in British-Columbien," 268; *Sessional Papers*, 1884, no. 4:108, Powell's report; 1885, no. 3:102, Blenkinsop's report; 1905, no. 27:256, DeBeck's report; 1906, no. 27:236, DeBeck's report.
5. *Sessional Papers*, 1882, no. 6:171, Blenkinsop's report; DIA, v. 1648, Pidcock to Vowell, Monthly report, Feb. 1895.
6. Wilson Duff, *The Indian History of British Columbia*, 38-40; *Sessional Papers*, 1873-1880.
7. Marie Mauzé, "Boas, les Kwagul et le potlatch," 25.
8. Ibid. These modifications were not twentieth-century scholarly discoveries. Everyone at all familiar with late nineteenth-century Kwakiutl life recognized it, not least the Kwakiutl themselves. See, for example,

Dawson, *Transactions of the Royal Society of Canada,* 1887, section II, 79; DIA, v. 3737, Pidcock to Vowell, 12 July 1895.

9. Kobrinsky, "Dynamics of the Fort Rupert Class Struggle," 40-42. See also Ruyle, "Slavery, Surplus, and Stratification on the Northwest Coast," 605, 617.

10. It should be noted that potlatch persistence among other groups, such as the Gitksan, cannot be explained this way.

11. Philip Drucker and Robert F. Heizer, *To Make My Name Good,* 52; Codere, "Kwakiutl," 434. Codere believes that the potlatch overshadowed the crests themselves, becoming "the central and all-encompassing institution."

12. Codere, *Fighting with Property,* 8; Drucker and Heizer, *To Make My Name Good,* 25-26, 33-34.

13. DIA, v. 1649, DeBeck to Vowell, 13 Nov. 1902; v. 1650, DeBeck to Vowell, 7 and 23 Jan. 1903; v. 3629, f. 6244-2, DeBeck to Vowell, 30 Oct. 1902; v. 1138, Vowell to DeBeck, 12 Nov. 1903.

14. BCARS, C. F. Newcombe Papers, Notebook 10 (2), "Dissatisfaction at Alert Bay," 1903; DIA, v. 3629, f. 6244-2, DeBeck to Vowell, Monthly report, Mar. 1904.

15. Or "Chief." So named by DeBeck "to the people's scorn," according to Codere, "Kwakiutl," 462.

16. DIA, v. 1650, DeBeck to Vowell, 11 Apr. 1904; ibid., DeBeck to Vowell, 8 June 1904.

17. DeBeck often found it difficult to recruit special constables from among the native people, since, regardless of their personal attitudes, "no Indian will act as a special in a case against the potlatch." DIA, v. 3629, f. 6244-2, DeBeck to Vowell, Monthly report, Feb. 1904.

18. Ibid., DeBeck to Vowell, Monthly report, Apr. 1904; ibid., DeBeck to Vowell, 17 Apr. 1904.

19. Ibid., DeBeck to Vowell, Monthly report, Apr. 1904.

20. Ibid., DeBeck to Vowell, 23 Jan. 1904; *Daily Times,* 23 Apr. 1904.

21. DIA, v. 3629, f. 6244-2, DeBeck to Vowell, Monthly report, Apr. 1904. The quotation refers more to Deasey's visit than to this article, which DeBeck described as a "mess of rubbish."

22. DIA, v. 1650, DeBeck to Superintendent General, 6 Dec. 1904; v. 3629, f. 6244-2, DeBeck to Vowell, 18 Oct. 1904.

23. DIA, v. 1650, DeBeck to Superintendent General, 6 Dec. 1904; ibid., DeBeck to Vowell, Monthly report, Nov. 1904.

24. Ibid., DeBeck to Superintendent General, 6 Dec. 1904.

25. DIA, v. 3629, f. 6244-2, Deputy Superintendent General to Vowell, 6 Dec. 1904; ibid., Deputy Superintendent General to Vowell, 5 Oct. 1905.

26. Ibid., Deputy Superintendent General to Vowell, 6 Dec. 1904; ibid., Vowell to Deputy Superintendent General, 22 Oct. 1904; ibid., DeBeck to Vowell, Monthly report, Apr. 1904.

27. Ibid., DeBeck to Vowell, Monthly report, Apr. 1904; ibid., DeBeck to Vowell, 30 Oct. 1903; v. 1650, DeBeck to Vowell, Monthly report, June 1904; v. 3629, f. 6244-2, DeBeck to Vowell, 7 Jan. 1903; *Sessional Papers,* 1881-1906.

28. DIA, v. 1650, DeBeck to Vowell, 4 Aug. 1904; *Sessional Papers,* 1907-08, no. 27:235, Halliday's report; DIA, v. 1654, Halliday to Secretary, 18 Feb. 1914.

29. DIA, v. 1650, DeBeck to various, 21 December 1904. This, though exceptional, is quite the opposite of the statement by Drucker and Heizer that agents compelled outlying groups to settle at Alert Bay. There is no evidence that this ever happened, though non-Nimpkish were allowed lots on the industrial school reserve if they abandoned the potlatch.

30. BCARS, "Memoirs of Dr. John Antle," unpublished manuscript, n.d., 96.

31. DIA, v. 1652, Stevens to Vowell, 9 June 1906.

32. DIA, v. 3629, f. 6244-2, Halliday to Vowell, 9 July 1907; v. 1653, Halliday to Vowell, 12 Mar. 1908.

33. Missionaries on the Nass, however, acting in their capacity as justices of the peace, had taken action. Charges had been laid under the tamananawas provision in 1889. In February 1889 the local magistrate was unable to gather the accused or witnesses, all of whom refused to attend court. The provincial constable, stationed at Metlakatla, was unable to intervene because of bad weather. Later charges against five were dismissed. The circumstances were in dispute, but it seems Rev. Green suggested such a course. They had, he said, promised to obey the law and he was certain they would keep their word. BCARS, S. Y. Wootton Letterbook, Wootton to Attorney General, 4 July 1889 and Wootton to Deputy Attorney General, 5 Aug. 1889.

34. AGP, Box 5, f. 4, Vowell to Deputy Attorney General, 10 Mar. 1900.

35. Christon I. Archer, "Cannibalism in the Early History of the Northwest Coast," 453-79; Joyce Wike, "A Reevaluation of Northwest Coast Cannibalism," 239-54.

36. The tamananawas provision seems to have been the result of "a petition prepared by Catholic clergy of Cowichan for certain Cowichan Indians," dated 2 Feb. 1881 and marked by Chief Ellos and forty-six Cowichan, and Powell's reports, especially that of 25 Apr. 1881. DIA, v. 3737, f. 27,590, Powell to Superintendent General; ibid., enclosed with Superintendent General to Powell, 30 Mar. 1881.

37. DIA, v. 1331, Powell to Lomas, 17 July 1885; v. 3737, f. 27,590, Powell to Superintendent General, 25 Apr. 1881; ibid., Pidcock to Vowell, 12 July 1895. The "red cedar bark" ceremony refers to the *tsleetsleka,* of which the hamatsa is a part.

38. DIA, v. 3628, f. 6244-1, Moffat to Deputy Superintendent General, 30 Aug. 1889, enclosing copy of Begbie's judgement.

39. *Sessional Papers,* 1883, no. 5:66; DIA, v. 1648, Pidcock to Vowell, 28 Apr. and 19 July 1894.

40. See Ira Jacknis, "George Hunt, Collector."

41. At the same time A-ki-ou-gu-luk (or Inguik), a Matilpi, was committed for trial for causing himself to be bitten. A-ki-ou-gu-luk went to trial in the case of Regina v. Kailukwirs (for Karlakwees, presumably), but left no record.

42. DIA, v. 1649, Pidcock to Vowell, 7 Mar. 1900.

43. *Province,* 11 Mar. and 18 Apr. 1900.

44. According to provincial records, Hunt served as constable thirteen days (at two dollars per diem) during the 1 July 1899 to 30 June 1900 fiscal year. Plan-Hettie is not listed, though another constable was simply enumerated as "Indian." British Columbia, *Sessional Papers,* 1900.

45. American Philosophical Society, Boas Professional Papers, Hunt to Boas, 27 Mar. 1900.

46. *Province,* 19 Apr. 1900.

47. DIA, v. 1649, Pidcock to Vowell, 10 Feb. 1901; Halliday, *Potlatch and Totem and the Recollections of an Indian Agent,* 10; Boas Professional Papers, Hunt to Boas, 28 Apr. 1900.

48. DIA, v. 3282, f. 64,535, Loring cited in Vowell to Deputy Superintendent General, 25 Feb. 1891; ibid., Pidcock to Powell, 3 Apr. 1889; ibid., Hall to Superintendent General, 5 Oct. 1889. The letter's left edge is torn, thus the bracketed extrapolations.

49. Boas Professional Papers, Macdonald to Boas, 22 Apr. 1890, responding to Boas's of 6 Apr.

50. DIA, v. 3282, f. 64,535, Vowell to Deputy Superintendent General, 25 Feb. 1891; Marjorie Mitchell and Anna Franklin, "When You Don't Know the Language, Listen to the Silence," 59; Boas Professional Papers, Macdonald to Boas, 22 Apr. 1890; DIA, v. 1355, Lomas to Vowell, 22 Nov. 1890. Nanaimo's "Uclataw Camp" was composed of Kwawkewlth Agency women.

51. DIA, v. 3282, f. 64,535, Vowell to Deputy Superintendent General, 25 Feb. 1891; ibid., Pidcock to Vowell, n.d. [1890?], copy. Apparently Vowell was correct in his assessment of the decline of native prostitution, at least in Victoria. Senator Macdonald felt that its extent was not as great as previous to 1890. Boas Professional Papers, Macdonald to

Boas, 22 Apr. 1890. But see Agent DeBeck's comments in DIA, v. 6809, f. 470-2-3, Pt. 6, DeBeck to Vowell, 2 Apr. 1906.

52. DIA, v. 1649, DeBeck to Vowell, Monthly report, May 1902.

53. DIA, v. 1652, Halliday to William Sloan, 7 Nov. 1907.

54. *Daily Colonist,* 8 May 1906 and 10 Apr. 1907; *Daily Times,* 5 June 1907; *Province,* 28 Aug. 1907.

55. Boas, *The Social Organization and the Secret Societies of the Kwakiutl Indians,* 358; Irving Goldman, *The Mouth of Heaven,* 77.

56. DIA, v. 1652, Halliday to Sloan, 7 Nov. 1907.

57. Ibid.

58. Boas, *Kwakiutl Ethnography,* 54-55.

59. Ibid., 75-76.

60. DIA, v. 1649, DeBeck to Vowell, 29 Dec. 1902.

61. DIA, v. 1652, Halliday to Superintendent General, 1 Feb. 1907.

62. Ibid., Halliday to Sloan, 7 Nov. 1907; ibid., Halliday to Vowell, 5 Sept. 1906; v. 1649, DeBeck to Vowell, 29 Dec. 1902.

63. Ibid., Halliday to Vowell, 5 Sept. 1906; ibid., Halliday to Provincial Secretary, 11 Mar. 1907.

64. DIA, v. 1649, DeBeck to Vowell, 29 Dec. 1902; v. 1652, Halliday to Vowell, 5 Sept. 1906.

65. *Sessional Papers,* 1911, no. 27:xxix-xxx.

66. The following is very dependent upon McIlwraith, *The Bella Coola Indians,* 373-74.

67. Olson, "The Quinault Indians," 223.

68. Edward Curtis, "The Kwakiutl," 131; Olson, "The Quinault Indians," 224. The rearing of children presented no problem; they were either placed within the new marriage or taken by grandparents, aunts or uncles.

69. Clellan S. Ford, *Smoke from Their Fires,* 203-04; Drucker and Heizer, *To Make My Name Good,* 84-85.

70. *Sessional Papers,* 1912-1913, no. 27:230.

Chapter 6   "Those Who Breach the Law Must Be Punished"

1. In 1917 Ditchburn became chief inspector for British Columbia, but retained responsibility for the old southwestern inspectorate; in 1923 he assumed the new post of Indian commissioner for British Columbia.

2. DIA, v. 3629, f. 6244-2, Ditchburn to Deputy Superintendent General, 27 Mar. 1913.

3. Ibid., D. C. Scott to Deputy Superintendent General, 14 Apr. 1913.

4. Sandra Gwyn, *The Private Capital,* 469.

5. E. K. Brown, "Memoir," xxvi.

6. A. J. M. Smith, "The Poetry of Duncan Campbell Scott," in S. L.

Dragland, *Duncan Campbell Scott,* 110. This paragraph and the following one draw upon the essays collected in Dragland's volume.

7. Brooke to Wilfred Gibson, 23 July 1913, in Geoffrey Keynes, *The Letters of Rupert Brooke,* 487.

8. Scott, "Indian Affairs, 1867-1912," 622-23; E. Brian Titley, *A Narrow Vision, 33.*

9. DIA, v. 6810, f. 470-2-3, Pt. 7, Scott's testimony before the parliamentary committee on Bill 14, 1920.

10. L. P. Weis, "D. C. Scott's View of History and the Indian," 28-29. Weis's remains the most sensitive and balanced interpretation of Scott and the Indians. We are also greatly indebted to Titley's *A Narrow Vision.*

11. S. D. Grant, "Indian Affairs under Duncan Campbell Scott," 37; Titley, *A Narrow Vision,* passim.

12. *Sessional Papers,* 1901, no. 27:xxxii; 1909, no. 27:xxxi.

13. DIA, v. 3629, f. 6244-2, Deputy Superintendent General to Halliday, 17 Apr. 1913. A similar letter went to Ditchburn, 17 Apr. 1913.

14. *Sessional Papers,* 1910, no. 27:246; 1907-08, no. 27:237; 1912-13, no. 27:229-30.

15. DIA, v. 3629, f. 6244-2, Halliday to Secretary, 26 Apr. 1913; ibid., Ditchburn to Secretary, 28 Aug. 1913.

16. Ibid., Green to Secretary, 14 May 1913.

17. Ibid., Deputy Superintendent General to Halliday, 20 May 1913.

18. Ibid., Perry to Secretary, 19 Jan. 1914, referring to February 1913; ibid., Rev. F. Ferrier to Deputy Superintendent General, 26 Jan. 1914.

19. *The Canada Year Book 1936* (Ottawa: Bureau of Statistics), 101, 1052.

20. DIA, v. 1653, Halliday to Deputy Superintendent General, 23 Feb. 1914; ibid., Halliday to Secretary, 13 June 1913; v. 1646, Halliday to Deputy Superintendent General, Monthly report, June 1913.

21. DIA, v. 1646, Halliday to Deputy Superintendent General, Monthly report, Aug. 1913; v. 1653, Halliday to Secretary, 30 Oct. 1913; v. 1646, Halliday to Deputy Superintendent General, Monthly report, Oct. 1913; v. 1653, Halliday to Ditchburn, 3 Nov. 1913.

22. DIA, v. 3629, f. 6244-2, Halliday to Secretary, 8 and 24 Nov. 1913.

23. Ibid., Halliday to Secretary, 24 Nov. 1913.

24. DIA, v. 1646, Halliday to Deputy Superintendent General, Monthly report, Jan. 1914; v. 1653, Halliday to Secretary, 16 Feb. 1914; ibid., Halliday to J. G. H. Bergeron, 19 Jan. 1914; BCARS, Newcombe Papers, Collections 6, Nowell to Newcombe, 13 Apr. 1914; DIA, v. 1646, Halliday to Deputy Superintendent General, Monthly report, Apr. 1914.

25. *Daily Colonist*, 7, 8, 9 May 1914. The judgement overlooked the Uslick conviction.

26. DIA, v. 3629, f. 6244-2, Maitland, Hunter and Maitland to Secretary, 8 May 1914; ibid., Halliday to Secretary, 12 May 1914; v. 1646, Halliday to Deputy Superintendent General, Monthly report, May 1914.

27. DIA, v. 3629, f. 6244-3, Halliday to Secretary, 2 Sept. 1914; ibid., Halliday to all chiefs of Kwawkewlth Agency, 26 Aug. 1914.

28. Newcombe Papers, Samuel A. Barrett to Newcombe, 3 Feb. 1915. Barrett's collecting went very well, probably because the Kwakiutl were more willing to sell ceremonial items when the ceremony itself was threatened. See Douglas Cole, *Captured Heritage*, 248-49.

29. *Province*, 10 Feb. 1915; *Vancouver World*, 10 Feb. 1915; *Nanaimo Free Press*, 10 May 1915; DIA, v. 3629, f. 6244-3, Halliday to Secretary, Monthly report, May 1915.

30. DIA, v. 3629, f. 6244-3, Comley to Secretary, 18 Nov. 1915; *Daily Times*, 17 Feb. 1916.

31. DIA, v. 1316, Ditchburn to Cox, 4 Oct. 1915; v. 3629, f. 6244-2, Secretary to Halliday, 2 Mar. 1915; v. 1646, Halliday to Deputy Superintendent General, Monthly report, Feb. 1916; v. 3629, f. 6244-3, Halliday to Secretary, 24 Mar. 1917; v. 1646, Halliday to Deputy Superintendent General, Monthly reports, Jan. and Dec. 1917.

32. Newcombe Papers, v. 43, Envelope 14a, "Alert Bay," 16 May 1921. Potlatches did, of course, continue.

33. DIA, v. 3629, f. 6244-3, Halliday to Secretary, 2 Mar. 1915.

34. Ibid.; v. 1316, Ditchburn to Cox, 4 Oct. 1915.

35. DIA, v. 3629, f. 6244-2, Maitland, Hunter and Maitland to Secretary, 8 May 1914; ibid., McInnis, reported in Halliday to Secretary, 20 Feb. 1915.

36. Ibid., Halliday to Secretary, 9 Jan. 1915; ibid., Clements to Deputy Superintendent General, 15 Mar. 1915; Boas Professional Papers, Sapir to Boas, 10 Feb. 1915; DIA, v. 3629, f. 6244-3, Sapir to Deputy Superintendent General, 11 Feb. 1915; ibid., Sapir to Deputy Superintendent General, 1 Mar. 1915, with enclosure of anthropologists' letters. Scott, it should be said, solicited a report on the potlatch from the anthropological divison of the museum: ibid., Deputy Superintendent General to R. G. McConnell, 8 Feb. 1915, cited in Deputy Superintendent General to Sapir, 11 Feb. 1915.

37. DIA, v. 3629, f. 6244-3, Deputy Superintendent General to Superintendent General, 18 Dec. 1916; v. 1653, Halliday to Secretary, 6 June 1913.

38. P. Capper of Lakalzap reported in October 1917 the biggest potlatch

since his arrival on the Nass, and J. J. Maroney wrote a few months later of "the general return to Indian dancing" among the Salish on the Chehalis reserve. DIA, v. 3629, f. 6244-3, Capper to Secretary, Field Matron's report, 31 Oct. 1917; ibid., Maroney to Secretary, 24 Jan. 1918.

39. House of Commons, *Debates,* 23 Apr. 1918, 1056. It received royal assent on 24 May.
40. DIA, v. 3630, f. 6244-4, Pt. 1, Deputy Superintendent General to J. G. Shearer, 23 Nov. 1920.
41. Halliday to Ditchburn, 19 Apr. 1919, quoted in Sewid-Smith, *Prosecution or Persecution,* 26.
42. We are indebted to lawyer Donald Phelps for his insights on these matters.

Chapter 7   *"The Potlatch Is Killed"*

1. *Sessional Papers,* 1920, no. 27:20; Deputy Superintendent General's report.
2. They were included in the national manpower registration, which caused some difficulties among the Nishga.
3. *Sessional Papers,* 1919, no. 27:10, Deputy Superintendent General's report; DIA, v. 1646, Halliday to Deputy Superintendent General, Monthly report, Apr. 1918.
4. DIA, v. 3086, f. 279,222-1C, Deputy Superintendent General to agents, 12 Feb. 1918, quoted in Titley, *A Narrow Vision,* 39; DIA, v. 3629, f. 6244-3, Deputy Superintendent General to all B.C. Indian agents, 21 Oct. 1918.
5. DIA, v. 1322, Ditchburn to Deputy Superintendent General, 15 May 1919.
6. DIA, v. 3629, f. 6244-3, Halliday to Deputy Superintendent General, 27 Dec. 1918.
7. Ibid.
8. DIA, v. 1646, Halliday to Deputy Superintendent General, Monthly report, Jan. 1919.
9. Ibid.; v. 3629, f. 6244-3, Frank Lyons to Deputy Superintendent General, 11 Feb. 1919; ibid., Halliday to Secretary, 13 Feb. 1919.
10. Clements to Halliday, 16 May 1919, in Sewid-Smith, *Prosecution or Persecution,* 27; DIA, v. 3629, f. 6244-3, Secretary to Rt. Rev. C. D. Scholfield, 26 Feb. 1919.
11. DIA, v. 3629, f. 6244-3, Halliday to Secretary, 13 Feb. 1919.
12. Lyons had been counsel to Cessaholis in the February 1915 case that had concluded with a suspended sentence.

13. DIA, v. 3630, f. 6244-4, Pt. 1, Senkler to Secretary, 26 Mar. 1919; ibid., Halliday to Secretary, 29 Mar. 1919.

14. Ibid., Halliday to Secretary, 29 Mar. 1919.

15. Ibid.; v. 1646, Halliday to Deputy Superintendent General, Monthly report, Mar. 1919.

16. Halliday to Clements, 28 May 1919, in Sewid-Smith, *Prosecution or Persecution,* 27.

17. DIA, v. 3629, f. 6244-3, Halliday to Secretary, 2 Mar. 1915, enclosing petition from the Indians of Kwawkewlth Agency to Secretary, 2 Mar. 1915; ibid., Charles Nowell to unaddressed, n.d. [June 1915?]; ibid., Indians of Kwawkewlth Agency to Deputy Superintendent General, n.d. [26 Dec. 1918]; ibid., Halliday to Deputy Superintendent General, 27 Dec. 1918; ibid., Deputy Superintendent General to Louie Ambers and others, 7 Feb. 1919.

18. DIA, v. 3630, f. 6244-4, Pt. 1, Criminal Court Proceedings, Rex v. Kwosteetsas and Rex v. Likiosa, 27 Mar. 1919; ibid., Cayley to Minister of Interior, 26 Sept. 1919; v. 3630, f. 6244-4, Pt. 1, Senkler to Secretary, 26 Mar. 1919.

19. Halliday to Deputy Superintendent General, 5 Feb. 1919, in Sewid-Smith, *Prosecution or Persecution,* 21; DIA, v. 1322, Ditchburn to Deputy Superintendent General, 15 May 1919.

20. DIA, v. 3630, f. 6244-4, Pt. 1, Deputy Superintendent General to Ditchburn, 11 June 1919; ibid., Ditchburn to Deputy Superintendent General, 22 May 1919.

21. Ibid., Clements to Deputy Superintendent General, telegram, 17 Dec. 1919; ibid., Deputy Superintendent General to Clements, telegram, 18 Dec. 1919; ibid., Lyons to Deputy Superintendent General, telegram, 22 Dec. 1919; ibid., Clements to Deputy Superintendent General, telegram, 22 Dec. 1919; ibid., Deputy Superintendent General to Clements, telegram, 23 Dec. 1919.

22. Ibid., Clements to Deputy Superintendent General, telegram, 22 Dec. 1919; ibid., Deputy Superintendent General to Clements, telegram, 23 Dec. 1919; ibid., Deputy Superintendent General to Superintendent General, 12 Jan. 1920; ibid., Halliday to Deputy Superintendent General, 15 Feb. 1920; ibid., Lyons to Deputy Superintendent General, 10 Mar. 1920.

23. DIA, v. 1646, Halliday to Deputy Superintendent General, Monthly report, Dec. 1919.

24. Ibid., Halliday to Deputy Superintendent General, Monthly report, Jan. 1920.

25. Again, Uslick excepted.

26. DIA, v. 3630, f. 6244-4, Pt. 1, Halliday to Deputy Superintendent General, 15 Feb. 1920.
27. DIA, v. 1646, Halliday to Deputy Superintendent General, Monthly report, Feb. 1920. The statement on church marriages is almost correct. Eight Indian couples were married in Christ Church between December 1919 and March 1920. The previous thirty-five years had seen between eight and eighteen, depending how one counts half bloods and names not readily identifiable. AADBC, Alert Bay, Marriage Register.
28. DIA, v. 3630, f. 6244-4, Pt. 1, John Antle to Deputy Superintendent General, 6 Jan. 1921; ibid., Matthews to Halliday, 28 Jan. 1921.
29. Agnes Alfred, quoted in Sewid-Smith, *Prosecution or Persecution,* 48; DIA, v. 3630, f. 6244-4, Pt. 1, Angermann to Assistant Commissioner [RCMP], B.C. District, 31 Jan. 1921.
30. Ford, *Smoke from Their Fires,* 218-24; DIA, v. 3630, f. 6244-4, Pt. 1, Angermann to "E" Division, RCMP, 26 Mar. 1921. Through Newcombe's intervention Nowell was released after serving about six weeks of his term.
31. The men were George Scow, Johnny Scow, Chief Dick, Lagis and Kesu. The copper was being passed from Chief Dick to George Scow. DIA, v. 3631, f. 6244-5, Angermann to "E" Division, RCMP, 28 Dec. 1921.
32. DIA, v. 3630, f. 6244-4, Pt. 1, Halliday to Secretary, 21 Dec. 1921.
33. Ibid.; Sewid-Smith, *Prosecution or Persecution,* 56-57.
34. We have three good accounts: Cranmer in Codere, "Kwakiutl"; DIA, v. 3630, f. 6244-4, Pt. 2, Angermann to "E" Division, RCMP, 1 Mar. 1922, and Herbert Martin's recollections in Sewid-Smith, *Prosecution or Persecution,* 55-57.
35. DIA, v. 3630, f. 6244-4, Pt. 2, McTaggart to Deputy Superintendent General, telegram, 21 Feb. 1922.
36. Ibid., Halliday to Deputy Superintendent General, 1 Mar. 1922.
37. Among the Nimpkish there were "a few small examples" of dancing property not surrendered and two owners of coppers, not having been at the Cranmer potlatch, felt they were not bound to enter the agreement.
38. DIA, v. 3630, f. 6244-2, Pt. 2, Halliday to Deputy Superintendent General, 10 Apr. 1922; ibid., Assistant Undersecretary of State to Deputy Superintendent General, 20 May 1922.
39. Hunt was paroled in June after serving the same two-month sentence as the others.
40. Sewid-Smith, *Prosecution or Persecution,* 4-6, 63.

41. Herbert Martin, quoted in Sewid-Smith, *Prosecution or Persecution,* 61. Cranmer and Emma had been married, according to Kwakiutl custom. He had sought to leave her in 1912 in order to marry Louisa Harris under provincial law, a move that was prevented by Halliday, acting as registrar of marriages and on the advice of Attorney General Bowser. Shortly after Emma's return from watching over the Oakalla prisoners, the marriage broke up. Emma married Herbert Martin in Christ Church in February 1930. She died 9 October 1935, age 42. In December 1935 Cranmer married Agnes Hunt in Christ Church. DIA, v. 11, 141, Secretary to Halliday, 17 Feb. 1912; Sewid-Smith, *Prosecution or Persecution,* 5-6; AADBC, Alert Bay, Marriage Register.

42. Sewid-Smith, *Prosecution or Persecution,* 63-64.

43. Often referred to as "confiscated," the word "surrendered" is probably more accurate. The ambiguities of the situation in which the Kwakiutl were placed, however, makes either usage more or less correct.

44. Deputy Superintendent General to Halliday, 6 June 1922, in Sewid-Smith, *Prosecution or Persecution,* 71; DIA, v. 3630, f. 6244-4, Pt. 2, Halliday to Secretary, 6 Sept. 1922; ibid., Secretary to Halliday, 20 Sept. 1922.

45. DIA, v. 3630, f. 6244-4, Pt. 2, Sapir to Deputy Superintendent General, 29 Jan. 1923; ibid., Halliday to Secretary, 1 May 1923; Sewid-Smith, *Prosecution or Persecution,* 69; Halliday, *Potlatch and Totem,* 192.

46. See Carol Henderson Carpenter, "Sacred, Precious Things," 64-70.

47. DIA, v. 3630, f. 6244-4, Pt. 2, Halliday to Deputy Superintendent General, 10 Apr. 1922.

48. Ibid.; Halliday to Secretary, Monthly report, Apr. 1922; ibid., Halliday to Secretary, 19 May 1922; ibid., Halliday to Secretary, 14 Apr. 1923; *Province,* 10 and 12 Apr. 1923.

49. DIA, v. 3630, f. 6244-4, Pt. 1, Sgt. H. E. Taylor to "E" Division, RCMP, 7 Jan. 1921; ibid., Robertson to Deputy Superintendent General, telegram, 29 Jan. 1921; ibid., McLaren to "E" Division, RCMP, 17 and 22 Feb. 1921.

50. DIA, v. 3630, f. 6244-4, Pt. 2, Cpl. D. Hall to "E" Division, RCMP, 6 Jan. 1922; *Omineca Herald,* 21 July 1922, in Leslie Allan Dawn, " 'Ksan: Museum, Cultural and Artistic Activity among the Gitksan Indians of the Upper Skeena, 1920-1973," 39.

51. DIA, v. 3630, f. 6244-5, Const. T. E. E. Greenfield to "E" Division, RCMP, 23 Feb. 1927; *Omenica Herald,* 31 Dec. 1930, 7 and 14 Jan. 1931; *Prince Rupert Daily News,* 3 and 4 Jan. 1931, in Dawn, " 'Ksan,"

40-42; DIA, v. 3631, f. 6244-5, Insp. J. M. Tupper to "E" Division, RCMP, 9 Feb. 1931; ibid., Mortimer to Secretary, 28 Mar. 1931 and 17 Apr. 1931.

52. DIA, v. 3630, f. 6244-4, Pt. 2, Fougner to Secretary, 22 Nov. 1922; ibid., Secretary to Fougner, 5 Dec. 1922.

53. McIlwraith Family Collection, McIlwraith to Family, 26 Mar. 1933; Cambridge University Library, A. C. Haddon Collection, McIlwraith to Ethel S. Fegan, 13 Oct. 1923; McIlwraith Family Collection, McIlwraith to Thomas F. McIlwraith, Sr., 13 Jan. 1924.

Chapter 8   "All We Want Is Justice"

1. DIA, v. 3629, f. 6224-2, Cox to Deputy Superintendent General, Monthly report, Nov. 1913; Boas Professional Papers, Sapir to Boas, 10 Feb. 1915; DIA, v. 1351, Robertson diary, 13 June 1914; *Ominica Herald,* 7 Jan. 1921, in Dawn, " 'Ksan," 23-24.

2. DIA, v. 3630, f. 6244-4, Pt. 1, Spruce Martin and Frank Walker to Clements, 14 Jan. 1920; v. 3629, f. 6244-3, West Coast Indian Chiefs to Deputy Superintendent General, 4 Dec. 1914; ibid., Indian Chiefs and Subchiefs of Squamish, Musqueam and Kwakiutl to Deputy Superintendent General, 7 Sept. 1914; v. 3629, f. 6244-4, Pt. 1, Chief Joseph of Clayoquot Sound to Deputy Superintendent General, 24 Jan. 1921; v. 3629, f. 6244-2, Chief Billy of Ahousat to Deputy Superintendent General, 25 Nov. 1915; v. 3629, f. 6244-3, Indians of the Kwawkewlth Agency to Secretary, enclosed with Halliday to Secretary, 2 Mar. 1915; v. 3629, f. 6244-2, Jim Quatel to Secretary, 14 May 1914; v. 3629, f. 6244-3, Charles Nowell to Clements, 28 Jan. 1915.

3. DIA, v. 3629, f. 6244-3, West Coast Indian Chiefs to Deputy Superintendent General, 4 Dec. 1914.

4. Ibid., Indian Chiefs and Subchiefs of Squamish, Musqueam and Kwakiutl to Deputy Superintendent General, 7 Sept. 1914; ibid., Indians of Kwawkewlth Agency to Deputy Superintendent General, n.d. [Dec. 1918].

5. Ibid., West Coast Indian Chiefs to Deputy Superintendent General, 4 Dec. 1914; ibid., Indian Chiefs and Subchiefs of Squamish, Musqueam and Kwakiutl to Deputy Superintendent General, 7 Sept. 1914; ibid., West Coast Indian Chiefs to Deputy Superintendent General, 4 Dec. 1914; v. 3630, f. 6244-4, Pt. 2, Dickie and DeBeck to Deputy Superintendent General, 27 Feb. 1922.

6. DIA, v. 3629, f. 6244-3, West Coast Indian Chiefs to Deputy Superintendent General, 4 Dec. 1914. This Nootka petition, signed by fourteen chiefs, was probably the one drafted, at their request, by Edward Sapir. Boas Professional Papers, Sapir to Boas, 10 Feb. 1915.

7. DIA, v. 3630, f. 6244-4, Pt. 1, Indians of Mamalillikulla Band to Clements, 10 Feb. 1920; ibid., Chiefs of the Ahousat Band to Deputy Superintendent General, 12 Jan. 1921; ibid., Chief Joseph of Clayoquot Sound to Deputy Superintendent General, 24 Jan. 1921; v. 3629, f. 6244-3, West Coast Indian Chiefs to Deputy Superintendent General, 4 Dec. 1914.

8. DIA, v. 3629, f. 6244-2, Quatel to Secretary, 14 May 1914; v. 3629, f. 6244-3, West Coast Indian Chiefs to Deputy Superintendent General, 4 Dec. 1914; ibid., Indian Chiefs and Subchiefs of Squamish, Musqueam and Kwakiutl to Deputy Superintendent General, 7 Sept. 1914; ibid., Indians of Kwawkewlth Agency to Deputy Superintendent General, n.d. [Dec. 1918].

9. DIA, v. 3629, f. 6244-2, Hanson and Milne to Clements, 14 Feb. 1914; v. 3630, f. 6244-4, Pt. 2, Dickie and DeBeck to Deputy Superintendent General, 27 Feb. 1922; ibid., H. I. Smith to Sapir, 16 Feb. 1915 and Boas to Sapir, 18 Feb. 1915; Boas, *Bulletin of the National Association on Indian Affairs* 3 (1924), 15.

10. DIA, v. 3629, f. 6244-3, Smith to Sapir, 16 Feb. 1915; ibid., Swanton to Sapir, 12 Feb. 1915; ibid., Sapir to Deputy Superintendent General, 11 Feb. 1915; ibid., Newcombe to Sapir, 16 Feb. 1915; v. 3630, f. 6244-4, Pt. 2, Dickie and DeBeck to Deputy Superintendent General, 27 Feb. 1922.

11. DIA, v. 3629, f. 6244-3, Sapir to Deputy Superintendent General, 11 Feb. 1915; *Daily Times*, 26 Aug. 1922; BCARS, Newcombe Papers, Misc. Ethnology, 35; Boas, "The Indians of British Columbia," transcript of an address before the Natural History Society, 28 Aug. 1922; DIA, v. 3629, f. 6244-3, Newcombe to Sapir, 16 Feb. 1915.

12. DIA, v. 3629, f. 6244-3, Sapir to Deputy Superintendent General, 11 Feb. 1915; ibid., Newcombe to Sapir, 16 Feb. 1915; ibid., Sapir to Deputy Superintendent General, 11 Feb. 1915.

13. Ibid., Indian Chiefs of Sechelt Band, enclosed with Peter Byrne to Secretary, 26 Jan. 1915.

14. DIA, v. 8481, f. 1/24-3, Pt. 1, Cook to Deputy Superintendent General, 1 Feb. 1919.

15. DIA, v. 3629, f. 6244-3, Missionaries of Vancouver Island Indians to Deputy Superintendent General, n.d. [1916]; *Western Methodist Recorder*, June 1922.

16. DIA, v. 3629, f. 6244-3, Deputy Superintendent General to Clements, 8 Feb. 1915; ibid., Nowell to Clements, 28 Jan. 1915; ibid., Halliday to Secretary, 2 Mar. 1915; v. 3630, f. 6244-4, Pt. 1, Ditchburn to Deputy Superintendent General, 22 May 1919, citing Deputy Superintendent General to Ditchburn, 18 Feb. 1919.

17. DIA, v. 3629, f. 6244-3, Deputy Superintendent General to Indians of Kwawkewlth Agency, 7 Feb. 1919; Deputy Superintendent General to E. K. Brown, 2 July 1941, in Robert L. McDougall, *The Poet and the Critic,* 26.

18. BCARS, E. K. DeBeck Papers, brief, 11 May 1921.

19. DIA, v. 3630, f. 6244-4, Pt. 1, Deputy Superintendent General to DeBeck, 11 June 1921; ibid., Kwakiutl petitions to Governor General, various dates, 7 Jan. 1922 to 30 Aug. 1922; ibid., Secretary to Dickie and DeBeck, 18 Mar. and 26 July 1921; ibid., Nowell to Clements, 11 Jan. 1921.

20. DIA, v. 3630, f. 6244-4, Pt. 2, Dickie and DeBeck to Superintendent General, 20 July 1922.

21. Ibid., Dickie and DeBeck to Deputy Superintendent General, 2 Aug. 1922.

22. See Darcy Anne Mitchell, "The Allied Tribes of British Columbia," 128.

23. See DIA, v. 6810, f. 470-2-3, Pt. 7, Moses Alfred, Charles Nowell, Peter Knox and Harry Mountain to Clements, 28 Mar. 1920. "We remember you told us when you was here that if we'd be franchised we could have our Potlash [*sic*]." If enfranchised, the Kwakiutl would have lost their native status, thus losing both the benefits and the penalties of the Indian Act. While Scott and the department encouraged (even sought to compel) the enfranchisement of "civilized and self-supporting" Indians, that route as a means to "have our Potlash" would not likely have been countenanced.

24. DIA, v. 3630, f. 6244-4, Pt. 1, Nowell to Clements, 11 Jan. 1921.

25. Ibid., Nimpkish Indians to Clements, n.d. [1920]; ibid., Mamalillikulla Indians to Clements, 10 Feb. 1920; ibid., Martin and Walker to Clements, 14 Jan. 1920.

26. House of Commons, *Debates,* 19 Jan. 1922, 3191-3192.

27. University of British Columbia Library, Leon J. Ladner Papers, Ladner to Stewart, 11 and 15 May 1922; ibid., Stewart to Ladner, 17 May 1922; ibid., Ladner to DeBeck, 31 May 1922; *Vancouver Sunday Sun,* 7 May 1922; "Potlatch," *Province,* 19 May 1922; Ladner Papers, DeBeck to Ladner, 20 May 1922.

28. Irving Abella and Harold Troper, *None Is Too Many.*

29. There is no evidence, however, for Paul Tennant's assertion that the potlatch law was used to stifle Indian political organizations by giving "agents and police a convenient means of discouraging assemblies of any sort, and the jailing of potlatch holders removed the Indian leaders with the most traditional authority." While it is true that "the commencement of prosecutions coincided with the first province-wide In-

dian political activity," the Allied Tribes movement of 1913-1926, the coincidence seems purely fortuitous. Tennant, "Native Political Organization in British Columbia, 1900-1969," 16.

30. DIA, v. 3630, f. 6244-4, Pt. 2, Seven Tribes to Lieutenant Governor, 13 May 1925; *Province*, 25 May 1925; *Daily Colonist*, 10 and 11 June 1925, J. R. Anderson and Charles St. Barbe to the editor.

Chapter 9   "Acts of Christian Charity"

1. DIA, v. 3631, f. 6244-5, Halliday to Deputy Superintendent General, 26 Feb. 1931; ibid., Perry to Secretary, 3 Dec. 1934; v. 8481, f. 1/24-3, Pt. 1, Todd to Secretary, n.d. [received 14 Apr. 1936]; v. 3826, f. 60,511 4A, Deputy Superintendent General to Thomas Murphy, 28 July 1931, cited in Katherine Ann Pettipas, "Severing the Ties That Bind," 326.

2. DIA, v. 3631, f. 6244-5, Halliday to Deputy Superintendent General, 26 Feb. 1931; Boas Professional Papers, Boas to Lieutenant Governor, 5 Mar. 1931; American Museum of Natural History, Anthropology Department, Newcombe to P. E. Goddard, 1 Jan. 1924; DIA, v. 8481, f. 1/24-3, Pt. 1, S. and J. Cook to J. S. Taylor, MP, 15 Apr. 1937.

3. DIA, v. 3631, f. 6244-5, Halliday to Secretary, 22 Mar. 1927; James Sewid, *Guests Never Leave Hungry*, 71.

4. DIA, v. 3631, f. 6244-5, Todd to Perry, 28 Nov. 1934; Ronald P. Rohner, *The People of Gilford*, 34. Rohner's account has "Robertson" instead of Halliday and "Chief Phillip" was probably Chief Dick Webber.

5. DIA, v. 8481, f. 1/24-3, Pt. 1, Cpl. Parsloe to Commissioner, RCMP, 10 Mar. 1936.

6. Bill Holm, *Smoky-Top*, 103, 104, 110, 115, 141. The quotation is from p. 109.

7. Ford, *Smoke from Their Fires*, 225-26.

8. DIA, acc. 80-81/18, Box 10, Newnham to Perry, 24 Jan. 1933; ibid., Supt. S. T. Wood to Perry, 9 Feb. 1933; ibid., Perry to Wood, 11 Feb. 1933; v. 3631, f. 6244-5, Todd to Perry, 28 Nov. 1934; Drucker and Heizer, *To Make My Name Good*, 32.

9. Sewid, *Guests Never Leave Hungry*, 106, 77, 82; Agnes Alfred quoted in Sewid-Smith, *Prosecution or Persecution*, 53.

10. Boas to Antonie Boas Wohlauer, 27 Oct. 1930, quoted in Franz Boas, *The Ethnography of Franz Boas,* 290; Christine Twince, quoted in Ida Halpern, *Indian Music of the Pacific Northwest Coast,* 12; Ford, *Smoke from Their Fires*, 237.

11. DIA, v. 3631, f. 6244-5, Halliday to Ditchburn, 10 June 1930; Ford, *Smoke from Their Fires*, 224-25, 227.

12. DIA, v. 8481, f. 1/24-3, Pt. 1, and Cook and Cook to Taylor, 15 Apr. 1937; Drucker and Heizer, *To Make My Name Good*, 47.

13. DIA, v. 3631, f. 6244-5, Halliday to Ditchburn, 12 and 27 Feb. 1931. The host at Karlakwees is referred to alternatively as Johnnie Speck and Henry Speck.

14. Ibid., Deputy Minister of Justice to Deputy Superintendent General, 18 Apr. 1931; ibid., Ditchburn to Deputy Superintendent General, 2 Apr. 1931; ibid., Halliday to Deputy Superintendent General, 26 Feb. 1931.

15. DIA, acc. 80-81/18, Box 10, Halliday to Ditchburn, 29 Mar. 1932; v. 3631, f. 6244-5, Halliday to Deputy Superintendent General, 26 Feb. 1931; ibid., Newnham to Secretary, Monthly report, Apr. 1933.

16. Sewid-Smith, *Prosecution or Persecution*, 54; DIA, acc. 80-81/18, Box 10, Todd to Perry, 7 Dec. 1934; George Manuel and Michael Posluns, *The Fourth World*, 79.

17. DIA, v. 8481, f. 1/24-3, Pt. 1, Todd to Deputy Superintendent General, Monthly report, Jan. 1935; Bell in Sewid-Smith, *Prosecution or Persecution*, 70-71.

18. DIA, acc. 80-81/18, Box 10, Clark to B.C. Police, 15 June 1931; ibid., Halliday to Ditchburn, 12 Feb. 1931; v. 3631, f. 6244-5, Halliday to Deputy Superintendent General, 26 Feb. 1931.

19. DIA, v. 3631, f. 6244-5, Perry to Secretary, 3 Dec. 1934.

20. *Daily Colonist*, 8 June 1929; *Log of the Columbia*, "The Potlatch," 1 (July 1930), 13 and 2 (Oct. 1931), n.p.; ibid., "Bishop Schofield Meets Indian Chiefs," 2 (Nov. 1931), n.p.; ibid., Rene Duncan, "The Potlatch: A Plea for the Modification of the Law Prohibiting Potlatches," 2 (Feb. 1932), 7-8.

21. DIA, v. 3631, f. 6244-5, Antle to Minister of Justice, 8 June 1931; ibid., Deputy Superintendent General to Ditchburn, 23 Nov. 1931.

22. AADBC, Bishop of Columbia (Schofield) Correspondence re: Potlatch, Accession 87-30, Box 15, Prosser to Schofield, 16 Mar. 1932.

23. DIA, v. 3631, f. 6244-5, Newnham to Secretary, Monthly report, Apr. 1933; AADBC, Synod of the Diocese of British Columbia, Synod Office Files, Text 63, Box 12, f. 13, A. F. Mackenzie to Schofield, 13 June 1933.

24. DIA, v. 8481, f. 1/24-3, Pt. 1, synod report on potlatch, n.d.; ibid., Archbishop, Bishops and Members of the Provincial Synod of B.C., Report on Synod, n.d. The resolution was reaffirmed, though in a weaker form, in April 1937, then more strongly in a circular by the bishops of Columbia and New Westminster in 1944. AAEPBC, Columbia Coast Mission, Kingcome, acc. 984-35P, Rev. Alan Greene to Kwakiutl chiefs, 29 Feb. 1944.

25. DIA, acc. 80-81/18, Box 10, Newnham to Perry, 17 Aug. 1933.

26. DIA, v. 3740, f. 39,675-2, Report of McInnis on visit to West Coast, 1934-35; acc. 80-81/18, Box 10, MacKay to Deputy Minister, 4 Mar. 1938.

27. DIA, v. 3631, f. 6244-5, Todd to Perry, 28 Nov. 1934; ibid., Perry to Secretary, 3 Dec. 1934.

28. Ibid., Perry to Secretary, 3 Dec. 1934; ibid., Todd to Perry, Monthly report, Dec. 1934; acc. 80-81/18, Box 10, Todd to Perry, 5 Jan. 1935. Some Kwakiutl remembered the bill to have included, in order to prevent large gatherings in a house, a restriction on the number of chairs a family could own. While not quite correct, the general idea is not inaccurate. Bill Holm to authors, March 1989.

29. DIA, v. 8481, f. 1/24-3, Pt. 1, Todd to Deputy Superintendent General, 27 Mar. 1935.

30. Ibid., marginalia on Todd to Deputy Superintendent General, 27 Mar. 1935; ibid., A. F. Mackenzie to Todd, 12 Feb. 1936.

31. In December 1936 the office of superintendent general of Indian affairs was abolished, with the department becoming the Indian affairs branch of the Ministry of Mines and Resources.

32. DIA, v. 3629, f. 6244-2, Neill to Vowell, 12 Feb. 1904 and 14 Apr. 1909. For a brief treatment of Neill's political career, see Gordon Hak, "The Socialist and Labourist Impulse in Small-Town British Columbia," 533-35.

33. House of Commons, *Debates*, 20 Mar. 1936, 1286-1300; 23 Apr. 1936, 2120-21.

34. DIA, v. 8481, f. 1/24-3, Pt. 1, Todd to Mackenzie, 11 Feb. 1936.

35. DIA, v. 11,143, f. 1, Todd to Neill, 5 Jan. 1937; ibid., Neill to Todd, 15 Jan. 1937.

36. DIA, v. 8481, f. 1/24-3, Pt. 1, Todd to Secretary, 18 Feb. 1937; v. 11,143, f. 1, Todd to Neill, 5 Jan. 1937; v. 8481, f. 1/24-3, Pt. 1, MacKay to Secretary, 22 Feb. 1938; ibid., Todd to Secretary, Monthly report, Jan. 1938.

37. DIA, v. 3631, f. 6244-5, Todd to Minister, Monthly report, Feb. 1939.

38. DIA, v. 8481, f. 1/24-3, Todd to MacKay, Monthly report, Mar. 1943; AAEPBC, Columbia Coast Mission, Kingcome, acc. 984-35P, Christmas to A. D. Greene, [illeg.] Apr. 1944; DIA, v. 11,143, Shannon CR10, Pt. D, Anfield to Todd, 7 Aug. 1944.

39. DIA, v. 3631, f. 6244-5, Todd to Minister, Monthly report, Feb. 1939; acc. 80-81/18, Box 10, MacKay to Deputy Minister, 22 Feb. 1938; ibid., MacKay to Secretary, 7 Mar. 1939.

40. *Prince Rupert Daily News*, 24 Jan. 1939, in Dawn, " 'Ksan," 45; DIA,

v. 6817, f. 486-8-4, Pt. 1, Bishop to R. A. Hoey, 6 Jan. 1939; ibid., Mortimer to MacKay, 25 Jan. 1939.

41. DIA, v. 3631, f. 6244-5, Chiefs of the Kitzegula Band to Deputy Minister, 20 Nov. 1939; ibid., Mallinson to Secretary, 20 Dec. 1939; see also *Omenica Herald*, 29 Nov. 1939, and *Smithers Interior News*, 6 Dec. 1939, in Dawn, " 'Ksan," 47.

42. *Prince Rupert Daily News*, 24 Jan. 1939, in Dawn, " 'Ksan," 44-45.

43. Duff, "A Potlatch Series at Kitsegukla, January 8-15, 1945," 2-3 (manuscript, University of British Columbia Museum of Anthropology, n.d.). We are indebted to Marjorie Halperin for making this available.

44. DIA, v. 8481, f. 1/24-3, Const. J. H. Ward to "E" Division, RCMP, 16 Jan. 1942.

45. Duff, "A Potlatch Series at Kitsegukla," 1; BCARS, Marius Barbeau Papers, B-F-428, Jan. 1945.

46. George Woodcock, *Ravens and Prophets,* 76-77.

47. DIA, v. 8481, f. 1/24-3, Pt. 1, MacKay to Deputy Minister, 4 Mar. 1938; v. 6817, f. 486-8-4, Pt. 1, MacKay to Secretary, 1 Feb. 1939; ibid., G. H. Barry to MacKay, 21 Jan. 1939.

48. Dan McCaskill, "Native People and the Justice System," 291.

Chapter 10   *"Advancing in a Civilized World"*

1. AAEPBC, Columbia Coast Mission, Kingcome, acc. 984-35P, Christmas to Greene, [illeg.] Apr. 1945; DIA, v. 8481, f. 1/24-3, F. Earl Anfield, "Personal Report on Two Conferences," n.d. [Apr. 1940]; Gitksan, cited in Duff, "A Potlatch Series at Kitsegukla," 60-61; House of Commons, *Debates,* 13 June 1938, 3814, 3813.

2. Ford, *Smoke from Their Fires,* 232, 228; AADBC, Bishop's Papers, unsorted, Text 203, Box 1, "Special Meeting Held at Alert Bay," 1 June 1936. Rohner recorded that the last Gilford Island arranged marriage occurred in the 1940s. *The People of Gilford,* 80.

3. Boas to various, Nov.-Dec. 1930, in Boas, *The Ethnology of Franz Boas,* 290-91, 293, 297. Boas, at the request of the Kwakiutl, wrote the lieutenant governor of B. C., asking that the law be changed. Boas Professional Papers, Boas to Lieutenant Governor, 5 Mar. 1931.

4. Sewid, *Guests Never Leave Hungry,* 109-10.

5. BCARS, Marius Barbeau Papers, B-F-428, cited in Adams, *The Gitksan Potlatch,* 13.

6. Codere, "Kwakiutl," 471; Drucker and Heizer, *To Make My Name Good,* 50-51.

7. Drucker and Heizer, *To Make My Name Good,* 65-66. They date it tentatively to the early 1920s, but Taylor mentioned it in the House of

Commons after his 1938 investigation as if it were a contemporary phenomenon.

8. Ibid., 62; Harry Assu with Joy Inglis, *Assu of Cape Mudge,* 57-58; *Native Voice,* Feb. 1952.
9. Codere,"Kwakiutl," 482-83; H. B. Hawthorn, C. S. Belshaw and S. M. Jamieson, *The Indians of British Columbia,* 110-11; DIA, *Annual Departmental Reports,* 1929, 91; 1933, 42; 1936, 49.
10. Codere, "Kwakiutl," 483.
11. Canada, Parliament, *Report of the Special Joint Committee of the Senate and House of Commons to Consider the Indian Act,* 443.
12. Rohner, *The People of Gilford,* 156, 153-54; Royal British Columbia Provincial Museum, Ethnology Division, photographs 15250: 21-41; Todd, quoted in Peter Camden Pineo, "Village Migrations of the Modern Kwakiutl," 35.
13. Adams, *The Gitksan Potlatch,* 94.
14. Susan Golla, "He Has a Name," 60-61, 67, 60.
15. *Native Voice,* March 1948 and Apr. 1948.
16. *Native Voice,* Jan. 1949; G. E. Mortimer, "Indian Artist Makes Eloquent Plea," reprinted from the *Colonist* in *Native Voice,* Dec. 1949; La Violette, *The Struggle for Survival,* 95.
17. DIA, v. 6811, f. 470-3-6, Pt. 2.
18. Ibid., 4th report, 22 June 1948, 186, 187.
19. Canada, House of Commons, *Debates,* 1950, 3936-51, 3962-81.
20. *Native Voice,* June 1950; *Daily Colonist,* 25 Mar. 1951; *News-Herald* (Vancouver), 11 and 15 July 1950; *Vancouver Sun,* 12 July 1950; *Victoria Daily Times,* 8 and 13 Nov. 1950; *Daily Colonist,* 12 Nov. 1950.
21. There is little evidence of immediate native reaction. The curious comment, which has gained some currency, that the potlatch law was dropped rather than repealed appears to be of more recent origin.
22. Sewid considered it "one of the biggest dances because all the big chiefs were there, the prominent and noble men of all the villages." Sewid, *Guests Never Leave Hungry,* 158-62.

Chapter 11   "What Is Best for the Indians"

1. Audrey Hawthorn, *Kwakiutl Art,* viii; Cameron, "The Collector," n.p.
2. Sewid, *Guests Never Leave Hungry,* 214-18, 224-26.
3. Assu with Inglis, *Assu of Cape Mudge,* 109-21.
4. Holm to authors, March 1989.
5. Hawthorn, *Kwakiutl Art,* x.
6. Golla, "He Has a Name," 58-63.
7. Ron Hamilton to authors, September 1989.

8. Golla, "He Has a Name," 222-36; Adams, *The Gitksan Potlatch,* vi, 13, 15; Jay Miller, "Feasting with the Southern Tsimshian," 27-28, 37; Stearns, *Haida Culture in Custody,* 14. For an analysis of contemporary Tlingit potlatches, see Sergei Kan, "Cohorts, Generations and Their Cultures."

9. See Francis Paul Prucha, *The Great Father,* 646-48; William T. Hagen, *Indian Police and Judges.*

10. Suttles, "Spirit Dancing and the Persistence of Native Culture among the Coast Salish," in Suttles, *Coast Salish Essays,* 207. Such dates are a little difficult since potlatch-like activity did continue. T. T. Waterman, writing in 1921, could talk of a potlatch by John Seattle of Auburn, given in "recent years," that cost $1400. Waterman, *Notes on the Ethnology of the Indians of Puget Sound,* 82.

11. For the Makah, see Elizabeth Colson, *The Makah Indians,* 15-18, 222-23; for the Quileute, see George A. Pettit, "The Quileute of LaPush," 83, 112.

12. Jacqueline Gresko, "White 'Rites' and Indian 'Rites,' " 178.

13. This was applied only twice in British Columbia: in the West Coast Agency in 1921 and in the Kwawkewlth Agency in 1935.

14. This account is taken from Gresko, "White 'Rites' and Indian 'Rites,' " 163-81; from Titley, *A Narrow Vision,* 162-83, and from Pettipas's excellent "Severing the Ties That Bind." The uncited quotations are from Titley, 166, 179 and 183.

15. DIA, v. 3628, f. 6244-1, Vowell to Deputy Superintendent General, 1 June 1897; v. 3629, f. 6244-2, Neill to Vowell, 12 Feb. 1904.

16. Knight, *Indians at Work,* 268.

17. Ibid., 268-69.

18. Hatch, *Culture and Morality,* 135; see Lucy Mair, "Comment," in Claude E. Stipe, "Anthropologist versus Missionaries," 171.

19. AADBC, Bishop's Papers, unsorted, Text 201, Box 1, "Special Meeting Held at Alert Bay," 1 June 1936; BCARS, Barbeau Papers, B-F-428, Jan. 1945; Adams, *The Gitksan Potlatch,* 118.

20. Hatch, *Culture and Morality,* 97.

21. Grant, *Moon of Wintertime,* 140.

22. DIA, v. 3629, f. 6244-2, DeBeck to Vowell, 7 Jan. 1903; v. 3630, f. 6244-4, Pt. 1, Deputy Superintendent General to C. F. Davie, 8 Jan. 1922.

23. BCARS, Marius Barbeau Papers, B-F-95.10, "Description of Hagwelgate potlatch, about July 18, 1920."

24. Drucker, *The Native Brotherhoods,* 121; DIA, f. 971/3-5-V, Charles Patsey and Charles Clifford to Mallinson, 6 Jan. 1940; ibid., Patsey and William Wale, statutory declaration, 1 Feb. 1946.

25. Adams, *The Gitksan Potlatch,* 12; Drucker and Heizer, *To Make My Name Good,* 33-34.

Bibliography

MANUSCRIPTS

American Museum of Natural History, Anthropology Department, New York.

Anglican Church of Canada. Columbia Mission Reports, London, 1869-1911. Archives of the Ecclesiastical Province of British Columbia, Vancouver.

———. Bishop of Columbia. Papers. Archive of the Diocese of British Columbia, Victoria.

———. Columbia Coast Mission, Kingcome, Archives of the Ecclesiastical Province of British Columbia, Vancouver.

———. Synod of the Diocese of British Columbia. Synod Office, Victoria.

Antle, Rev. John. "Memoirs of John Antle." Unpublished manuscript. BCARS.

Barbeau, Marius. Papers. BCARS. Microfilm.

Boas, Franz. Professional Papers. American Philosophical Society, Philadelphia.

British Columbia. Attorney General. Papers. BCARS.

———. Provincial Police. Papers. BCARS.

Canada. Department of Indian Affairs. (RG10). Western (Black) Series. NAC.

———. Privy Council Office. Minutes. (RG 2). NAC.

———. Census of Canada, 1881. NAC.

Cowichan Indian Agent (W. H. Lomas) Correspondence. BCARS.

Dawson, George M. Papers. McGill University Archives, Montreal.

DeBeck, E. K. Papers. BCARS.

DeBeck Family. Papers. BCARS.

Duff, Wilson. "A Potlatch Series at Kitsegukla, January 8-15, 1945." University of British Columbia Museum of Anthropology, Vancouver.

Haddon, A. C. Collection. Cambridge University Library, Cambridge.

Ladner, Leon J. Papers. Special Collections, University of British Columbia Library, Vancouver.

Loring, R. E. Papers. NAC.

McIlwraith, T. F. Family Papers. Private.

[Magee, Bernard]. "Log of the *Jefferson*." Copy in Special Collections, University of British Columbia Library, Vancouver.

Newcombe, C. F. Papers. BCARS.

Tate, C. M. Diaries. BCARS.

Wastell, A. M. "Alert Bay and Vicinity, 1870-1954." Unpublished manuscript compiled by Major J. S. Matthews. BCARS.

Wooton, S. Y. Letterbook. BCARS.

PUBLISHED SOURCES

Documents

Anglican Church of Canada. Annual Reports of the Columbia Coast Mission, 1936-1950.

British Columbia. *Papers Relating to the Commission Appointed to Enquire into the Condition of the Indians of the North-West Coast.* Victoria: Richard Wolfenden, [1888].

Canada. Annual Report of the Department of Indian Affairs. *Sessional Papers*, 1873-1919.

Canada. Department of Indian Affairs. Annual Departmental Reports, 1929-1940.

————. House of Commons. *Debates.*

————. *Indian Acts and Amendments, 1868-1950.* 2d ed. Treaties and Historical Research Centre, Corporate Policy, Department of Indian and Northern Affairs, 1981.

————. Parliament. *Report of the Special Joint Committee of the Senate and House of Commons to Consider the Indian Act,* 1946-1948.

Books

Abella, Irving, and Troper, Harold. *None Is Too Many: Canada and the Jews of Europe, 1933-1948.* Toronto: Lester & Orpen Dennys, 1986.

Adams, John W. *The Gitksan Potlatch: Population Flux, Resource Ownership and Reciprocity.* Toronto and Montreal: Holt, Rinehart & Winston of Canada, 1973.

Assu, Harry with Joy Inglis. *Assu of Cape Mudge: Recollections of a Coastal Indian Chief.* Vancouver: University of British Columbia Press, 1989.

Blackman, Margaret B. *During My Time: Florence Edenshaw Davidson, a Haida Woman.* Vancouver: Douglas & McIntyre; Seattle: University of Washington Press, 1982.

Boas, Franz. *The Ethnography of Franz Boas: Letters and Diaries of Franz Boas Written on the Northwest Coast from 1886 to 1931.* Compiled and edited by Ronald P. Rohner. Translated by Hedy Parker. Chicago: University of Chicago Press, 1969.

————. *Kwakiutl Ethnography.* Edited and abridged by Helen Codere. Chicago: University of Chicago Press, 1966.

————. *The Social Organization and the Secret Societies of the Kwakiutl Indians.* Report of the United States National Museum for 1895. Washington: Government Printing Office, 1897.

Brink, J. H. Van den. *The Haida Indians: Cultural Change Mainly Between 1876-1970.* Leiden, The Netherlands: E. J. Brill, 1974.

Codere, Helen. *Fighting with Property: A Study of Kwakiutl Potlatching and Warfare, 1792-1930.* Monographs of the American Ethnological Society. New York. J. J. Augustus, [1950].

Cole, Douglas. *Captured Heritage: The Scramble for Northwest Coast Artifacts.* Vancouver: Douglas & McIntyre; Seattle: University of Washington Press, 1985.

Collison, W. H. *In the Wake of the War Canoe.* London: E. P. Dutton, 1915.

Colson, Elizabeth. *The Makah Indians: A Study of an Indian Tribe in Modern American Society.* Manchester: Manchester University Press, 1952.

Crosby, Rev. Thomas. *Among the An-Ko-Me-Nums or Flathead Tribes of Indians of the Pacific Coast.* Toronto: William Briggs, 1907.

De Laguna, Frederica. *Under Mount Saint Elias: The History and Culture of the Yakutat Tlingit.* 3 vols. Washington: Smithsonian Institution Press, 1972.

Dragland, S. L., ed. *Duncan Campbell Scott: A Book of Criticism.* Ottawa: Tecumseh Press, 1974.

Drucker, Philip. *The Native Brotherhoods: Modern Intertribal Organizations on the Northwest Coast.* Bureau of American Ethnology Bulletin no. 168. Washington: U.S. Government Printing Office, 1958.

————. *Cultures of the North Pacific Coast.* San Francisco: Chandler, 1965.

Drucker, Philip, and Heizer, Robert F. *To Make My Name Good: A Reexamination of the Southern Kwakiutl Potlatch.* Berkeley and Los Angeles: University of California Press, 1967.

Duff, Wilson. *The Indian History of British Columbia: The Impact of the White Man.* Anthropology in British Columbia, Memoir No. 5. Victoria: Provincial Museum of Natural History and Anthropology, 1964.

Fisher, Robin. *Contact and Conflict: Indian-European Relations in British Columbia, 1774-1890*. Vancouver: University of British Columbia Press, 1977.

Ford, Clellan S. *Smoke from Their Fires: The Life of a Kwakiutl Chief*. New Haven: Institute of Human Relations by Yale University Press, 1941.

Freemen, Rev. B. C. *The Indians of Queen Charlotte Islands*. Toronto: Methodist Young People's Forward Movement for Missions, n.d.

Goldman, Irving. *The Mouth of Heaven: An Introduction to Kwakiutl Religious Thought*. New York: John Wiley & Sons, 1975.

Grant, John Webster. *Moon of Wintertime: Missionaries and the Indians of Canada in Encounter Since 1534*. Toronto: University of Toronto Press, 1984.

Gwyn, Sandra. *The Private Capital: Ambition and Love in the Age of Macdonald and Laurier*. Toronto: McClelland & Stewart, 1984.

Hagen, William T. *Indian Police and Judges*. New Haven: Yale University Press, 1966.

Halliday, W. M. *Potlatch and Totem and the Recollections of an Indian Agent*. London and Toronto: J. M. Dent & Sons, 1935.

Halpern, Ida. *Indian Music of the Pacific Northwest Coast: Kwakiutl*. New York: Ethnic Folkways, 1981. Sound recording and booklet.

Harrison, Charles. *Ancient Warriors of the North Pacific*. London: H. F. & G. Witherby, 1925.

Hatch, Elvin. *Culture and Morality: The Relativity of Values in Anthropology*. New York: Columbia University Press, 1983.

Hawthorn, Audrey. *Kwakiutl Art*. Vancouver: Douglas & McIntyre; Seattle: University of Washington Press, 1979.

Hawthorn, H. B.; Belshaw, C. S.; and Jamieson, S. M. *The Indians of British Columbia: A Study of Contemporary Social Adjustment*. Toronto: University of Toronto Press; Vancouver: University of British Columbia, 1960.

Hinckley, Ted C. *Alaskan John G. Brady: Missionary, Businessman, Judge, and Governor, 1878-1918*. Columbus: Ohio State University Press for Miami University, 1982.

Holm, Bill. *Smoky-Top: The Art and Times of Willie Seaweed*. Vancouver: Douglas & McIntyre; Seattle: University of Washington Press, 1983.

Jewitt, John R. *A Journal Kept at Nootka Sound. . . .* Boston: John R. Jewitt, 1807.

Keynes, Geoffrey, ed. *The Letters of Rupert Brooke*. New York: Harcourt, Brace & World, 1968.

Knight, Rolf. *Indians at Work: An Informal History of Native Indian Labour in British Columbia, 1858-1930*. Vancouver: New Star Books, 1978.

La Violette, Forrest E. *The Struggle for Survival: Indian Cultures and the Protestant Ethic in British Columbia.* Reprinted with additions. Toronto: University of Toronto Press, 1973.

Leslie, John, and Maguire, Ron, eds. *The Historical Development of the Indian Act.* 2d ed. Treaties and Historical Research Centre, P.R.E. Group. Ottawa: Indian and Northern Affairs, 1978.

McIlwraith, T. F. *The Bella Coola Indians.* 2 vols. Toronto: University of Toronto Press, 1948.

McLean, Rev. John. *The Indians: Their Manners and Customs.* Toronto: William Briggs, 1889.

Manuel, George, and Posluns, Michael. *The Fourth World: An Indian Reality.* Don Mills, Ont.: Collier-Macmillan Canada, 1974.

Moziño, José Mariano. *Noticias de Nutka: An Account of Nootka Sound in 1792.* Translated and edited by Iris Higbie Wilson. Toronto: McClelland and Stewart, 1970.

Murray, Peter. *The Devil and Mr. Duncan.* Victoria: Sono Nis Press, 1985.

Patterson, E. Palmer, II. *Mission on the Nass: The Evangelization of the Nishga (1860-1890).* Waterloo, Ont.: Eulachan Press, 1982.

Pierce, Rev. William Henry. *From Potlatch to Pulpit.* Vancouver: Vancouver Bindery Limited, 1933.

Prucha, Francis Paul. *The Great Father: The United States Government and the American Indians.* 2 vols. Lincoln: University of Nebraska Press, 1984.

Rohner, Ronald P. *The People of Gilford: A Contemporary Kwakiutl Village.* National Museum of Canada Bulletin no. 225, Anthropological Series no. 83. Ottawa: National Museum of Canada, 1967.

Rosman, Abraham, and Rubel, Paula G. *Feasting with Mine Enemy: Rank and Exchange among Northwest Coast Societies.* New York: Columbia University Press, 1971.

Scott, Duncan Campbell. *The Poet and the Critic: A Literary Correspondence between D. C. Scott and E. K. Brown.* Edited by Robert L. McDougall. Ottawa: Carleton University Press, 1983.

Scott, Robert C. *My Captain Oliver: A Story of Two Missionaries on the British Columbia Coast.* Toronto: The United Church Publishing House, 1947.

Sewid, James. *Guests Never Leave Hungry: The Autobiography of James Sewid, A Kwakiutl Indian.* Edited by James P. Spradley. Montreal: McGill-Queen's University Press, 1972.

Sewid-Smith, Daisy (My-yah-nelth). *Prosecution or Persecution.* [Cape Mudge?]: Nu-yum-balees Society, 1979.

Stearns, Mary Lee. *Haida Culture in Custody: The Masset Band.* Vancouver: Douglas & McIntyre; Seattle: University of Washington Press, 1981.

Suttles, Wayne. *Coast Salish Essays.* Vancouver: Talonbooks; Seattle: University of Washington Press, 1987.

Titley, E. Brian. *A Narrow Vision: Duncan Campbell Scott and the Administration of Indian Affairs in Canada.* Vancouver: University of British Columbia Press, 1986.

Usher, Jean. *William Duncan of Metlakatla: A Victorian Missionary in British Columbia.* Publications in History, no. 5. Ottawa: National Museum of Canada, 1974.

Waterman, T. T. *Notes on the Ethnology of the Indians of Puget Sound.* Indian Notes and Monographs, Miscellaneous Series no. 59. New York: Museum of the American Indian Heye Foundation, 1973.

Williams, David R. *". . . The Man for a New Country": Sir Matthew Baillie Begbie.* Sidney, B.C.: Gray's, 1977.

Woodcock, George. *Ravens and Prophets: An Account of Journeys in British Columbia, Alberta and Southern Alaska.* London: Allan Wingate, 1952.

Articles

Archer, Christon I. "Cannibalism in the Early History of the Northwest Coast: Enduring Myths and Neglected Realities." *Canadian Historical Review* 61 (December 1980): 453-79.

Blackman, Margaret B. "Totems to Tombstones: Culture Change as Viewed through the Haida Mortuary Complex, 1877-1971." *Ethnology* 12 (January 1973): 47-56.

―――. "Creativity in Acculturation: Art, Architecture and Ceremony from the Northwest Coast." *Ethnohistory* 23 (Fall 1976): 387-413.

―――. "Ethnohistoric Changes in the Haida Potlatch Complex." *Arctic Anthropology* 14 (1977): 39-53.

Boas, Franz. "The Indians of British Columbia." *Popular Science Monthly* 32 (1888): 628-36.

―――. "The Houses of the Kwakiutl Indians, British Columbia." *Proceedings of the United States National Museum* 11 (1888): 197-213.

―――. "Reisen in British-Columbien." *Verhandlugen der Gesellschaft für Erdkunde zur Berlin* 6 (1889): 257-68.

―――. "Tamanos." In *Handbook of American Indians,* edited by Frederick W. Hodge, 681. Bureau of American Ethnology Bulletin no. 3, part 2. Washington: U.S. Government Printing Office, 1912.

Brown, E. K. "Memoir." In *Selected Poems of Duncan Campbell Scott,* xi-xlii. Toronto: Ryerson Press, [1951].

Cameron, Silver Don. "The Collector," *Vancouver Sun* Weekend Magazine, 6 December 1975.

Carpenter, Carol Henderson. "Sacred, Precious Things: Repatriation of Potlatch Art." *artscanada* 12 (May-June 1981): 64-70.

Codere, Helen. "Kwakiutl Society: Rank Without Class." *American Anthropologist* 59 (June 1957): 473-86.

———. "Kwakiutl." In *Perspectives in American Indian Culture Change*, edited by E. H. Spicer, 431-516. Chicago: University of Chicago Press, 1961.

Curtis, Edward. "The Kwakiutl." In *The North American Indian* 10: 141-242. Norwood, Mass.: Plimpton Press, 1915.

Dawson, George M. "Notes and Observations on the Kwakiool People of Vancouver Island and Adjacent Coasts, Made during the Summer of 1885." *Transactions of the Royal Society of Canada*, Section 2, 1887: 63-98.

Donald, Leland, and Mitchell, Donald H. "Some Correlates of Local Group Rank Among the Southern Kwakiutl." *Ethnology* 14 (October 1975): 325-46.

Drucker, Philip. "Rank, Wealth, and Kinship in Northwest Coast Society." In *Indians of the North Pacific Coast*, edited by Tom McFeat, 135-46. Seattle: University of Washington Press, 1967.

———. "Comment." *Arctic Anthropology* 14 (1977): 89-93.

Duff, Wilson. "Contributions of Marius Barbeau to West Coast Ethnology." *Anthropologica* 6 (1964): 63-96.

Dundes, Alan. "Heads or Tails: A Psychoanalytic Study of Potlatch." *Journal of Psychological Anthropology* 2 (1979): 395-424.

Gibbs, George. "Tribes of Western Washington and Northwestern Oregon." In United States Geographical and Geological Survey of the Rocky Mountain Region, *Contributions to North American Ethnology*, I, 157-361. Washington: U.S. Government Printing Office, 1877.

Gough, Barry M. "A Priest Versus the Potlatch: The Reverend Alfred James Hall and the Fort Rupert Kwakiutl, 1878-1880." *Journal of the Canadian Church Historical Society* 24, no. 2 (1982): 75-89.

Grant, S. D. "Indian Affairs under Duncan Campbell Scott: The Plains Cree of Saskatchewan 1913-1931." *Journal of Canadian Studies* 18 (Fall 1983): 21-39.

Gresko, Jaqueline. "White 'Rites' and Indian 'Rites': Indian Education and Native Responses in the West, 1870-1910." In *Western Canada Past and Present*, edited by Anthony W. Rasporich, 163-81. Calgary: McClelland & Stewart West, 1975.

Grumet, Robert Steven. "Changes in Coast Tsimshian Redistributive Activities in the Fort Simpson Region of British Columbia, 1788-1862." *Ethnohistory* 22 (1975): 295-318.

Hak, Gordon. "The Socialist and Labourist Impulse in Small-Town British

Columbia: Port Alberni and Prince George, 1911-1933." *Canadian Historical Review* 70 (December 1989): 519-42.

Hall, David J. "Clifford Sifton and Canadian Indian Administration, 1896-1905." In *As Long as the Sun Shines and Water Flows: A Reader in Canadian Native Studies*, edited by Ian A. L. Getty and Antoine S. Lussier, 120-44. Vancouver: University of British Columbia Press, 1983.

Jacknis, Ira. "George Hunt, Collector." In *Chiefly Feasts*, edited by Aldona Jonaitis. New York: American Museum of Natural History, in press.

Kan, Sergi. "Cohorts, Generations, and Their Culture: The Tlingit Potlatch in the 1980s." *Anthropos* 84 (1989): 405-22.

Kobrinsky, Vernon. "Dynamics of the Fort Rupert Class Struggle: Fighting with Property Vertically Revisited." In *Papers in Honor of Harry Hawthorne*, edited by V. Serl and H. Taylor, 32-59. Bellingham: Western Washington State College Press, 1975.

La Violette, Forrest E. "Missionaries and the Potlatch." *Queen's Quarterly* 58 (Spring 1951): 237-51.

Leighton, Douglas. "A Victorian Civil Servant at Work: Lawrence Vankoughnet and the Canadian Indian Department, 1874-1893." In *As Long as the Sun Shines and Water Flows: A Reader in Canadian Native Studies*, edited by Ian A. L. Getty and Antoine S. Lussier, 104-19. Vancouver: University of British Columbia Press, 1983.

McCaskill, Dan. "Native People and the Justice System." In *As Long as the Sun Shines and Water Flows: A Reader in Canadian Native Studies*, edited by Ian A. L. Getty and Antoine S. Lussier, 288-98. Vancouver: University of British Columbia Press, 1983.

Macnair, Peter. "From Kwakiutl to Kwakwa̱ ka'wakw." In *Native Peoples: The Canadian Experience*, edited by R. Bruce Morrison and C. Roderick Wilson. Toronto: McClelland & Stewart, 1986.

Mauzé, Marie. "Boas, les Kwagul et le potlatch: éléments pour une réévaluation." *L'Homme* 100 (October-December 1986): 21-63.

Miller, Jay. "Feasting with the Southern Tsimshian." In *The Tsimshian: Images of the Past, Views of the Present,* edited by Margaret Seguin, 27-39. Vancouver: University of British Columbia Press, 1984.

Mitchell, Marjorie, and Franklin, Anna. "When You Don't Know the Language, Listen to the Silence: An Historical Overview of Native Women in British Columbia." In *History of British Columbia: Selected Readings*, edited by Patricia E. Roy, 49-68. Toronto: Copp Clark Pitman, 1988.

Olson, Ronald L. "The Quinault Indians." In *University of Washington Publications in Anthropology,* no. 2: 1-190. Seattle: University of Washington Press, 1927.

———. "The Social Life of the Owikeno Kwakiutl." *Anthropological Records* (1954): 213-60.

Patterson, E. Palmer, II. "A Decade of Change: Origins of the Nishga and Tsimshian Land Protests in the 1880s." *Journal of Canadian Studies* 18 (Fall 1983): 40-54.

Pettit, George A. "The Quiluete of LaPush." *Anthropological Records* 14 (1960): 1-118.

Ray, Verne F. "Lower Chinook Ethnographic Notes." In *University of Washington Publications in Anthropology,* no. 7: 29-165. Seattle: University of Washington Press, 1938.

Ringel, Gail. "The Kwakiutl Potlatch: History, Economics, and Symbols." *Ethnohistory* 25 (Fall 1979): 347-62.

Ruyle, Eugene E. "Slavery, Surplus, and Stratification on the Northwest Coast: The Ethnoenergetics of an Incipient Stratification System." *Current Anthropology* 14 (December 1973): 603-31.

Sapir, Edward. "The Social Organization of the West Coast Tribes." In *Indians of the North Pacific Coast,* edited by Tom McFeat, 28-48. Seattle: University of Washington Press, 1966.

Scott, Duncan Campbell. "Indian Affairs, 1867-1912." In *Canada and its Provinces,* vol. 7, edited by Adam Shortt and A. G. Doughty, 593-626. Toronto: Glascow, Brook & Company, 1914.

Stipe, Claude E. "Anthropologist Versus Missionaries: The Influence of Presuppositions." *Current Anthropology* 21 (April 1980): 165-79.

Suttles, Wayne. "Post-Contact Culture Changes among the Lummi Indians." *British Columbia Historical Quarterly* 18 (1954): 29-102.

Swanton, John. "Social Conditions, Beliefs and Linguistic Relationship of the Tlingit Indians." In *26th Annual Report of the Bureau of American Ethnology for 1905-1906,* 391-486. Washington: U.S. Government Printing Office, 1904.

Tennant, Paul. "Native Indian Political Organization in British Columbia, 1900-1969: A Response to Internal Colonialism." *BC Studies* 55 (Autumn 1982): 3-49.

Tobias, John L. "Protection, Civilization, Assimilation: An Outline History of Canada's Indian Policy." *Western Canadian Journal of Anthropology* 6 (1976): 13-30.

Weis, L. P. "D. C. Scott's View of History and the Indian." *Canadian Literature* 111 (1986): 27-39.

Wike, Joyce. "A Reevaluation of Northwest Coast Cannibalism." In *The Tsimshian and Their Neighbors on the North Pacific Coast,* edited by Jay Miller and Carol M. Eastman, 239-54. Seattle: University of Washington Press, 1984.

Wyatt, Victoria. "Alaskan Indian Wage Earners in the 19th Century." *Pacific Northwest Quarterly* 78 (January-April 1987): 43-49.

Newspapers and Journals

Canada Gazette.
Daily Colonist (also known as *The Colonist*).
The Daily Columbian (also known as *The Columbian*).
Log of the Columbia.
Missionary Bulletin.
Nanaimo Free Press.
Native Voice.
News Advertiser.
News-Herald.
Omineca Herald.
Prince Rupert Daily News.
Vancouver Daily Province (before 1898, *The Province*, Victoria).
Vancouver Sunday Sun.
Vancouver World.
Victoria Daily Times (also known as *The Victoria Times*).
Wesleyan Missionary Notices.
Western Methodist Recorder.

Films

Potlatch!: A Strict Law Bids Us Dance. 16 mm, 53 min. Alert Bay: U'mista
    Cultural Society, 1975.

Unpublished Sources

Barnett, H. G. "The Nature and Function of the Potlatch." Anthropology
    Department, University of Oregon, 1948. Mimeo.
Dawn, Leslie Allan. " 'Ksan: Museum, Cultural and Artistic Activity
    among the Gitksan Indians of the Upper Skeena, 1920-1973." Master's
    thesis, University of Victoria, 1976.
Golla, Susan. "He Has a Name: History and Social Structure Among the
    Indians of Western Vancouver Island." PhD diss., Columbia Univer-
    sity, 1987.
Hajda, Yvonne P. "Regional Social Organization in the Greater Lower Co-
    lumbia, 1792-1830." PhD diss., University of Washington, 1984.
Krueger, Jan K. "Masset, Aiyansh, Tahl Tan: A Comparative Study of An-
    glican Missions to the Indians of British Columbia." Master's thesis,
    University of Western Ontario, 1987.
Langdon, Steve. "The Development of the Nootkan Cultural System." Pa-
    per presented at the Northwest Coast Studies Conference, Simon Fraser
    University, May 1976.

Leighton, J. Douglas. "The Development of Federal Indian Policy in Canada, 1840-1890." PhD diss., University of Western Ontario, 1975.

McNeary, Stephen A. "Where Fire Came Down: Social and Economic Life of the Niska." PhD diss., Bryn Mawr College, 1976.

Mitchell, Darcy Anne. "The Allied Tribes of British Columbia: A Study in Pressure Group Behaviour." Master's thesis, University of British Columbia, 1977.

Pettipas, Katherine Ann. "Severing the Ties That Bind: The Canadian Indian Act and the Repression of Indigenous Religious Systems in the Prairie Region, 1896-1951." PhD diss., University of Manitoba, 1989.

Pineo, Peter Camden. "Village Migrations of the Modern Kwakiutl." Bachelor of Arts essay, University of British Columbia, 1955.

Index